THE BOOK OF
GENESIS

THE BOOK OF
GENESIS

J. Van Rietschoten

Published by The Study
Box 445, Fergus, Ontario
Canada N1M 3E2

www.thestudy-books.com

The Book of Genesis: A Workbook
J. VanRietschoten, Minister Emeritus in the Canadian Reformed Churches

1st Edition, 2021

Copyright © 2021 The Study. All rights reserved. No part of this publication may be reproduced in any manner without permission in writing from the publisher, except brief quotations used in connection with a review in a magazine or newspaper.

All Scripture quotations, unless otherwise indicated, are taken from English Standard Version (ESV)., electronic ed. (Crossway, 2010).

All quotations from liturgical forms, confessions, and Psalms are taken from the Book of Praise: Anglo-Genevan Psalter (Winnipeg: Premier, 2014).

Library and Archives Canada Cataloguing in Publication

Title: The book of Genesis / J. Van Rietschoten.
Names: Van Rietschoten, J., author.
Description: 1st edition.
Identifiers: Canadiana 20220226814 | ISBN 9780886661304 (softcover)
Subjects: LCSH: Bible. Genesis—Commentaries.
Classification: LCC BS1235.53 .V36 2022 | DDC 222/.1107—dc23

Printed in Canada
Published by The Study
Box 445, Fergus, Ontario
Canada N1M 3E2
www.thestudy_books.com
ISBN-13 978-0-88666-

Cover Design: @VanveenJF

Publisher's Note:
The following book is a great additional resource to the library of books published by The Study. It is both accessible for many readers, while also striving to be scholarly. An honest effort has been made to ensure that scholarly details are included in the footnote while the flow of the books remains accessible to a wider audience.

Preface

"In the beginning God created the heavens and the earth…" (Gen 1:1). The entire book of Genesis is about so many beginnings. It introduces us to the almighty God, the Creator and Governor of the world, of time, and of purpose. Genesis teaches us about the beginnings of man's disobedience, of the enmity God established between the Seed of the Serpent and the Seed of the Woman, and of God's love towards fallen creatures. It does not take long and Genesis also tells us about the effect of sin: shame, murder, and evil intentions always, leading to the worldwide flood. Again, God demonstrates his goodness in new beginnings: a new covenant with Noah and creation and his formal covenant of grace with Abraham and his posterity through whom the whole world would be blessed. We read through Genesis and learn how God cared for his people, kept them safe and distinct in Egypt while they grew into a nation, and how he remains faithful to his promises while guiding the world's history to achieve his purposes.

Rev. John VanRietschoten has prepared this Study Guide as a way to help Christians explore these beginnings. He does so with a pastoral heart, with careful study, and with many helpful questions. He guides users of this Study Guide to see Genesis in the context of the whole of scripture, but also, and somewhat uniquely, in the context of Israel's historical redemption from Egypt. He helps readers understand the original context while exploring the broader implications and applications. While the format of the book is unique, its insights, questions, and observations are well worth the effort for adult group bible studies to learn from.

I've already alluded to the many questions – not each question needs to be worked through as a group. May I make the following suggestion: Members of the study group should read the scripture passage that will be studied (and perhaps the accompanying study notes), and this Study Guide. The leader of the session might want to highlight a few of the pertinent questions they found to be intriguing, challenging, or applicable. Once the discussion is started, other members would contribute comments about other questions they were wondering about or struggled with. I would like to encourage study groups to avoid using this Study Guide as a textbook, but as it is intended, as a guide through your study.

May the Lord bless you as you study the book of beginnings, Genesis. May this Study Guide be of support as you navigate through the book, and may the Lord add his blessings on your study.

In Christ,

Dr. Chris DeBoer (Ed.D.)

Publishing Manager – The Study

March 2022

Introduction

MOSES AND THE BOOK OF GENESIS

Moses was born in the Egyptian Delta in approximately 1530 B.C. The happenings recorded in the book of Genesis stretch from the time of creation to the death of Joseph in Egypt. Moses was born a few centuries after the death of Joseph, so he did not personally witness the times and events described in the book of Genesis. Moses wrote the book at about the time of Israel's exodus from Egypt. Since he had no personal knowledge of that time period, where then did Moses get to know all that is written in the book of Genesis? Part of the answer to this question must be that God personally revealed to Moses much of what he had to write. For other parts Moses could fall back on writings written earlier by men who were guided by God the Holy Spirit.

THE ART OF WRITING WAS KNOWN EARLY

Writing was a skill known as early as 4000 B.C. Writing was already known to Abraham. Abraham originated from the Babylonian city of Ur. A contemporary of Abraham was the Babylonian king Hammurabi at Ur[1], who wrote a book of laws consisting of a Preface, 282 commandments, and an epilogue. Another possible source for Moses is the book of Jashar. Joshua 10:13 records: "Is this not written in the Book of Jashar?" This book is also mentioned in 2 Samuel 1:18. In translation the Book of Jashar means "the Book of the Righteous." The righteous were Seth, Enoch, Noah, Abraham, Isaac, Jacob and Joseph. Among the writings of the time of Moses the so-called *Proto-Sinaitic writings* must also be included. In the Sinai desert, and near Thebes in Egypt, writings were found that proved to be a mixture between Egyptian hieroglyphics and Semitic letters. Since it was first discovered in the desert of Sinai this writing became known as *Proto-Sinaitic* writing. This script is considered a forerunner of the Hebrew script of the Bible. Some scientists date this writing as early as 3000 B.C., others as approximately 2000 B.C.[2] Since Moses was educated at the court of Pharaoh (Acts 7:22) and lived in the Sinai desert for forty years, he must have been able to read and write the Proto-Sinaitic script.

The book of Genesis certainly is the oldest of all the books of the Bible. Besides recognizing Genesis as the oldest book in the Bible we must take into account the time period wherein it pleased God to have this book written by Moses.

---

[1] K.R. Veenhof, in The World of the Bible, A.S. Van der Woude ed., Grand Rapids MI, 1986, p. 210. Appr. 1800 B.C.

[2] Joseph Lam, The Invention and Development of the Alphabet. In: Visible Language Inventions of Writing in the Ancient Middle East and Beyond Edited by Christopher Woods with Emily Teeter, Geoff Emberling. Oriental Institute Museum Publications. Number 32. The Oriental Institute of the University of Chicago. P. 189; M. Sandman Holmberg, The God Ptah, Lund 1946 pp. 220/1; Jan Assmann, Religion and Cultural Memory, Stanford CA 2006 p. 66

THE TIME PERIOD

At the time God gave this book to Moses the LORD God was waging war against Egypt. It was the time of "Let my people go". Two possible time periods are presented by scholars. These are usually indicated as the early date of the Exodus (ca. 1450 B.C.) and the late date of the Exodus (ca. 1210 B.C.) The time line presented in the Bible calls for the early date of the Exodus (1 Kings 6:1). The early date places the Exodus in the Late Bronze Age while the late date places the Exodus at the beginning of the Iron Age. However, when we read the LORD's instructions to Moses to rob the Egyptians, we do not find any mention of iron among the metals named. The reason is that at the early time-slot Egypt did not have mass production of iron. It was the Hittites who lived at the North end of Canaan who had mass production of iron.[3] The Hittites had iron chariots. Though the Hittites had iron, the Iron Age had not yet started. The time of the Exodus was still in the Late Bronze Age. The book of Genesis fits the position of Moses and the Hebrews in the Egypt of the Thutmosid Pharaohs of the New Kingdom era. It does not fit the era of the Ramesside Pharaohs as claimed by those who hold to the late date of the Exodus.

THE BOOK OF GENESIS AS GOD'S TRUTH OVER AGAINST THE LIE OF EGYPTIAN IDOLATRY

During our study of the book of Genesis we must take into account that the LORD God was teaching his chosen people Israel his truth over against the lie of the idolatry they had witnessed and even practiced in Egypt (Josh 24:14; Ezek. 20:2-8). The same holds true for the idolatry of the Canaanites (Lev. 18:3). One of the main differences between Genesis and Egyptian idolatry is that Genesis is *revelation from the God who speaks and acts* while the gods of Egypt are silent and a product of man's imagination. Modern science of Darwinian evolution has fallen prey to the same imagination. Darwinian evolution recognizes no revelation by the God who acts and speaks. There is only silence and man's imagination. With Darwinian evolution we have in some form returned to the idolatry of Egypt. Both are 'nature religions.'

As an additional purpose, the Book of Genesis was to encourage the enslaved Hebrews who cried out to the God of their fathers in their distress. In Exodus 3, it is revealed that the LORD God had heard the cry of his people. In Deut. 26:7 Moses refers to the same: "Then we cried to the LORD, the God of our fathers, and the LORD heard our voice and saw our affliction, our toil, and our oppression."

QUESTIONS

1. The book of Genesis belongs to the canonical books of the Bible (2 Timothy 3:16). Where in the Three Forms of Unity do we confess this?
2. What does "canonical" mean?
3. Should we study the book of Genesis independently from the rest of the Bible? How could the rest of the Bible benefit us in the study of the book of Genesis?
4. Genesis is the first book of the Bible. Is it therefore also the basis on which the whole Bible rests? If so, how so? If not, why not?

---

[3] Redford, Donald B. Egypt, Canaan, and Israel in Ancient Times 1992, Princeton Univeristy Press. p. 210 "Ancient Egypt: Iron was still quite rare and used only for luxury items; and both production and market had long since been cornered by the Hittites".

Genesis 1:1 – The Beginning

In the beginning, God created the heavens and the earth.

The title "Genesis" means birth or becoming. It is taken from the Septuagint, which is the Greek translation of the OLD TESTAMENT. The Hebrew title of the book is *berëshit*. This is also the first word in the book. *Berëshit* means in "the beginning" or "at the head". [4]

TO CONSIDER

- Which title would fit the book better, "Genesis" or "In the Beginning" (*Berëshit*)?
- *Berëshit* – beginning - has as its opposite *acharit* – which means last or end. Would this "Berëshit" and its opposite *"acharit"* have anything to do with "in the beginning" and its aim "in the last days" – or "latter days" (See John 6:39-54 and Joel 2:23 and 28, Acts 2:17 and 2 Timothy 3:1)?

For the answer to these questions read the section that follows below:

The first verse in the Bible reads, "In the beginning God created the heavens and the earth". The words "In the beginning" is a translation of the original Hebrew *berëshit* – *be* means in and *rëshit* means beginning. Within the word *berëshit* (= beginning) we find the word *rësh* which means *head*. Just as the English word "head" has a variety of meanings, so the Hebrew word *rësh* has a variety of meanings. We speak of the father as the head of the household. We also speak of the beginning of a document as the header, and of the issue of a river as the head of the river. *Berëshit* in Genesis 1 can then be translated as, "At the head". At the head of everything God created the heavens and the earth. In myths, stories, and fantasies weird things are said about the beginnings. Taking into account that the basic meaning of *berëshit* is "at the head" helps us to deal with the many and different speculations about "the beginning". One of the most frequent speculations about Genesis 1:1 is calling the beginning *chaos*. The contrary is the case. There is no chaos here but order. Genesis 1:1 reveals to us God standing at the head of his Way on the way to the end: the "Last Day" of Revelation 21 & 22. The following quote will show this abundantly.

> When it means "beginning," *rëshit* is the opposite of *acharit*, "end," in
> the sense of final situation. In this it differs from its synonym *tehilla* which stands in

---

[4] TWOT Number 193 ב (bĕ) A very common preposition with a wide range of meanings. BDB list mainly: in, at or by, with (of accompaniment or of instrument), a verbal complement of specialized meaning, and, used with the infinitive construct, to introduce a temporal clause. Currently the Hebrew prepositions are recognized as having an even wider range of meaning. Ugaritic evidence indicates that bĕ also often means "from," as does the preposition lĕ (Gordon, UT 19: no. 435; AisWUS 486).

contrast only to subsequent situations. Thus *rëshit* refers to the beginning of a process with a definite end or goal, or to a specific limited period of time, whereas *tehilla* means simply the first in a series of events without a definite end.[5]

In Genesis 49:1, Jacob uses the word *acharit (beacharit hayom)* "in the last day". Verse ten of that chapter foretells of the sceptre that will not depart from Judah until Shilo comes to whom will belong the gathering of the nations. In Jacob's prophecy we meet God's going forth from "in the beginning" of Genesis 1 towards the "last days". The *berëshit* of Genesis 1:1 tells us of God standing at the "head" of his way. He is the opener of the way that runs from creation to recreation.

The NEW TESTAMENT word for *end* is *telos*. The OLD TESTAMENT word *acharit/end* is in the NEW TESTAMENT Greek *telos/end*. Matt. 24:13 "But the one who endures to the end (*telos*) will be saved". Just like our word "end" has a variety of meanings, so the biblical Greek word "telos" has a variety of meanings. One aspect of our word "end" is goal, or final result. The same applies to the words "acharit" and "telos"; it is a goal, final result. This shows that the end of God's history is the result of God beginning his history.

Conclusion

In the beginning *(Berëshit)* is not just a start without a definite end *(tehila)*. Rather, "in the beginning" has the "end-goal" *(telos)* in view. In other words, God knows the roadway of his creation from the "head" *(rësh)* to the "end" *acharit* (O.T.) / *telos* (N.T.) or from Genesis 1:1 to Revelation 22:21.

Visual Timeline

Creation – Adam, Seth, Enoch, Noah, Moses, David, Christ, the Church, Restoration

Berëshit ———————————————————————▶ *acharit hayom*

At the head   **The Way**   **latter / last day**

As the Head, God is the Header. He pushes forward from the beginning to the finish line. He accomplishes what he has purposed from eternity. No one and nothing can stop him. God's "In the beginning" guarantees his "At the last day". It is the same God, Spirit, and Word of Genesis 1 who completes his Way in Revelation 21-22. In other words, the God, Spirit, and Word who created is the same God, Spirit and Word who recreates at the last Day.

Questions

1. Are there two creation accounts? Is chapter two repeating chapter one?

2. The following questions may help to answer the previous question.
   1. Which human being was present in chapter one?
   2. Which human being was present in chapter two?

---

[5] G.J.Botterweck et al. TDOT Vol. XIII p.269, s.v. berëshit.

3. Does it make a difference that in chapter one we find that God / Elohim created and in chapter two that the LORD God / YAHWEH Elohim created? (We will come back to this distinction when we deal with chapter two.)

Genesis 1:2 - The "Deep" and the "Waters"

The earth was without form and void, and darkness was over the face of the deep. And the Spirit of God was hovering over the face of the waters.

TO CONSIDER

- Is God to be identified with the waters?
- What do you know about the water of the creation myths of Babylon and Egypt and their nature gods?
- What does Proverbs 3:20 and 8:27-28 tell you of God's relation to the waters?
- Is the Darwinian evolution theory correct when it credits the waters with a natural power to produce life?
- What does 2 Peter 3:5 teach us regarding the created waters of the earth? Compare this to the lie of the nature religions.
- Do you think we will have to come back to 2 Peter 3:5 as we continue through chapter one?
- What was the Spirit of God doing while he hovered over the face of the waters?
- The words used for the Spirit in the Old and New Testament are *ruach* and *pneuma*. Both words can mean wind or spirit or Spirit. Some translate Genesis 1:2 "and a wind of God hovered across the waters." Is it correct to speak of the "wind of God" instead of the "Spirit of God"? See Zechariah 4:6-7.
- Some maintain that darkness and waters are evil primordial powers of death and disorder. According to some theologians God had to wage war against these evil powers and subdue them in order to perform his work of creation. What is your answer to this theory? (Compare the Babylonian myth of Enûma Elish in which we find Marduk's fight with Tiamat).

AN EARTH WITHOUT LIGHT IS AN EARTH WITHOUT LIFE

In outer space it is dark, and no living thing exists in outer space. Before God brought light, the earth was one of the dark objects in space. No life was possible until God said, "Let there be light".

In 2010 the Canadian astronaut Robert Frisk spent six months at the international space station. When he returned to earth one of his remarks was, "I'm also looking forward to feeling the warm rays of sunshine on my skin…". Astronauts in outer space need to imitate conditions on earth by creating artificial surroundings so that they will not die. In spite of living in a space capsule "Astronauts who travel in space are at risk for bone loss in much the same way that cancer patients who receive radiation therapy are, and both groups are more likely to develop fractures than the general population".[6]

---

[6] Science Daily July 17, 2006

The hovering work of the Spirit of God together with the Word God spoke, brought light and life to the earth. God took the earth out of the lifeless dark of outer space when he spoke, "let there be light," and when the Spirit of life hovered over the waters (Psalm 33:6; Psalm 104:30).

QUESTIONS

1. Was it merely a spirit of power hovering over the waters?
2. The Spirit of God hovered over the waters. What does that tell you about the theory that life evolved from ammonia/nitrogen?
3. Considering that Moses wrote the book of Genesis at the time Israel had seen God at work with wonders in Egypt, who would the God of Genesis 1 be to Israel?
4. In Egypt, Ptah was the waters. Ptah made the gods and earth and man by the thought of his heart and the words of his mouth. Ptah put his "vital power" into the statues of the gods. Had the Hebrews been exposed to this and tainted by it? Exodus. 32:4.
5. "The thoughts of Ptah's heart and the words of his mouth"; This sounds like Genesis 1, but if you apply Romans 1:20 ff. is it the same?
6. From where does the light, that makes our life on earth possible, come? Is the sun the source of that light? If not who is? The following verses from Scripture may help to answer this question:

Daniel 2:22 "He reveals deep and hidden things; he knows what is in the darkness, and the light dwells with him".

Isaiah 60:19,20 "The sun shall be no more your light by day, nor for brightness shall the moon give you light; but the LORD will be your everlasting light, and your God will be your glory. Your sun shall no more go down, nor your moon withdraw itself; for the LORD will be your everlasting light, and your days of mourning shall be ended".

Revelation 21:23-25 "And the city has no need of sun or moon to shine on it, for the glory of God gives it light, and its lamp is the Lamb. By its light will the nations walk, and the kings of the earth will bring their glory into it, and its gates will never be shut by day – and there will be no night there."

7. How is God able to withhold light and bring darkness? (e.g. Exodus 10:21 ff. and many other occasions.)
8. What effect does your answer have on the scientific study of nature?

Genesis 1:3-5 – The First Day

And God said, "Let there be light," and there was light. And God saw that the light was good. And God separated the light from the darkness. God called the light Day, and the darkness he called Night. And there was evening and there was morning, the first day.

TO CONSIDER

- God saw that the light was good. What does that tell you about the darkness? (Take into account ancient myths and modern theories).
- Why did God separate the light from darkness?
- Does the daily alternation from light to darkness *absolutely* depend on the sun and the moon?
- How was it possible for God to create a day and a night without the sun and the moon?
- What happens when God withholds light? Or should we say his light? Consider: Exodus 14:20; 2 Samuel 22:29; Isaiah 45:7; God against Egypt in Ezekiel 32:8.

GOD'S REVELATION ABOUT HIS LIGHT AND DARKNESS TO YOUNG ISRAEL TAINTED BY THE IDOLATRY OF EGYPT.

The ancient Egyptians observed the sun going down in the West toward the Libyan desert and rise in the East from the Sea of Reeds. To them, the going down of the sun was the Sun-Boat of the sun god Ra going down into the darkness underneath the Sea of Reeds. Underneath the Sea of Reeds were the powers of darkness trying to prevent the sun (that is Ra) from rising high into the sky once more to bring life-giving light. The storm-god Seth would strive to hamper the progress of the boat of Ra. The boat and its occupants were also threatened by the serpent Apophis. In the end, Seth would change from being an enemy to a defender and conquer Apophis. Ra would rise and would once more be received in the heavens to bring light and life.

Ra supposedly was the "face" of the opener of the way: Ptah. As the face of Ptah, Ra would continue what Ptah began. By the "vital power" of Ptah within him, Ra would create and re-create in endless circle. The face of the invisible Ptah supposedly was seen in the light of the sun, that is Ra. Ptah's breath, (or wind,) of power to bring life was invisible and therefore represented by the god Amon whose name means "hidden". Amon's real name was not known and could not be known.
Throughout her history Israel remained tainted with similar idolatrous practices of worshiping the invisible true God as if he were present in the sun, Asherah poles and manmade images.

God weaned Israel away from the Egyptian distortion by revealing himself as the God who is present, who is light and who creates day and night. As the *Head of the Way*, the God of creation governs the day and the night. He is the living God who never is threatened by darkness. His divine Spirit and Word bring life and light. He may never be distrusted as life-giver. He is also able to make himself known. In spite of God revealing himself to the Hebrews as the life-giver who is near, Israel did not trust him as the God who is near. They treated him as a distant god unable to make himself known.

QUESTIONS

1. Which Bible Book shows how quickly Israel treated the God of Genesis 1 in the manner of the Egyptian idolatry?
2. Deism[7] of the 19th century was also the age of rediscovering ancient Egypt with amazement. Is there a link between Deism and the idolatry of ancient Egypt?
3. In what ways could the idolatry of the distant god be a danger to us Christians?

TO CONSIDER: SIX DAYS OF CREATION

- Does the Bible really give us reason to doubt whether the six days of creation were days of evening and morning, i.e. 24 hours?

When we looked at 1:1 we found that the beginning stretches forward with the end or the purposed end in view [*berëshit* and *acharit/telos*]. The end will be in the same style as the beginning.

⁹ remember the former things of old; for I am God, and there is no other; I am God, and there is none like me, ¹⁰ declaring the end from the beginning and from ancient times things not yet done, saying, 'My counsel shall stand, and I will accomplish all my purpose,'
   Isaiah 46: 9-10

QUESTIONS

1. Apply what we found in Isaiah 46:9-10 to the whole of God's history, beginning at the six days of creation. An example is 1 Corinthians 15:51-52. Are there any other texts?
2. How does "in the twinkling of an eye, in a moment" help you to accept God's time span of six days of creation?
3. How does Matt. 24:44 confirm what we found regarding the six days of creation?
4. How would the message of God's six days of creation encourage the enslaved Hebrews when God sent Moses to them with the book of Genesis?
5. Did the Hebrews have any similar difficulty with the six days of creation to that which many of our generation have?
6. How can we be encouraged by God's six days of his beginning as we face the tribulation of the last days?

---

[7] Deism: the view of those who reduced the role of God to a mere act of creation in accordance with rational laws discoverable by man and held that, after the original act, God virtually withdrew and refrain from interfering in the processes of nature and the ways of man. It is also known as a natural religion: the acceptance of a certain body of religious knowledge that is inborn in every person or that can be acquire by the use of reason and the rejection of religious knowledge when it is acquired through either revelation or the teaching of any church. (Manuel, F. & Pailin, D. (November, 2017) *Deism*. Encyclopedia Britannica. Access Date: December 17, 2019).

Genesis 1:6-8 – The Second Day

And God said, "Let there be an expanse in the midst of the waters, and let it separate the waters from the waters." And God made the expanse and separated the waters that were under the expanse from the water that were above the expanse. And it was so. And God called the expanse Heaven. And there was evening and there was morning, the second day.

The separation of the waters by means of a firmament (or expanse) reveals to us the sovereign power of God over the waters that until then had covered the earth. God is not part of the waters but master of the waters.

TO CONSIDER

- In Egypt, the Hebrews were confronted with the myth that the god Ptah was himself the waters as Ptah Nun. What does the creation of a firmament, separating the waters, reveal to Israel and us about the relation of our God to nature? Is the Christian faith a "nature" religion?
- God called the firmament "heaven". God could have left the firmament unnamed, but he did not. He gave the firmament the name "heaven". What does this tell you of God's home in relation to the earth?
- Genesis 1:8 lays the basis for later revelation about heaven. Can you find in the Bible an example of later revelation about heaven?
- Is heaven just an idea or is heaven a place?

VERSES 9-13 - THE THIRD DAY

And God said, "Let the waters under the heavens be gathered together into one place, and let the dry land appear." And it was so. God called the dry land Earth, and the waters that were gathered together he called Seas. And God saw that it was good. And God said, "Let the earth sprout vegetation, plants yielding seed, and fruit trees bearing fruit in which is their seed, each according to its kind, on the earth." And it was so. The earth brought forth vegetation, plants yielding seed according to their own kinds, and trees bearing fruit in which is their seed, each according to its kind. And God saw that it was good. And there was evening and there was morning, the third day.

After God revealed the creation and the naming of heaven, he now reveals the creation and naming of the dry land. God gathered the waters that covered the earth in places so that dry land could appear. God named the land "earth" and the contained waters "sea". On this land God caused vegetation to grow and bear fruit.

TRUTH OF GOD

We now have in the verses 1-9 the following **truths**:
    God is the Head of all things separate from his creation,
    the life-giving Spirit of God,
    the light-giving God,

God separating light from darkness,
God separating the waters below from the waters above by a firmament,
God calling the firmament heaven,
God gathering the waters calling it sea,
God making the dry land appear calling it earth,
God making a separation between heaven and earth.
God causing grass and herbs yielding seed and also fruit trees to grow on the earth.

LIE OF EGYPTIAN IDOLATRY

In Egypt, Israel had been tainted by the **lie** of Egypt's gods.
Egyptian idolatry placed the gods in the sky, especially the sun and the moon.
They believed that the statues of their gods on earth had a vital power within them.
They dressed their gods in the secret part of their temples and put food out before them.
They believed the dead to be judged under the Sea of Reeds before the mummified god Osiris.
They believed vegetation to grow upon the gods of the underworld.

DISCUSSION

Compare the truths of the verses 1-9 with the lie of Egypt and figure out how God through Moses' writing of Genesis 1:1-9 weaned the Israelites away from the lie of Egypt.

Genesis 1:14-19 – The Fourth Day

And God said, "Let there be lights in the expanse of the heavens to separate the day from the night. And let them be for signs and for seasons,[a] and for days and years, and let them be lights in the expanse of the heavens to give light upon the earth." And it was so. And God made the two great lights—the greater light to rule the day and the lesser light to rule the night—and the stars. And God set them in the expanse of the heavens to give light on the earth, to rule over the day and over the night, and to separate the light from the darkness. And God saw that it was good. And there was evening and there was morning, the fourth day.

TO CONSIDER

Many a sceptical comment has been made about these verses. It is considered impossible that there was light and dark, day and night on the earth if there were no light bearers, no sun, no moon, and no stars. There seems to be an unacceptable contradiction. But is there really an irreconcilable contrast?

QUESTIONS

1. Do the light bearers (sun moon and stars) have light of themselves? Are they independent entities?
2. God is the source of light. What happens when God withholds his light? [Look back to Genesis 1:3-5]
3. What added function are the light bearers given by God besides giving light?

4. Do these questions help to show that there is no contrast here?

In Egypt the Israelites became tainted with the idolatrous worship of the sun and the moon.

DISCUSSION

- How does God's truth regarding the light bearers wean Israel away from the worship of heavenly objects?
- What, in this space age, can we learn from God's revealing authority and power over sun, moon, and stars?

Genesis 1:20-23 – The Fifth Day

And God said, "Let the waters swarm with swarms of living creatures, and let birds fly above the earth across the expanse of the heavens." So God created the great sea creatures and every living creature that moves, with which the waters swarm, according to their kinds, and every winged bird according to its kind. And God saw that it was good. And God blessed them, saying, "Be fruitful and multiply and fill the waters in the seas, and let birds multiply on the earth." And there was evening and there was morning, the fifth day.

TO CONSIDER

After God had created an environment able to sustain life, God created living sea creatures after their kind, and living land and air creatures after their kind.

QUESTIONS

1. What did this environment, able to sustain life, consist of?
2. The bone structure of fish and birds are very much alike. Does that show support for the Darwinian evolution theory?
3. Is there any likeness between water pressure and air pressure?
4. What does being fruitful and the multiplication of life have to do with God's blessing? Was it in their make up so that they would pair and multiply?
5. This is the first time that we hear the revelation that God blesses. Find in the Bible other occasions where God blesses. What is the significance of being blessed?
6. In the verses of the fifth day we do not read that God saw what he had created and said that it was very good. Could God blessing the sea and air creatures mean the same as saying that it was very good? Is there a common line between "blessing" and "good"?
7. If the answer is "yes" may we apply this to the whole of the Bible where blessing appears?
8. The sea and air creatures were to be fruitful and multiply in perpetuity. Does God's blessing also have the perspective of perpetuity in it?
9. Does future growth depend on God's blessing?

10. When God says "be fruitful and multiply," is that a command or an instruction? Or in other words, is it prescriptive or descriptive?

Genesis 1:24-31 – The Sixth Day

And God said, "Let the earth bring forth living creatures according to their kinds—livestock and creeping things and beasts of the earth according to their kinds." And it was so. And God made the beasts of the earth according to their kinds and the livestock according to their kinds, and everything that creeps on the ground according to its kind. And God saw that it was good.

Then God said, "Let us make man in our image, after our likeness. And let them have dominion over the fish of the sea and over the birds of the heavens and over the livestock and over all the earth and over every creeping thing that creeps on the earth."
So God created man in his own image, in the image of God he created him; male and female he created them.
And God blessed them. And God said to them, "Be fruitful and multiply and fill the earth and subdue it and have dominion over the fish of the sea and over the birds of the heavens and over every living thing that moves on the earth." And God said, "Behold, I have given you every plant yielding seed that is on the face of all the earth, and every tree with seed in its fruit. You shall have them for food. And to every beast of the earth and to every bird of the heavens and to everything that creeps on the earth, everything that has the breath of life, I have given every green plant for food." And it was so. And God saw everything that he had made, and behold, it was very good. And there was evening and there was morning, the sixth day.

TO CONSIDER

God's work of creation on the sixth day is recorded for us in two parts. The first part covers the verses 24-25. Here we learn of God's creation of the land animals. That section ends with the now familiar: *And God saw that it was good.* One might expect that these words would mean the end of God's creation work on the sixth day. However, that work does not end here. God continued his work of creation on the sixth day by creating man.

The fact that zoological beings, both animal and man, were created on the same day seems to give credence to some form of evolution of the species. But is this so?

QUESTIONS

1. Land animals and man were created on the same day yet not at the same time. What does that tell us about the similarity and also the distinction between land animals and man?
2. In the science of biology land animals and man are both classified in the category of zoology. Is that correct?
3. Does the similarity between the two justify the Darwinian theory of evolution of the species?
4. Land animals and man were created separately. Does that disqualify the theory of evolution of the species?

5. In ancient Egypt animals often functioned as a kind of mediator between man and the invisible god. Example: The goddess Hathor was often represented as a golden cow. Where do we find the same idolatry in Israel?
6. In Egypt the king Pharaoh was the embodiment of the god. Is this a corruption of man created in the image of God? (See Romans 1:20 ff.)
7. Are we allowed to interpret the creation of man in the image of God in the light of what is revealed about the image in the New Testament?
8. Can you distil from Ephesians 4:23-24 and Colossians 3:10 what the image of God consists of?
9. When animals and man were both created on the sixth day does this make the animal also an image of God?
10. In verse 28, we read for the second time "and God blessed them". In verse 22 we met this phrase for the first time (see page 11 above). Are you able to apply the aspect of perpetuity to verse 28 where God blesses man? Link this to verse one "In the beginning…" and "God's road".

ADDITIONAL POINTS

We cannot leave chapter one yet. There remain two points. First, there is the question whether in chapter one man and woman had already been created or not. This question presents itself to us because of chapter two where God makes man from the dust of the earth and woman even later.

It is my conviction that time and again in the Scriptures the "that" is revealed to us and not (yet) the "how". In chapter one God reveals "that" he created man and woman. In chapter two God reveals "how" he made man and later woman.

The second point that remains to be discussed is the "us" and the "our" in verse 26. For that we must go back to the beginning of chapter one. There it is revealed that God created. He did that together with the life-giving Spirit hovering over the waters and the life-giving Word that he spoke. They are the "us". We will meet the "us" again in chapter two just like in the beginning of chapter one.

Frankfort et. al. *The Intellectual Adventure of Ancient Man p. 55* "One of the texts which comments incidentally on creation states that mankind was made in the image of god. This text emphasizes the goodness of the creator-god in caring for his human creatures (~ 2000 B.C.). *'Well tended are men, the cattle of god. He made heaven and earth according to their desire, and he repelled the water monster (at creation). He made the breath (of) life (for) their nostrils. They are his images that have issued from his body. He arises in heaven according to their desire. He made for them plants and animals, fowl and fish, in order to nourish them. He slew his enemies and destroyed (even) his (own) children when they plotted rebellion (against him))'.*"
(See also ANET p. 417, The Instruction for King Merikare, trsl. J.Wilson, 130-135.) [8]

The Hebrews sojourned in Egypt since the time of Joseph. During that time they were exposed to this idolatrous belief that man issued from the body of the god and thereby became the image of the god.

---

[8] James B. Pritchard, *Ancient Near Eastern Texts Related to the Old Testament,* Third edition with supplement. Princeton NJ 1969

Discussion

1. Did Israel ever treat God as if he were a man?
2. Who were the "us" when God spoke "let us make man in our image"?
3. Evaluate this statement: God must be a man for man is the image of God.

Chapter 2:1-3 – The Seventh Day

Thus the heavens and the earth were finished, and all the host of them. And on the seventh day God finished his work that he had done, and he rested on the seventh day from all his work that he had done. So God blessed the seventh day and made it holy, because on it God rested from all his work that he had done in creation.

MATTERS IN GENESIS CHAPTER TWO THAT SHOULD BE DISCUSSED

A. God's works were finished from the foundation of the world
B. The Day of Rest today
C. The matter of God / Elohim in chapter one and LORD / YAHWEH in chapter two
D. The matter of man and woman being created as helpmeet (counterpart)

A. GOD'S WORKS WERE FINISHED FROM THE FOUNDATION OF THE WORLD

Heb. 4:3-10

*3 For we who have believed enter that rest, as he has said, "As I swore in my wrath, 'They shall not enter my rest,'" **although his works were finished from the foundation of the world.** 4 For he has somewhere spoken of the seventh day in this way: "And God rested on the seventh day from all his works." 5 And again in this passage he said, "They shall not enter my rest." 6 Since therefore it remains for some to enter it, and those who formerly received the good news failed to enter because of disobedience, 7 again he appoints a certain day, "Today," saying through David so long afterward, in the words already quoted, "Today, if you hear his voice, do not harden your hearts." 8 For if Joshua had given them rest, God would not have spoken of another day later on. 9 So then, there remains a Sabbath rest for the people of God, 10 for whoever has entered God's rest has also rested from his works as God did from his.*

QUESTIONS

1. What would it mean that God's works were finished from the foundation of the world?
   a. Would that have any bearing on our life today?
2. In what way do we, who believe in Christ, have rest?
   a. In Heidelberg Catechism, Lord's Day 38 we confess, "and so begin in this life the eternal Sabbath". How do we do that?

3. "Finished". Today mankind is still developing the earth and even tries to develop outer space. That leads to the question whether God's work of creating the heavens and the earth then really was finished – or maybe not? In answering this question is it helpful to use Heb. 4:3-4?
4. In Genesis 2:1, the NIV has "in all their vast array" instead of "host". Which is the better translation and why?
5. Here, for the first time, we find the number seven. Would you agree that the use of the number seven throughout the Scriptures is based on this first use of the number seven in Genesis 2:1-3?
6. When God made the seventh day holy did he then also make the number seven holy?

B. THE DAY OF REST TODAY

TO CONSIDER

- The Lord Jesus Christ rose from the dead on the first day of the week. Every week we celebrate this day as the Lord's Day and we rest. Is that legalistic?
- What must we teach our children regarding resting on the Lord's Day?
- Some teach that the Day of Rest was not kept until the LORD gave the Ten Commandments as recorded in Ex. 20. They then teach that we do not need to observe a Day of Rest since the Ten Commandments have been fulfilled by Christ. How should we deal with that teaching?
- Was there any observance of the seventh Day of Rest before Exodus 20?

STYLE OF SPEAKING AND WRITING

In the style of speaking and writing similar sounding words are often grouped together to bring a point across. We can do this in English. For example: *Battling for first place the batter batted the ball into orbit of higher spheres but the opposing team battered them into second place.*

This was also done in Hebrew. In Genesis 2:1-3 God the Holy Spirit made use of this style. The words "rest" and "seven" sound very much alike and also look somewhat alike in spelling. The word for "rest" looks and sounds somewhat like **shabat** and the word for "seven" somewhat like **shava**.

To bring this point across let us paraphrase verse two: And on day **shava** God finished his work that he had done, and he **shabatted**. That is, on day seven God finished his work that he had done, and he rested. By using this style of writing, God the Holy Spirit laid the basis for his later speaking of God's Seventh Day as the Sabbath. *'Seven' and 'Rest' plus 'Day of Rest' belong together.*

DOES GOD GIVE US A COMMANDMENT IN GENESIS TWO?

Another way of putting that is: Are the words in verse three, *"So God blessed the seventh day and made it holy"*, descriptive or prescriptive? This point is often debated.
When God blesses, he approves, calls it good, and allows it into his presence and communion. What God blesses belongs to his road, his future. When God makes something, or somebody, holy he sets it apart for himself and at peace with his own Holiness.

DISCUSSION

Before we go on please have a look at the wording of this verse (Genesis 2:3) and see if you can form your own opinion. Is it descriptive or prescriptive? See if Exo. 16:22-26 can help you decide.

Genesis 2:4

4 "These are the generations of the heavens and of the earth when they were created, in the day that the LORD God made the earth and the heavens".

DIFFERENCES IN TRANSLATION OF THE WORD TOLEDOT

"Generations" in 2:4 is a translation of the Hebrew word *toledot.*
The NIV translates, "This is the account of the heavens and the earth."
The NKJ translates," This is the history."
The ESV and KJV translate, "These are the generations."

The translation "generations" comes the closest to the Hebrew *toledot*. The word *toledot* is a plural derived from the Hebrew verb *jalad* to give birth, to bring forth. The word generations, pictures what the LORD God is causing the earth and heavens to bring forth. As such it has the element of continuation, of future, in it. This brings the word generations/toledot in line with words of continuation we already met like in 1:1, "in the beginning", "blessing" 3x, and 2:1-3 "seventh day".

QUESTIONS

1. How many times do you find sections in the book of Genesis that begin with "these are the generations of" / "these are the *toledot* of"?
2. What does this tell you of God progressing in his road?
3. Please reread page 1 comments on *"in the beginning"* as "head" and consider the impact this phrase has on the whole of the Bible and God's history, "in the generations" pp. 3-4.
4. Which of the three translations of *toledot* do you prefer and why?

C. THE MATTER OF GOD / ELOHIM IN CHAPTER ONE AND LORD / YAHWEH IN CHAPTER TWO

Earlier we briefly touched on this matter and promised to come back to it when dealing with chapter two. In chapter one it is revealed that the life-giving God by his Spirit and Word created the heavens and the earth while there was no one beside him.

In chapter one God was not speaking to man. From chapter 1:1 to 2:3 God was not yet in communication with man. That does not come until chapter 2:4. From then on it is revealed that God is in communication with man, appears to man, speaks with man, gives commands to man, and acts for man. All that is expressed by the now added Name of God: "YAHWEH". The Name YAHWEH means: **HE IS**. God lets himself be seen and heard to man in acts and words so that we could say and confess: **"HE IS"**.

Before the fall into sin there was unhindered knowledge of God for there was perfect holiness and blessedness. Adam and Eve knew God by Name.

FURTHER EXPLANATION ON THE NAME LORD / YAHWEH

Exodus 3:14 *"God said to Moses, 'I AM WHO I AM' this is what you are to say to the Israelites: 'I AM has sent me to you'."*
At the burning bush God appeared to Moses in the light of fire and glory. There God sent Moses to Egypt to lead into freedom the descendants of Abraham the Hebrew. God commanded Moses to tell the Hebrews: I AM has sent me to you.

Exodus 6:2-3
² God also said to Moses, "I am the LORD. ³ I appeared to Abraham, to Isaac and to Jacob as God Almighty, but by my name the LORD I did not make myself known to them. (God Almighty is El Shaddai). The words *I am the LORD* read in the Hebrew *I am YHWH*. This is pronounced as YAHWEH and usually translated into English as LORD. The literal meaning of the name YHWH is *"HE IS"*.

At first glance it seems as if it says in Exod. 6:3 that Abraham did not know the name YHWH. This raises the question how from Genesis 2:4 on the name YHWH appears in the book of Genesis. It has been suggested that Moses inserted the name YHWH with hindsight. There is however a better explanation.

The key to understanding lies in the similarity and difference in which God appeared to Abraham and to Moses. In Genesis 17:1 we read that God appeared to Abraham. The word 'appeared' tells us that God made himself visible to Abraham. God is on his way to judge Sodom and Gomorrah as El Shaddai, the Judge of all the earth. Abraham sees three men and calls one of the men LORD, YHWH (Genesis 18 and 19). In Exod. 3 and 6 God appears to Moses. Also to Moses God makes himself visible; thus far the similarity.

Now the difference: Abraham sees a man but Moses sees fire, burning light. Moses is commanded to take his shoes off his feet for the ground he stands on is holy ground. In this burning light is a person who is God communicating with man in light of fire. Ever since the fall into sin it has never happened that God made himself visible to a man in a presence of burning light so that man could say "See, there HE IS, there is YHWH". **Before the fall into sin God made himself visible to Adam. Adam could fully say "there he is" or "there is YHWH".** This is the tragedy of the fall into sin; the holy, unrestricted, covenant bond between God and man was no longer there. Men continued to remember that YHWH exists, that there is a HE IS, but this YHWH no longer allowed man to see the living God, in the burning light of fire.

It still could be said of Enoch, Noah, Abraham, that YHWH spoke to them but they did not see him in his burning light of holiness. That is why God said in Genesis 6 that he made himself visible to Abraham as El Shaddai but did not make himself known to Abraham as HE IS, as YHWH. That did not happen to himself visible to Moses appearing in the light of the burning bush. There is progress on God's road from Abraham to Moses.

As a rule the Bible versions give us 3:14 as *"I am who I am"*. This translation does not show that in the original Hebrew there is repetition. Literally it says *"I am and I am"*. W. Gispen in his commentary on Genesis deals with these words of God as he spoke them to Moses. Gispen considers these words of God a **solemn declaration;** almost in the climate of the oath. Gispen translates God's words in the following manner: *I most certainly am HE.* In other words God said, I most certainly am HE who before the fall into sin appeared to Adam as YHWH so that Adam could say "He Is". God is indicating that he is opening the Way that was closed by the fall into sin. Once again he is opening the living Bond of Covenant between him and his people. Once again he is seen, not yet in his full Glory, but at least in the burning light of his holiness. This means that the Opener of the Way has come in holy power and presence to break open the Way for his enslaved people. God is setting his enslaved, landless, people free to bring them to inherit the land promised to Abraham.

DISCUSSION

1. Would you say that, contrary to common opinion, the Name "God the LORD / Elohim YAHWEH" was known to Adam and Eve?
2. The Name YAHWEH indicates that for Adam and Eve this was already the Name of God in the Bond of the Covenant. See Hosea 6:7 *"Like Adam they transgressed the covenant"*. Is this our speculation or is this revelation and therefore true?

Through Moses the LORD God sent the book of Genesis to Israel at the time of the Exodus to teach them truth about YAHWEH because they were tainted by the idolatry of ancient Egypt.

Egypt did not know God as YAHWEH. The Egyptians had no revelation. All that idolaters have is their own foolish imagination. There was no bond between the imaginary creator god and the Egyptians. The imaginary creator god was distant and out of reach. This had affected the Hebrews in Egypt. To them YAHWEH, the Creator, had become far away and hidden. Even in the days of the prophet Isaiah, Israel fell back into the same idolatry. Through Isaiah YAHWEH Elohim reminded them of who he was from the very beginning of creation:

27 Why sayest thou, O Jacob, and speakest, O Israel,
My way is hid from the LORD,
And my judgment is passed over from my God?
28 Hast thou not known? hast thou not heard,
That **the everlasting God, the LORD,**
The Creator of the ends of the earth, fainteth not, neither is weary?

Here the LORD God reminds Israel of the truth. He is not hidden as the gods of the nations are hidden. He is the same from the time of creation. He is still "God the LORD / Elohim YAHWEH.

QUESTIONS

1. Could you explain how in our time of human pride God has been replaced by other gods?
2. Is it of vital necessity to make known to the nations that God is the Creator, and how God the LORD is the Creator from of old?
3. Is God indeed the life-giver and is he known only in the Bond of the Covenant?

4. Is it correct to put this in New Testament terms: Known in the Bond of the Covenant through Jesus Christ and the life-giving Spirit?
5. How far away is God for the world population today?
6. Do you know of any world religions that have a so-called "god" but who is only a nature god imagined by men?
7. Do you know of any eastern religion that has infiltrated the West?
8. Do Judaism and Islam really live in the Bond of the Covenant the Lord God has with Christ's believers today? If not, why not?

Genesis 2:4-17

In chapter 1-2:4 we found revealed **THAT** God created.
Now in chapter 2 we find revealed **HOW** the LORD God created.

TO CONSIDER

- Is chapter two a repetition of chapter one?
- The LORD God planted a garden where he made trees, vegetation, to spring up and there he put the man. What does that tell us about the rest of the world? What condition was that in?
- Does the mandate given in 1:28 to subdue the earth help you in answering this question?
- The mandate is wide and awesome. What in man's make-up enabled him to do all this perfectly? In other words, what had the LORD God given to man so that he could do this wisely, rightly and knowledgable?
- In verse 17 the LORD God gives the threat that eating of the Tree of Knowledge of Good and Evil would result in death. What would that tell you about God as the Opener of the Way of Life? What is the opposite of Opener?
- Can you find any other examples in the Bible of God opening and/or closing?
- Who today is the Holy One that opens and no one closes and who closes and no one opens?
- Where in the Bible do we find that revealed?

Genesis 2:10-14

THE RIVERS

QUICK QUESTION

1) A river flowed out of the garden the LORD God had made. This river divided into four rivers that are known by name. Is there a reason why the LORD God did not reveal the name of the initial river?

The enslaved Hebrews in Egypt looked around and from the far South down to the far North they saw the River Nile. That exposed them to the lie of Egypt's idolatry. To the Egyptians the Nile Valley was the original habitat of gods and men. The River Nile came down the cataracts from inner Africa. The Egyptians were ignorant of that. They thought that the Nile came up out of the earth as part of the primeval waters called Ptah (see Appendix I). The ground that opened to flood the valley with life-giving water came from Ptah, the so-called "Opener of the Way of Life". The LORD God sent Moses to Egypt to reveal the truth over against Egypt's lie. The original habitat of man is not to be found in the Nile Valley of Egypt. The original and perfect habitat for man was created by the LORD God who is the true Opener of the Way of life and its continual Provider.

QUESTIONS

1. Through Moses the LORD God exposed the false pride of Egypt pertaining to the origins of the Way of Life. How would the exposing of the lie of Egypt by God have helped the Hebrews to trust the LORD God to bring them life and freedom from the land of their slavery and death?
2. In what terms did the LORD God describe the land he was bringing the Israelites to?
3. The LORD God told them that he would give them a land stretching from the South – the River of Egypt- to the North –the River Euphrates. Does that tell you anything of the LORD God progressing on the road he started *"in the beginning"*?
4. We are on our way to the promised inheritance with Christ on the New Earth. Should the progression from the Garden of Eden to the land the LORD God gave Israel between the Brook of Egypt and the River Euphrates help us to trust our God to bring us into the inheritance with Christ?

Genesis 2:18-25

The LORD God shows Adam pairs of animals, has Adam name them, and then pairs also Adam, for the LORD God says that it is not good for man to be alone. The LORD God made "a helper fit for him" (ESV). The Hebrew text literally has "a helper across from him" or "close to him". The meaning could be that the LORD God made for Adam his *"Counterpart"*.

ADAM NAMING THE ANIMALS

The act of giving animals names seems quite simple. In reality, naming the animals required wisdom and insight. Adam understood the animals fully which we are no longer able to do because we live after the fall into sin. Adam had the necessary wisdom and insight to understand because he was created " Ephesians 4:24).

QUESTIONS

1) Where in the letters of Paul is it revealed that New Testament believers are being restored to this wisdom and insight?
2) How does this restoration apply to our scientific pursuit of understanding the world around us?
3) Explain why unbelief makes a person blind and unable to properly name the world around us? What is it that unbelievers miss?
4) Apply this to the stubborn adherence to the theory of Darwinian evolution.

God created Adam and Eve as each other's Counterpart

QUESTIONS

1. Was there to be intercourse and birth of children in the state of righteousness?
2. Are we doing justice to God our Creator if we consider "sex" to be a result of sin?
3. Man in the Hebrew is *Ish* woman *Isha*. What does the likeness of the two names tell you about the relationship God intended ish and isha to practice? See also verse 24.
4. Adam said *"This at last is bone of my bones and flesh of my flesh; she shall be called woman (isha) for she was taken out of man (ish)"*. What does that tell us about the man as head of his wife?
5. What does this tell us about the responsibility of man for his wife?
6. Note how the titles Ish and Isha are alike and of the same root. Were ish and isha created in such unity that together they were the image of God?
7. It pays to look up what our God reveals about the image of God in Eph. 4:24 and Col. 3:10. From these passages explain how ish and isha were able to live in total unity.
8. The words in these two New Testament passages are addressed to Christians. How could husbands and wives make use of these words to strive to live together in total unity?
9. How could we use these last two discussion points to pastorally counsel Christian husband and wives who experience difficulty to be one in their marriage? What assets have they been given by God to maintain or restore unity?
10. God's road is one of which God is the beginning and the end. Use this line to discuss the following point:
11. In verse 24 we read that; *"a man shall leave his father and his mother and hold fast to his wife, and they shall become one flesh"*. How does this instruction of the LORD God fit into his forward movement on his Way of Life?
12. How does today's marriage of a Christian husband and wife fit into God's forward movement on his Way of Life?
13. Show why the legalization of same-sex marriage could not fit into God's forward movement on his Way of Life.
14. Does our strong God leave a husband and wife, whom he did not give children, outside of his forward movement on his Way of Life?

NAKEDNESS BEFORE AND AFTER THE FALL INTO SIN

What was nakedness before the fall into sin like? How did our first parents experience being naked? The only source to satisfy our curiosity is the Bible. However, the Bible only tells us that our first parents were naked and not afraid. The ability to be naked and not afraid is now lost. We cannot retrieve it and cannot recall what it was like. Fear is part of man's life. We are unable to regain the ability to be naked and without fear. That is what the next chapter teaches us. Chapter three also teaches us that only the LORD God, who created us without fear, is able to recreate us so that we might have our nakedness covered and live without fear.

Genesis 3

INTRODUCTION TO CHAPTER THREE

In Chapter 1:1-2:3 our God reveals to us **that** he is the **"Opener of the Way of Life"**. As the Opener of the Way of Life our God by his Word and Spirit created the environment for living creatures and for mankind. Our God created mankind male and female and in his image. *²⁸ And God blessed them. And God said to them, "Be fruitful and multiply and fill the earth and subdue it, and have dominion over the fish of the sea and over the birds of the heavens and over every living thing that moves on the earth."*

In Chapter 2:4-25 our God reveals **how** he created male and female and how he placed them in a good and perfect environment. In this environment our God enabled male and female to fulfill the mandate spelled out in 1:28. Male and female were able because God created them as his image. In this section we see Adam at work as image of God with perfect knowledge, holiness and righteousness.

The Bond of the Covenant, in the time when all was "good", contained a promise, a demand, and the threat of the curse. The demand is seen in the mandate of 1:28. The promise is seen in the Tree of Life. The threat of the curse is seen in the admonition not to eat from the Tree of Knowledge of Good and Evil because doing that would bring the curse of death.

Study of chapter three must be done with relation to chapters one and two. As we study chapter three some questions must be asked.

QUESTIONS

1. As life on the earth progressed what happened to the Bond of the Covenant between God and man?
2. Did our first parents, Adam and Eve, continue to trust God, to believe the promise, to obey the demand, and to stay far away from curse and death?
3. Did they continue to perfectly function in the image of God?
4. Did they remain one as counterparts?
5. Did they continue to be secure in their nakedness?

Genesis 3:1-6

*3 Now the **serpent** was more **crafty** than any other beast of the field that the LORD God had made. He said to the woman, "Did God **actually** say, 'You shall not eat of any tree in the garden'?" ² And the woman said to the serpent, "We may eat of the fruit of the trees in the garden, ³ but God said, 'You shall not eat of the fruit of the tree that is in the midst of the garden, neither shall you touch it, lest you die.' " ⁴ **But** the* *serpent said to the woman, "You will not surely die. ⁵ **For** God knows that when you eat of it your eyes will be opened, and you will be like God, **knowing** good and **evil**." ⁶ So when the woman saw that the tree was good for food, and that it was a delight to the eyes, and that the tree was to be desired to make one **wise**, she took of its fruit and ate, and she also gave some to her husband who was with her, and he ate."*

In the verses quoted some words have been highlighted to guide us through the passage.

"Crafty"- knowing – wise

These three words belong to the same field of meaning. The meaning of the Hebrew word for crafty must be determined from the context in which it is used. In other places it may mean clever, sensible, and even wise. Here the context shows that the word must be understood as unfavorable: crafty. The serpent is crafty for he uses his wisdom and his knowledge to deceive.

TO CONSIDER

1. Did God create the serpent with good wisdom and knowledge?
2. What must have happened to the serpent so that he became the enemy of God and his Way?
3. The Holy Spirit reveals in 2 Peter 2:4 and Jude:6 the rebellion and judgment of angels. Let us take these verses into account as we discuss the serpent as the enemy of God and his Way.
4. In the cult of the ancient Egyptians the serpent-god is both defender and enemy. Does our true God also have two sides: good and evil?
5. First nations culture views the serpent and the turtle as the creatures closest to the earth, endued with all wisdom and understanding everything we need to know to live our lives – hence a god, and object of worship.

"Actually"

In some versions the Hebrew is translated "has God indeed". The way the serpent phrases his question to our first mother Eve aims to sow distrust. The serpent's words seem mild but are in fact sharp and hateful towards God. The Hebrew text has a wee little word that has the effect of taunting. The serpent is taunting. The effect is like: *Nah nah nahna God did not say this to you. Try to contradict me. Woman, you are being fooled.*

QUICK QUESTION

What title did the God the Holy Spirit give God's adversary in Matt. 4:3 and 1 Thes. 3:5?

"But"

The word "but" shows contrast and often shows adversity. Adverse, that is what the serpent means it to be. The serpent uses the word "but" to indicate that he is going to contradict God. He is going to turn God's true words into a lie. According to the serpent God has lied when He threatened with the curse of death.

"For"

With this word the serpent does not first of all introduce what he has to say about God. The word for introduces the pounding impact of what the serpent wants our first mother Eve to believe. The serpent wants our first mother to believe that eating from the Tree of Knowledge of Good and Evil will bring her and our first father Adam eternal life. The impact of the serpent's words is, *Go ahead! Rebel against God! You will be just like God knowing good and evil.* ***And you will live for ever!***

DISCUSSION TIME

1. What kind of eternal life would it be knowing good and evil? Would it be the kind of eternal life God had promised?
2. Look around. Look at the history of mankind. Where, now and in the past, do we see rebellion against God and man trying to live forever?
3. In what manner was the serpent trying to close God's Open Road?
4. The serpent aimed at closing God's Road of Life. What would be the end-result if he succeeded?

"Wise" in verse six

In the Hebrew of the Old Testament there exists another word for wisdom that is used here in verse 6. The word used here must be read in connection with the lie of the serpent who promises knowledge. Because the context is about knowledge, the ESB has in the margin a note with an alternate translation. The note reads, *"Or to give insight"*. Our first mother saw that the tree could give knowledge, namely insight into good and evil. She believed the serpent and ate from the fruit of the tree. She also gave some to our first father and he ate. They expected to be like God.

QUESTIONS

1. In verse five the serpent says that God knows good and evil. Later in verse 22 the LORD God himself said *"Behold, the man has become like one of us knowing good and evil"*. Is God evil? 2 Peter 2:4 and Jude verse six can help us to unravel this so-called problem.
2. Who are the "us" in verse 22?
3. The book of Job shows Satan present before God among the angels in heaven. Do they belong to the "us"?
4. Could it be that there was good and evil present among God's court in heaven?
5. Consider whether the rebellion among God's angels had spread to God's good creation?
6. What happened to man, created in the image of God, when he and his wife became rebels against God?
7. What happened to the Bond of the LORD God to which he had bound our first parents? Hosea 6:7 may help us.
8. The serpent/tempter called evil good. Is there good in evil?
9. Has the serpent/tempter ever given up on convincing people that there is good in evil?
10. The lie that there is good in evil was believed throughout past history. Is this lie also believed and practiced in our world?
11. Is it even practiced in our nation?

NAKED/AROM

2:25 "And the man and his wife were both *naked* (arom) and were not **ashamed**."
3:1 "Now the serpent was more *crafty* (arom) than any other beast of the field that the LORD God had made."
3:7 "Then the eyes of both were opened, and they knew that they were *naked* (arom). And they sewed fig leaves together and made themselves loincloths."
3:10-11 "And he said, "I heard the sound of you in the garden, and I was **afraid**, because I was *naked* (arom), and I hid myself." He said, "Who told you that you were *naked* (arom)? Have you eaten of the tree of which I commanded you not to eat?"

"Naked" is the English translation of the Hebrew word, "arom". When you vertically go down these verses you find that in the Hebrew text of these verses the Hebrew word "arom" is used in all five verses. There is no variation. In the English translation there is variation. In 3:1 arom is translated with the word "crafty". I venture the thought that the Serpent is "arom", "naked" in the sense of slippery. This is supported by the fact that in the LORD's dietary laws Israel was forbidden to eat anything that has no scales such as water snakes.

Since the book of Genesis is foundational for the whole of Scripture we find that the concept "naked" continues throughout the Bible. Here are a few examples from the New Testament. Let us study these verses in the light of God clothing Adam and Eve, covering their nakedness.

Romans 13:14 *"But put on the Lord Jesus Christ, and make no provision for the flesh, to gratify its desires".*
2 Corinthians 5:1-5 *"For we know that if the tent that is our earthly home is destroyed, we have a building from God, a house not made with hands, eternal in the heavens. ² For in this tent we groan, longing to put on our heavenly dwelling, ³ if indeed by putting it on we may not be found naked. ⁴ For while we are still in this tent, we groan, being burdened—not that we would be unclothed, but that we would be further clothed, so that what is mortal may be swallowed up by life. ⁵ He who has prepared us for this very thing is God, who has given us the Spirit as a guarantee".*
Revelation 3:17 *"For you say, I am rich, I have prospered, and I need nothing, not realizing that you are wretched, pitiable, poor, blind, and naked".*
Revelation 16:15 *"Behold, I am coming like a thief! Blessed is the one who stays awake, keeping his garments on, that he may not go about naked and be seen exposed!"*

REGRESSION IN CHAPTER THREE

It is important to note the progression – or regression – in chapter three. From being naked and not ashamed there is the regression to being naked and afraid. Here the Holy Spirit reveals to us the change from being good and in God's image to becoming evil and unable to function as the good image of God. Our first parents had knowledge from God that was to them a joy. Now the knowledge they have brings them fear. Before they listened to the Serpent they lived in the Bond of communion with God. Now they hide from him in fear. Earlier they lived in harmony with each other as husband and wife. Now they refuse to accept personal blame and our first father put the blame on our first mother and even on God for Adam says, "the woman whom you gave to be with me, she gave me fruit of the tree and I ate". Our first mother blames the Serpent who deceived her and she ate.

THE LORD GOD CLOSES AND OPENS THE WAY OF LIFE. 3:14-24

The first to be addressed by the LORD God is the Serpent. Though the Serpent is cursed in terms of an animal from vs. 15 it becomes clear that the Serpent is a person. There will be enmity between the offspring of the woman and the offspring of the Serpent. The offspring of the woman shall bruise the head of the Serpent and the offspring of the Serpent will bruise the heel of the offspring of the woman. The LORD God did not reveal when that would happen. The concept "offspring" indicates future events. The future event will definitely bring the downfall of the Serpent and the victory of the offspring of the woman. The coming downfall of the Serpent means that the LORD God is closing the Way of Life for the Serpent and the offspring of the Serpent. This, however, does not mean that the Serpent has succeeded in closing God's Way of Life for men that God began. The Opener of the Way of Life (1:1) continues what he started..

This is clear from the verses 16-24. The LORD God does not make a full end with our first parents. Our first mother will give birth to children with increased pain. No longer will there be harmony between her and her husband. Her desire will be for him but he will rule over her. Our first father will no longer till the ground in joy and ease. The ground is to be cursed because of man's breaking of the Bond of the Covenant. Thorns and thistles will obstruct growth of vegetation and impede man's labor. The life of man will be subject to death, *"for you are dust and to dust you shall return"*.

IN SPITE OF ALL THIS THERE IS A FUTURE FROM GOD

That future will bring war between the offspring of the woman and the offspring of the serpent. The outcome of that war will be victory for the Seed of the Woman and defeat for the Serpent. *"I will put enmity between you and the woman, and between your offspring and her offspring; he shall bruise your head, and you shall bruise his heel."* (Genesis 3:15) These words of God have often been called **"The First Gospel"**.

GOSPEL MEANS GOOD NEWS OR GLAD TIDINGS

Throughout the Scriptures this means the glad tidings of the victory of God over his enemies. Genesis 3:15 is assurance of the victory of God over the Serpent fulfilled in the birth and life of Jesus Christ, the Seed of the Woman. Luke 2:11-12 reveals to us *"And the angel said unto them, Fear not: for, behold, I bring you good tidings of great joy, which shall be to all people. 11 For unto you is born this day in the city of David a Saviour, which is Christ the Lord"*. God has made true the good news of Genesis 3:15.

Vs. 20 brings us **a remarkable revelation.** God the Holy Spirit shows us here that our first father understood what the LORD God was doing. In ch. 2:23 our first father spoke with joy of the Woman – Isha. God had made her bone of Adam's bones and flesh of his flesh. He spoke those words while he still was good, the image of God. In 3:20 our first father speaks again. Because of his and his wife's sin death has come into the world. Our first father heard the verdict, *"for you are dust and to dust you shall return"*. God closes the Way of Life and immediately opens the Way in grace. It is then that our first father speaks words of insight into the grace of the LORD God. " *The man called his wife's name Eve, because she was the mother of all living"*. Our first father called our first mother by a name of life, of opening: Eve, mother of all living. Praise be to God for his infinite mercy!

Then in **3:21** the LORD God puts his seal on this in caring grace,*" And the* LORD *God made for Adam and for his wife garments of skins and clothed them"*. In spite of our first parents breaking the Bond of the Covenant with the LORD God their nakedness is covered, they are clothed. The LORD God did not withdraw from the man and woman whom he created in his image. The Way of Life remained open for the LORD God was present to save! With that revelation Moses is sent to deliver Abraham's offspring from slavery in Egypt.

THE LIE THAT GOD HAS WITHDRAWN FROM THE EARTH AND MANKIND

For several centuries Abraham's descendants had been exposed to the Egyptian lie of the withdrawal of the gods because of the rebellion of mankind against the gods.
Jan Assmann, *The Search for God in Ancient Egypt.* p. 6 middle, *"The Egyptian concept of "divine presence" is the theme of this volume. It proceeds from the impression that this divine presence was something special, that is, that the Egyptians felt especially close to their deities. It also proceeds from the fact that the time when the sun god ruled over deities and humankind together, both groups dwelling on earth, was over, and that with the withdrawal of the gods to the sky, the world, which was now subject to history, was in need of kingship as a second best solution in the struggle against the gravitational pull of the alienation of meaning.*

JVR: If I understand Assmann correctly then the Creator has withdrawn leaving mankind to the corruption that came about because of rebellion. No longer is there communication between the gods and mankind. The next best thing is to have a king who takes the place of the Creator by enforcing and enacting "Maat", universal order and prosperity. (Compare this with Israel asking for a king as revealed in the Book of Samuel.)

THE TRUTH THAT THE LORD (YHWH) CONTINUES TO BE PRESENT

During the centuries that Abraham's descendants sojourned in Egypt their lives had become hard; they were enslaved and forced to endure the death of their sons. During that time is indeed seemed that the LORD God of their father Abraham had withdrawn. There was no word, nor help from him.
When YHWH sent Moses with Word and Wonder to deliver them he also sent them the truth that from the beginning the LORD had been present to open the Way of Life in the face of death. Genesis three assures them, and us, that the LORD is present to save and to clothe the naked.

The good news that the LORD is present and never forsakes the work of his hands should always have caused the people to trust him. Throughout Scripture we find that God's people acted as if he were not there. Just follow the pattern of deformation and reformation throughout history. Follow also the pattern of the LORD God never leaving his Way of Life which he had begun in the beginning, *berëshit!*

Our strong God has "made full" the promise he made in Genesis 3:15 : The Seed of the Woman has come. He has defeated Satan, sin and death. He is Jesus Emmanuel, God with us. God is present to clothe the naked by incorporating the believers into Jesus Christ. However, in our New Testament times many continued the pattern of treating God as an absentee landlord and rebelled against him (See Matt. 21:33 ff. the Parable of the Tenants).

THE CHERUBIM WITH THE FLAMING SWORD

The same light of God's Glory that brought life to a dead planet earth (Genesis 1:1 ff.) now bars the way to the Tree of Life.

QUESTIONS

1. Why would God not want man to live forever?
2. Do you know examples of mankind searching for the tree of life?
3. Describe some of the modern efforts made to enable man to live forever.
4. Why is death still the "last enemy"? (1 Corinthians 15:26)
5. When the LORD sent Moses to deliver his people from Egypt by doing God's wonders the LORD repeatedly stated concerning the Hebrews that he did this so **"That you may know that I am YHWH"** Exodus 6:6-7; 7:5; 7:17; 8:22; 10:2; 14:4 and 18.
6. What does this tell you about the state of Israel's faith?

4 *Now Adam knew Eve his wife, and she conceived and bore Cain, saying, "I have gotten a man with the help of the LORD."*

TO CONSIDER

1. How does verse one show that Eve trusted the presence of the LORD?
2. Where did Eve base her trust on?
3. Whom did Eve expect her firstborn son to be?

4:-2-7 The LORD was not pleased with Cain's offering but He was pleased with Abel's offering. It seems that the text does not tell us what the difference between the two offerings was. The context, however, does show us the difference. The LORD God told Cain why his offering had not been accepted. The words, *"If you do well"* tell us that Cain was not doing well. Cain is warned that if he continues not to do well he may go all the way and let sin be his master. The opposite of doing well is doing evil. Proverbs 15:8 may shed light on the matter of the two sacrifices: *"The sacrifice of the wicked is an abomination to the LORD, but the prayer of the upright is acceptable to him"*. See also 1 Samuel 15:22 *"... to obey is better than sacrifice."*

God the Holy Spirit reveals in the following three New Testament verses that Abel was righteous and Cain was of the evil one. Moreover, Israel's sin at Baal Peor was like the sin of Cain.

Matthew 23:35 *"so that on you may come all the righteous blood shed on earth, from the blood of innocent Abel to the blood of Zechariah the son of Barachiah, whom you murdered between the sanctuary and the altar"*.

1 John 3:12 *"We should not be like Cain, who was of the evil one and murdered his brother. And why did he murder him? Because his own deeds were evil and his brother's righteous"*.

Jude 11 *"Woe to them! For they walked in the way of Cain and abandoned themselves for the sake of gain to Balaam's error and perished in Korah's rebellion"*.

DISCUSSION POINT

In these first verses of chapter 4 is the LORD God absent or present from the family of Adam and Eve?

Verses 8-24

QUESTIONS

1. The LORD God deals with Cain in a covenantal manner. What do we mean by that? How is that revealed in the verses 3-16?
2. Which two things in the judgment of the LORD weighed heavy for Cain?
3. Cain married, had children, his children produced practical scientific firsts. Where was the worship of the LORD God in all that?
4. What filled the life of Cain and his offspring?
5. Do we find the style of Cain and his offspring in the culture, society, and productivity of our present world?
6. In connection with that let us discuss the position of Christian believers taking part in the present race for achievement in science and technology. Is it a blessing from God when the research of people has positive results when they deny the presence of God to bless?
7. What is the consequence of living without the presence of the LORD God?
8. Was killer Lamech merely the first gang-buster? How should we qualify him?
9. It often is expressed that the line of Seth is the line of the Seed of the Woman and the line of Cain the line of the Seed of the Serpent. How do you react to that?

Verses 25-26

SETH

QUICK QUESTION

1) Eve bore another son and honoured God as the giver. What does that tell you of the presence of God in Adam's household?

In **verse 26** it is revealed that at the time of Enos people *"began to call upon the name of the LORD"*. The most current understanding of verse 26 is that at the time of Enos people began worship services with formal calling on the Name of YHWH. This certainly is not excluded but is not the first or most important. Here is stark contrast between the style of the offspring of Cain and the style of the offspring of Seth. In Cain's line there was success outside the presence of the LORD. In Cain's line there was human achievement. No help from the LORD was needed nor prayed for.

The offspring of Seth believed with the heart that God, though far away, is present to hear prayer. His Name YHWH means HE IS! Calling upon the Name of the God WHO IS was done in trust that *"Our help is in the Name of the LORD the maker of heaven and earth"* (Psalm 121). See also Deut. 4:6. Throughout God's history with his people this line is continued in Scripture. It always concerns the presence of the LORD who opens and closes the Way. While opening the Way for his own the LORD closes the Way for those who belong to the Serpent.

QUESTIONS

1. Why is the LORD God present among his believers today?
2. How is the LORD God present among his believers today?
3. What did our Saviour promise before he ascended into heaven? Matt. 28.
4. When did Israel forget about calling upon the Name?
5. What does the LORD withhold from us when we do not call upon his Name, thereby denying his presence?

Genesis 5

This chapter contains a list of generations spanning from Adam to Noah. Seemingly this is an intermezzo without special meaning. However, at least two things should be taken into consideration. For the first we go back to chapter three. For the second we look ahead in chapter five.

In chapter three God the Holy Spirit reveals enmity between the seed of the Woman and the seed of the Serpent. The Seed of the Woman will ultimately be victorious over the seed of the Serpent. There will be an Opener of the Way of Life born of the woman but without the will of man. The generations of chapter five show the line of the seed of the Woman. The fact that this list ends with Noah, whose name means 'rest', makes us look ahead to chapters six and following. With Noah, God keeps the Way of Life open.

The second item that the list of generations in chapter five shows is the growth of population. This is the line of Seth and Enosh in whose days they trusted the presence of the LORD and called upon his Name. This is the time of which chapter six reveals that man multiplied upon the earth but not for the better. Deformation, corruption, sets in.

W.H. Gispen in his commentary on Genesis[9] concludes from the Masoretic Hebrew Text that the Flood took place 1656 years after Adam was created. The year of the flood was also the year Methuselah died.
In 5:21-24 it is Enoch who is singled out. Twice we read that Enoch "walked with God". It is impossible to walk with God unless God is pleased to walk with you. The preposition "with" tells us that there is a walking together. Enoch was the seventh from Adam and prophesied (Jude:14). That means that the time of corruption was proceeding in his time. His walk with God certainly was noticed as a witness for the Opener and Closer of the Way. God took righteous Enoch out of this corrupt world. (Heb. 11:5)

QUESTIONS

1. What does the length of life of Adam and his descendants tell you about the passing on of the knowledge of YHWH as the Opener and Closer of the Way of Life?
2. In 5:1-3 we twice meet the words likeness, image. Is there a difference between the two?
3. What kind of likeness, image, would Adam pass on to Seth?
4. Could this already harbour the seeds of deformation that was to come?
5. What does this tell us about our sons and daughters whom we today father in our likeness?
6. In whose likeness do we, sinners, need to be created?
7. In 5:21-24 we are told of Enoch the great-grandfather of Noah. Above, I stated that Enoch was a witness in his day for the Opener and Closer of the Way. What do you find about this in Jude:14-16?
8. Upon whom did, and does this judgment come?

---

[9] W.H. Gispen, Genesis, COT, p. 198, Kampen, 1974

9. What does Heb. 11: 5-6 reveal to us about faith?
10. How is the case of Enoch used in these verses to teach us about faith?

Genesis 6:1-8

6 *When man began to multiply on the face of the land and daughters were born to them,* **2** *the sons of God saw that the daughters of man were attractive. And they took as their wives any they chose.* **3** *Then the LORD said, "My Spirit shall not abide in man forever, for he is flesh: his days shall be 120 years."* **4** *The Nephilim were on the earth in those days, and also afterward, when the sons of God came in to the daughters of man and they bore children to them. These were the mighty men who were of old, the men of renown.*
5 *The LORD saw that the wickedness of man was great in the earth, and that every intention of the thoughts of his heart was only evil continually.* **6** *And the LORD regretted that he had made man on the earth, and it grieved him to his heart.* **7** *So the LORD said, "I will blot out man whom I have created from the face of the land, man and animals and creeping things and birds of the heavens, for I am sorry that I have made them."* **8** *But Noah found favour in the eyes of the LORD.*

In the verses 6-8 of chapter six YHWH reveals himself as the Closer of the Way of Life for the wicked. The words about Noah show YHWH as the one who keeps the Way of Life open.
Several points need our attention:
1. There is the matter of the sons of G(god) and the Nephilim.
2. Then there is the matter of the 120 years.
3. Lastly there is the matter of favour or grace in verse eight.

THE SONS OF (G)GOD

The sons of G(god) saw the daughters of man, found them attractive, took them as their wives, came in to them and they bore children to them. Writing G(god) forces us to make a decision. Are these sons of the only true God or are they men who act as gods?

Whenever a Bible Version has sons of *God* with the capital G, this indicates that apparently the translators decided that these "mighty men" were in the sphere of the only true God. This would raise the possibility that they were angels. In most commentaries on the book of Genesis the position is indeed taken that angels, or fallen angels, had children by "the daughters of man". The mixing of these divine beings with human beings would then result in a race of giants. However, are angels and humans compatible? Are angels able the copulate and conceive children? The Lord Jesus Christ revealed that angels do not marry (Mat. 22:30). The first chapter of Genesis reveals that God created all living things "according to their kind" (Genesis 1; and I Corinthians 15:35-41). The angels are created of a different kind than men.[10] Angels are "ministering spirits" (Heb. 1:13-14). The spirit kind of angels is incompatible with the corporeal kind of women. Since the sons of god cannot be angels who were they? It is our conviction that these were not sons of God but sons of god. We make that choice based on Genesis 6:4 and Num. 13:33 and many other passages referred to below. [11]

Genesis 6:4 *"The Nephilim were on the earth in those days, and also afterward, when the sons of God came in to the daughters of man and they bore children to them. These were the mighty men who were of old, the men of renown".*
Numbers 13:33 *"And there we saw the Nephilim (the sons of Anak, who come from the Nephilim), and we seemed to ourselves like grasshoppers, and so we seemed to them."* (For Anakim see also Dt 1:28; 2:10; 9:2; Jos. 11:21; 14:12)

From these verses we learn that Nephilim, or sons of god, were on the earth **both before the flood as well as after the flood**. That is what the word "afterward" indicates. It is important to note that the Nephilim, or sons of god, existed both before the flood and after the flood. The Nephilim that were observed in Canaan by the spies Moses sent in were called *"sons of Anak who come from the Nephilim"*. Biblical revelation draws a line from the wicked Nephilim, or sons of god, from before the flood to the wicked Nephilim, or Anakim, in Canaan after the flood. The wickedness of the Nephilim from before the flood was so great that God destroyed them by the flood. The wickedness of the Nephilim in Canaan after the flood was so great that God destroyed them and dispossessed them as he had promised to Abraham (Genesis 15:16).

An example of a "son of god" after the flood is Gilgamesh the king of Uruk in Mesopotamia. Gilgamesh is partly historical and partly mythical. [12]The saga about him is called the Gilgamesh Epic. Parts of this Epic date as far back as 2600 B.C. In the Epic, Gilgamesh is called divine. In later history this trend of being divine continued. Vivid examples are Nebuchadnezzar, king of Babylon and Darius, king of the Medes (see the book of Daniel). A mark of all these "sons of god" was that they rose up against the only true God and his people, and defied him in utter wickedness. Remember Goliath whom David slew because he defied the living God of Israel (1 Samuel 17). One more example of a so-called son of god is the king of Tyre. In Ezekiel 28: 1-10, we find the following,

28 *The word of the LORD came to me:*
² "Son of man, say to the prince of Tyre, Thus says the Lord GOD:
"Because your heart is proud,
and you have said, 'I am a god,
I sit in the seat of the gods,
in the heart of the seas,'
yet you are but a man, and no god,
though you make your heart like the heart of a god—

---

[10] I thank Dr. A.J.Pol for pointing this out to me.

[11] M.G. Kline Divine Kingship and Genesis 6.1-4 WTJ 24:2 (May 62) p. 188 Libronix dig. Ed.
W.H. Gispen, Genesis, COT, p. 220 ff. Kampen, 1974

[12] D.B.Redfort, Egypt, Canaan and Israel in Ancient Times, p. 38. Princeton N.J. 1992

³ you are indeed wiser than Daniel;
no secret is hidden from you;
⁴ by your wisdom and your understanding
you have made wealth for yourself,
and have gathered gold and silver
into your treasuries;
⁵ by your great wisdom in your trade
you have increased your wealth,
and your heart has become proud in your wealth—
⁶ therefore thus says the Lord GOD:
Because you make your heart
like the heart of a god,
⁷ therefore, behold, I will bring foreigners upon you,
the most ruthless of the nations;
and they shall draw their swords against the beauty of your wisdom and defile your splendor.
⁸ They shall thrust you down into the pit,
and you shall die the death of the slain
in the heart of the seas.
⁹ Will you still say, 'I am a god,'
in the presence of those who kill you,
though you are but a man, and no god,
in the hands of those who slay you?
¹⁰ You shall die the death of the uncircumcised
by the hand of foreigners;
for I have spoken, declares the Lord GOD."

[For those of you who have knowledge of the Hebrew language I am inserting an entry from the Theological Wordbook of the Old Testament. The importance of this entry is the reference to the verb *fala*, to be wonderful. Throughout the OLD TESTAMENT the attribute "wonderful" is used for YHWH. The wonderful deeds of the LORD are the "niflaoth". The Nephilim considered themselves "wonderful" as the LORD is "wonderful". The Nephilim were not products of angels copulating with humans but pretenders. Pretending to be divine they defied the living God in the line of Lamech the descendant of Cain.]

[**Nephilim TWOT 1393a** נְפִילִים (*nĕpîlîm*) **giants, the Nephilim** (Gen 6:4; Num 13:33, only). While some scholars attempt to relate this term etymologically to *nāpal*, I, via the noun *nēpel* "untimely birth" or "miscarriage" (as productive of superhuman monstrosities), think a more likely reconstruction is the proposal of a root *nāpal* II, akin to other weak verbs, *pûl* II "be wonderful, strong, mighty," *pālā'* "be wonderful," and even *pālâ* "separate, distinguish," *pālal* "discriminate." This pattern of semantically related groups of weak verbs with two strong consonants in common is a notably recurrent phenomenon in Hebrew lexicography. Actually, the translation "giants" is supported mainly by the LXX and may be quite misleading. The word may be of unknown origin and mean "heroes" or "fierce warriors" etc. The

RSV and NIV transliteration "Nephilim" is safer and may be correct in referring the noun to a race or nation.] M.C.F.[13]

THE LINE OF THE "SONS OF GOD" PRETENDERS CONTINUED IN THE NEW TESTAMENT

Some examples are: Acts 13:6-12 Elymas, the magician; a false Jewish prophet who opposed the Gospel and was blinded. The antichrist(s) mentioned in I and II John; the Son of Lawlessness spoken of in 2 Thessalonians 2:3-4 who will sit in the temple of God proclaiming himself to be God. The line ends with the defeat of Antichrist foretold in Revelation 20.

THE 120 YEARS

There are two possible interpretations. The 120 years may be the time allowed for repentance before the flood. Mostly the 120 years are taken as the average length of a person's life after the flood.

BUT NOAH FOUND FAVOR IN THE EYES OF THE LORD (VS. 8-9)

To interpret the word favor in this verse we are forced to proceed to the verses 9-12. The adversative "but" tells us that Noah was different from all the corrupt people around him. " ... *all flesh had corrupted their way on the earth*" ...but ... "*Noah was a righteous man, blameless in his generation. Noah walked with God.*" Try to picture Noah "*in his generation*". Around Noah were the "sons of god", the Nephilim, who considered themselves as powerful as God and opposed to God. Noah occupied the lonely position of a man who is *righteous, blameless, walking with God*. The words *righteous* and *blameless* are best understood if we turn to the time when YHWH spoke with Abraham. Genesis 15:6 "*And he believed the LORD, and he counted it to him as righteousness*". That is how Noah was righteous. Noah believed the LORD and the LORD accounted righteousness to Noah in his favor. Let us do the same with the word *blameless*. Genesis 17:1, "*walk before me and be blameless*". Both with Noah and with Abraham the word *blameless* is the translation of a Hebrew word that first of all means "*whole*" *(tam)*. Our English word "wholeheartedly" excellently fits what God says about Noah and to Abraham. When you walk with the LORD you must do that wholeheartedly, or loyally, with an undivided heart. Noah walked with God in faith, believing him and practicing that in his walk of life among a corrupt population. In that walk he did not turn to the left or to the right for he was loyal to God with an undivided heart.

What God the Holy Spirit reveals in verse three about God's favor upon Noah is foundational for the whole of the Bible. A Christian must walk with God with a believing heart, be loyal to Christ, and practice serving him with an undivided heart.

---

[13] Fisher, M. C. (1999). 1393 נפל. In R. L. Harris, G. L. Archer, Jr. & B. K. Waltke (Eds.), Theological Wordbook of the Old Testament (R. L. Harris, G. L. Archer, Jr. & B. K. Waltke, Ed.) (electronic ed.) (587). Chicago: Moody Press. Walvoord, J. F., Zuck, R. B., & Dallas Theological Seminary. (1985). The Bible Knowledge Commentary: An Exposition of the Scriptures (Ge 5:3–6:4). Wheaton, IL: Victor Books.

Genesis 6:1-8

DISCUSSION TIME

1. Do angels have bodies or are they spirits?
2. Are angels able to copulate?
3. Are angels of the same created "kind" as mankind?
4. Which translation do you think is better, "sons of God" or "sons of god"?
5. Which other name is used for the "sons of god"?
6. This name shows that these "sons of god" considered themselves "wonderful". Who alone is truly "wonderful"?
7. Using the word "*afterward*" in verse four, decide whether there were also Nephilim on earth after the flood.
8. After the flood the Nephilim were also called by another name. Which name is that?
9. Gilgamesh was a historic king of early Uruk about whom a long saga was written. What word is used for Gilgamesh that shows that he was one of the "sons of god"?
10. The Nephilim chose for themselves from all fair women whomever they chose. That is a typical "harem" description. Which book in the OLD TESTAMENT relates a similar situation?
11. Give examples of men who sat on thrones as if they were God.
12. Who will sit in the temple of God as if he is God (N.T.)?
13. Can Psalm 90 help us to decide to what the 120 years refer?
14. The sin of mankind before the flood was full. So was the sin of the Canaanites at the time of the Exodus. What was the character of this sin?
15. Describe Noah's position among the men of his generation.
16. Using what is revealed about Abraham, describe why Noah was "righteous in the eyes of the LORD".
17. What does it mean to be "blameless"?
18. Understanding what "righteous" and "blameless" means, examine whether Noah found favor in the eyes of the LORD because of works or because of grace and faith.
19. Noah "walked with God". How is it possible to walk with divine Majesty?
20. What does Noah's walk with God tell you about the presence of God?
21. Having read those notes decide how YHWH used his presence with Noah to convince the enslaved Hebrews in Egypt of his power to be present to save them.

Genesis 6:10-14; 17-18

(These are the generations of Noah.)
10 *"And Noah had three sons, Shem, Ham, and Japheth. Now the earth was corrupt in God's sight, and the earth was filled with violence. And God saw the earth, and behold, it was corrupt, for all flesh had corrupted their way on the earth. And God said to Noah, "I have determined to make an end of all flesh, for the earth is filled with violence through them. Behold, I will destroy them with the earth. Make yourself an ark of gopher wood. Make rooms in the ark, and cover it inside and out with pitch".* **17***"For*

behold, I will bring a flood of waters upon the earth to destroy all flesh in which is the breath of life under heaven. Everything that is on the earth shall die. But I will establish my covenant with you, and you shall come into the ark, you, your sons, your wife, and your sons' wives with you."

I combined these verses because, together, they represent the core of the account of the flood.

QUESTIONS

1. The first part of the core shows the reason why God brought about the destruction of mankind by means of a flood. What was that reason?
2. The second part of the core in verse eighteen shows the reason why God saved Noah and his family. What was the reason for this?
3. God's promise to Noah to save him and his family was sealed by covenant. What do you know about the parts of God's covenant?
4. Can you find those parts in verse eighteen?
5. Is God present here in closing and opening the Way of Life?
6. Where in the Heidelberg Catechism do you also find the terms "opening and closing".
7. Can you see a line from Genesis 6 to church censure today?

Genesis 6:18-22

18 But I will establish my covenant with you, and you shall come into the ark, you, your sons, your wife, and your sons' wives with you. 19 And of every living thing of all flesh, you shall bring two of every sort into the ark to keep them alive with you. They shall be male and female. 20 Of the birds according to their kinds, and of the animals according to their kinds, of every creeping thing of the ground, according to its kind, two of every sort shall come in to you to keep them alive. 21 Also take with you every sort of food that is eaten, and store it up. It shall serve as food for you and for them." 22 Noah did this; he did all that God commanded him.

QUESTIONS

1. What position did Noah have in his family with respect to the Covenant?
2. Who were included in God's covenant with Noah?
3. What does that tell you of God's covenant with his believers today?
4. Compare the words "come" in verse 18 regarding men, and "bring" regarding animals in verse 19. What does this tell you of the distinction between men and animals in the sight of God?
5. Look at all the provisions Noah was told to take along. Was that just to keep them alive in the ark? Or was this also with respect to the future?

Genesis 7

7 Then the LORD said to Noah, "Go into the ark, you and all your household, for I have seen that you are righteous before me in this generation. ² Take with you seven pairs of all clean animals, the male and his mate, and a pair of the animals that are not clean, the male and his mate, ³ and seven pairs of the birds of the heavens also, male and female, to keep their offspring alive on the face of all the earth. ⁴ For in seven days I will send rain on the earth forty days and forty nights, and every living thing that I have made I will blot out from the face of the ground." ⁵ And Noah did all that the LORD had commanded him. ⁶ Noah was six hundred years old when the flood of waters came upon the earth. ⁷ And Noah and his sons and his wife and his sons' wives with him went into the ark to escape the waters of the flood. ⁸ Of clean animals, and of animals that are not clean, and of birds, and of everything that creeps on the ground, ⁹ two and two, male and female, went into the ark with Noah, as God had commanded Noah. ¹⁰ And after seven days the waters of the flood came upon the earth.

DISCUSSION TIME

1. This is the second time that YHWH uses the word *righteous* for Noah. The first time was in Ch. 6:9. There the words *righteous* and *blameless* are used side by side. Apparently righteous and blameless are two similar concepts. Please go back to p. 35 and again study the section, "But Noah found favor in the eyes of the LORD (vs. 8-9)". What do we learn there about 'righteous' and 'blameless'?
2. Another word the LORD uses is *"generation"*. Does the LORD use this in general or did He use "this generation" as Judge and judgmentally?
3. In the book of Leviticus the LORD gives instructions about clean and unclean animals with respect to sacrifices and to eating. Was that totally new or did the LORD make this known much earlier already?
4. Why would there be seven pairs of clean animals preserved in the ark and only one pair of unclean animals?

7:11-12 In the six hundredth year of Noah's life, in the second month, on the seventeenth day of the month, on that day all the fountains of the great deep burst forth, and the windows of the heavens were opened. ¹² And rain fell upon the earth forty days and forty nights.
In 7:11-12, and throughout chapter Eight, we find exact dating of years and months and days of the flood as well as of Noah and his family. What does this tell you about writing and record keeping in those early days of history? Were Noah and his family underdeveloped Neanderthals?

In 7:16 we read *"And those that entered, male and female of all flesh, went in as God had commanded him. And the LORD shut him in"*.

QUICK QUESTION

- YHWH was personally present to safeguard Noah, and all that were with him in the ark, by closing the ark. This carried a message to the descendants of Abraham enslaved in Egypt. What was that message?

7:22 to 8:1a

*22 Everything on the dry land in whose nostrils was the breath of life died. 23 He blotted out every living thing that was on the face of the ground, man and animals and creeping things and birds of the heavens. They were blotted out from the earth. Only Noah was left, and those who were with him in the ark. 24 And the waters prevailed on the earth 150 days. **8:1a** But God remembered Noah and all the beasts and all the livestock that were with him in the ark".*

DISCUSSION TIME

- The biblical revelation of the world-wide flood is denied and attacked by many a person. In these notes I accept the account of the world-wide flood as revealed by God himself. The truth of the Word of God about which we confess in the Reformed Confessions stands firm and our adherence to that truth must not waver. Does any one of you object?
- The transition from chapter seven to chapter eight is characterized by the verb *"remembered"*. When you read of Noah and his family shut in the enclosure of the ark for almost a year, knowing they were not just alone in the world but alone without a "world", put yourself in their place. How do you feel?
- Lost? Forsaken? Now read 8:1 and let the glory of what God did sink in: "**BUT GOD REMEMBERED**"! What we read here of the LORD remembering is again foundational for the whole of the Bible. The LORD is the Opener of the Way of Life. The LORD also is the Closer of the Way of Life. The LORD God sent the flood closing the Way of Life for every one on earth, **but the LORD God remembered the covenant He had made with Noah and his family. When the LORD God remembers HE ACTS AND DOES WHAT HE PROMISED.** I repeat: That is foundational. We find this in our personal lives. The LORD God remembers his own. He keeps his own on his Way of Life and leads them forward through time into eternity.
- Is remembering only an action of storing information in your brain?
- Can you find instances in the Bible of the LORD God remembering?
- Can you find instances of the LORD God remembering in the history of the Church?
- Can you find instances of the LORD your God remembering you in the course of your life?
- God remembered Noah. Were Noah's sons and their wives forgotten?

Genesis 8

TO CONSIDER

- In 8:7-8, what is the difference between a raven and a dove? Clue: Pay attention to the dove needing to come back for seven days and to what the dove finally had in its beak. Notice the raven going to and fro. What did the raven in the meantime subsist on?
- How long were Noah and his family in the ark?
- In 8:15 God said to Noah, *"Go out of the ark"*. Was a command needed?
- 8:19, *"All went out by families."* Compare this with Genesis 1:21 and 6:20. There we find a word that virtually is the same as family. What is that word?
- Can you use this to show that the theory of common origin of men and other creatures is false?
- What does Noah's sacrifice tell you about God as the owner of all the earth?
- Almost all versions of the Bible translate that *"God smelled the pleasing aroma"*. Later on in Exo. 29:18 the same translation "pleasing aroma" is given. Noah's name means "rest". The Hebrew word for "pleasing" is related to Noah's name. The LORD God smelled an aroma that brought "rest". The destruction because of the curse on wickedness had ended. What had been laid to rest with God? His
- God spoke this *"In His heart"*. What does this tell you about your God?
- 8:22 *"While the earth remains"*. Does this herald the possibility that at one time in the future the earth would not remain?
- In 8:21 the LORD states *"I will never again curse the ground because of man"*. Does this mean that the LORD takes back what he said to Adam in Genesis 3:17? Is there a difference?
- In 8:21 the LORD says, *"for the intention of man's heart is evil from his youth"*. What does this tell us about our heart?
- What did the Lord Jesus say about the heart?
- What did the LORD God promise through the prophet Ezekiel in 36:26?
- For the first time we hear of sequence of four consecutive seasons. Was this new or old? In other words, were there already seasons before the flood? Could it be that the conditions had changed because of the flood?
- Is the LORD God still Master of the four seasons?
- What should man's attitude be before God regarding the four seasons?
- Have you ever heard of the possibility that the flood changed the vapor shield around the earth? Add to this the formation of mountain ranges etc.

Contrast between Noah's sacrifice to the LORD (YHWH) and Egyptian placating of Hathor

Noah's sacrifice

- Going back to chapter 6:8-9 we read the following: *⁸ But Noah found favor in the eyes of the LORD. ⁹ These are the generations of Noah. Noah was a righteous man, blameless in his generation. Noah walked with God.*
- It was this Noah who after the flood brought a sacrifice to the LORD. His sacrifice was pleasing to the LORD, just like Abel's sacrifice had been pleasing to the LORD. Noah was not placating an angry God. Noah was honoring the LORD who carried Noah and his family through on the LORD's Open Way of Life and in his presence. Noah's sacrifice was like the later *"Peace Offerings"*. The peace offerings were a celebration of restored peace between the LORD and the forgiven sinner and his family. If the LORD still was angry he would not have accepted Noah's sacrifice.

Egyptian placating of Hathor

The Egyptians, and also the idolaters among Israel, poured out a libation of alcoholic drink to placate Hathor, the Queen of Heaven.

The goddess Hathor had been instructed by her "father" Re (the sun) to destroy rebellious mankind. She was successful but had to sleep before she could finish her task. Re regretted his decision and found a way to save a remnant of mankind. He ordered red ochre to be mixed with seven thousand jugs of beer so it would look like blood. The blood thirsty Hathor drank herself into a stupor. Hathor forgot about destroying the remnant of men. Re decided that he no longer could cope with wicked man and decided that he and his gods would withdraw from the earth. Re ascended up on the back of Hathor who took the form of a cow with fierce horns but also with a nourishing udder. The underside of Hathor became the sky and in and around her body gods supported her as stars. Hathor continued to be a threat to mankind and needed to be placated repeatedly. For centuries fierce, angry, Hathor was placated on the "Feast of Hathor" by baking cakes for her and by pouring out libations of strong drink to her. Besides being portrayed as a cow Hathor also was portrayed as a woman curved as the sky. The festivities for Hathor became occasions for revelry and drunkenness. The placated side of Hathor was portrayed by the softness of the gold of a golden calf. Instead of a cow with fierce horns she was also portrayed in the way of a golden calf.

See: H. Frankfort Kingship and the Gods p. 170, "Elsewhere the late king as son of Re attempts to establish his relationship with the heavenly family by calling himself a calf – and a golden one, at that – thus sharing the sun's substance*: 'Pepi comes to thee, O father of his! Pepi comes to thee, O Re! A calf of gold, born of heaven, The soft one of gold, formed by the Hesa-cow {Pyr. 1028-30}*
(n. 53 p.385) "the Hesa-cow is here the heavenly cow, in Heliopolis she counts as the mother of the Mnevis bull". [14]

---

[14] H. Frankfort Kingship and the Gods, Chicago 1948, 1978

THE PLACATING OF HATHOR AS THE QUEEN OF HEAVEN BECAME CUSTOMARY IDOLATRY IN ISRAEL EVER SINCE THE SOJOURN IN EGYPT

The cult of Hathor was prominent throughout Egypt and the Sinai desert. In the Sinai desert are the ruins of a temple to Hathor dating back to the 12th Dynasty of Egypt. Taking into account that Israel's Exodus from Egypt was during the Eighteenth Dynasty it becomes clear that the Hebrews in Egypt were tainted with the placating of Hathor in the cult of Hathor. They practiced the cult of Hathor in the desert at Mount Sinai. There they made themselves a calf of gold and danced with revelry. (Exo. 32). In 1 Kings 12 we read that Jeroboam upon his return from Egypt made two golden calves calling them Israel's gods. The link from Jeroboam to Egypt is telling. In Canaan the cult of Hathor had as equivalent the cult of Astarte. Reading through the Old Testament one repeatedly comes across Israel's apostasy with the cult of Astarte. A very clear example of Israel and the cult of the "Queen of Heaven" is found in the book of Jeremiah (One time in 7:18 and four times in 44:17-19 and 25). After the deportation to Babylon a small remnant is left. They fear the Babylonians and make ready to flee to Egypt. They do so defying the promise of the LORD to protect them. Instead of trusting the LORD they trust in the Queen of Heaven. They say, *"But we will do everything that we have vowed, make offerings to the queen of heaven and pour out drink offerings to her, as we did, both we and our fathers, our kings and our officials, in the cities of Judah and in the streets of Jerusalem. For then we had plenty of food, and prospered, and saw no disaster."* It is significant that they mention the Queen of Heaven while seeking refuge in Egypt. It is also significant that they refer to "their fathers".

THE LONG STANDING SIN OF PLACATING THE QUEEN OF HEAVEN IN SPITE OF MOSES' ACCOUNT OF THE LORD'S ANGER AND MERCY REVEALED IN GENESIS 6-9

Although it is revealed that there were those among the Hebrews who were faithful to the God of Abraham, the majority apparently served the idols of Egypt including the cult of Hathor. The LORD sent Moses to them to call them away from this idolatry.

The account of the LORD's covenant of grace with Noah, all mankind, even creatures and nature, should have convinced them to trust in the mercy and power of the LORD (YHWH) to deliver them from slavery in Egypt and to bring them out to the promised land. This, above all, should have brought them on their knees before the LORD to serve him alone and trust his everlasting Covenant and walk on his Way of Life.

(See also the added Appendix "The Myth of the Heavenly Cow and the Queen of Heaven.)

The Heavenly Cow after the outermost shrine of Tutankhamun The Destruction of Mankind - the New World Order & the Magic of Re by Wim van den Dungen Antwerp, 2006 - 2008.

Erik Hornung, Der Eine und die Vielen p.59 Darmstadt 1973

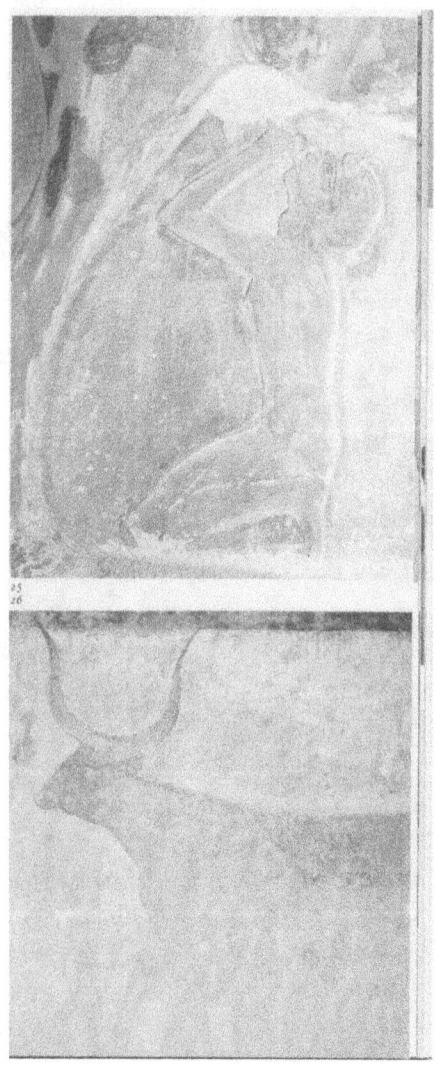

The goddess Hathor. An ancient sky goddess, she was first represented as a cow; later she was as a woman with a cow's head, and then as a goddess as in the preceding picture, myths she and Isis are often confused: Hathor in some traditions is the mother of Horus, though the stronger and more important myth of Isis and Osiris gives the mother's part to Isis,. But confusion is further increased by the habit of iconographers of portraying Isis with cow's horns. However the cow attribute is principally Hathor's and she was often described as the nurse of Horus, which led to the pictures of her as a cow suckling the pharaoh. The one thus engaged is Amehotep II, in a wall painting from his tomb.

Hathor was also believed to suckle the dead, to them on their journey to the next world, a function depicted in the mural from the tomb of Rameses VI in the Valley of the Kings. Hathor was goddess of light-hearted pleasure and love, music and dancing. R. Patrick, All Color Book of Egyptian Mythology, New York, 1972, p. 31

Noah's sacrifice to the LORD (YHWH) and Egyptian placating of Hathor.

Discussion Point

1. Why would the Egyptians offer Hathor strong drink?
2. What does "placating" mean?
3. Why would the remnant in Jeremiah's day choose for the Queen of Heaven (Hathor) instead of the LORD (YHWH)?
4. Since when did the wicked among God's people pour out libations of strong drink to Hathor?
5. Did God's covenant people ever try to placate the LORD their God?
6. Did the LORD God give his people sacrifices to placate him?
7. What does Psalm 50 teach us about placating the LORD God (Micah 6:6-8)?
8. Who was foreshadowed by the sacrifices of the LORD?
9. The Son of God, our Saviour Jesus Christ, died on the cross to take away our sin and guilt. Did he placate his Father?

Genesis 9

QUESTIONS

1. Can you find the LORD's new beginning in 9:1-3?
2. Which earlier words of the LORD do these verses remind you of?
3. There is a difference. What is that difference?
4. Verse four contains a prohibition: "… do not eat flesh with its life, that is it's blood". Is there a special reason for this?
5. Consider scalp hunters and head hunters. Why did they do that (Animism)?
6. Verse 5 and 6 contain what we call the principle of capital punishment. Is this an instruction from God or a command from God?
7. Is this command obeyed in our society?
8. Is capital punishment a safe procedure in any society?
9. How can capital punishment be made safer?
10. Whom do we dishonour if we murder willfully?
11. Could the second half of verse 6 help us in answering the previous point?
12. Genesis 9:7 repeats Genesis 1:28. Is there a difference in circumstances?
13. Did the command to be fruitful and multiply have anything to do with the coming of the promised Seed of the Woman?
14. Is the command to be fruitful and multiply valid today?
15. Does that have anything to do with God's Open Way of Life?
16. What is the difference between the maximum and optimum number of children procreated by parents today?
17. The first meaning of covenant is 'bond'. To what did the LORD God bind himself in the verses 8-11?
18. Has the LORD God always been true to this covenant?
19. The nature gods of ancient Egypt were capricious, willful. The Hebrew slaves needed to know that the God of Noah was not capricious. How did the rainbow teach them the steadfast love and faithfulness of the LORD?
20. Who sees the rainbow first?
21. What does the LORD God remember when he sees the Rainbow?
22. What must we remember when we see the Rainbow?
23. The covenant given by the LORD God concerned humans, animals and vegetation. Did this make it a lesser covenant?
24. How does this covenant fit into the whole of God's Open Way of Life?

(ESV) reads," *Whoever sheds the blood of man, by man shall his blood be shed, for God made man in his own image*".

This is the third time that God the Holy Spirit refers to man being made in the image of God. This time we are reminded of the fact so that we will not murder. God the Holy Spirit apparently deems it necessary to repeatedly remind mankind that man was created in the image of God. The way we are instructed about the life and the blood of our neighbour refers back especially to Genesis 1:26-27 and 2:7. Both passages reveal that man at his creation was not made part of God. Man is separate from God. God *"formed the man from the dust of the ground and breathed into his nostrils the breath of life, and the man became a living creature."* (Genesis 2:7)

The image of God can never mean that men came forth from the body of God. Here we touch on God's necessary correction of the pagan teaching of ancient Egypt. From olden times the Egyptian teaching of the origin of man was that man had come forth from the body of the god Ra. Here follows a quote from the *"Instruction of King Merikare"*. This Instruction is from the Old and Middle Kingdom and copies are found in the time of the New Kingdom. This covers the time of the sojourn of the Hebrews in Egypt. **M.Lichtheim**[15] on p. 106 records this line from the Instruction, *"They are his images, who came from his body, he shines in the sky for their sake."*

For centuries the Hebrews in Egypt were exposed to the falsehood that men came forth from the body of the god. This falsehood was blasphemous toward God for it lowered uncreated God to the level of created man. It was equally blasphemous toward God for this falsehood elevated mortal man to the level of the eternal living God. Throughout the history of Israel in the Old Testament many of the Israelites never came loose from the falsehood learned in Egypt. They made images of God looking like mortal man just like the pagans of whom we find written in Rom. 1:23, *"and exchanged the glory of the immortal God for images resembling mortal man and birds and animals and creeping things"*.

Today the biblical revelation that man is created in the image of God unmasks the falsehood of the theory that man evolved from gases and cells billions of years ago. This is not only an untruth about the origin of man, it is blasphemous toward God for it denies him the honour of being the Creator of mankind in his image.

QUICK QUESTION

How are the falsehoods about the origin of man of Egypt and the Darwinian Evolution Theory alike? They both…

---

[15] Miriam Lichtheim, Ancient Egyptian literature Vol. I University of California Press, Berkely, 1976, 2006

Genesis 9:18-28.

QUESTIONS

1. Verse 19 reveals that from the three sons of Noah *"the people of the whole earth were dispersed."* What is anticipated by this verse?
2. Noah became drunk. Noah was the first one to plant a vineyard. Possibilities are that he was ignorant of the potency of fermented grapes. The other possibility is that Noah was a drunkard. What does the Bible indicate?
3. What is so special about the nakedness of a father?
4. Noah curses Canaan and not Ham. Ham repeatedly is called the father of Canaan instead of just Ham. What does this tell you about the responsibility of a father for his son within the family unit?
5. Ham told his brothers. Was this mere telling? It merited a curse.
6. Did the curse on Canaan take effect later on?
7. The feast for Hathor, the Queen of Heaven, involved imbibing and drunkenness. How would Genesis 9:18-28 be a warning to Israel? See pages 45-46.
8. Noah does not first bless Shem. Whom does he first bless?
9. God blesses us. Is it not rather strange for us to bless God? Yet throughout the Bible we find that the believer blesses God.
10. Some Bible translations change "blessed be the God etc" to "praised be the God etc." Let's take into account that in Genesis 1 and 2 "bless" and "good" are synonymous. What are we really saying of God when we bless him? We say that he is totally ……..
11. How did the blessing of Shem take effect in later times?

Foundation Lines in chapters 10 and 11

Beginning from Genesis 1:1 we have maintained that the book of Genesis is God's foundation book. Genesis 1:1 immediately reveals to us God at the beginning of his Way of Life. We are told that God created man in his image and placed him on his Way of Life, man and woman. God's Way of Life is attacked by the Serpent who as an anti-god lures man and woman from the Way of Life to the Serpent's way of death. The Bond with YHWH God is broken. The presence of YHWH God in his own creation is challenged by the Serpent. The LORD God shows that no one and nothing can stop him from completing his Way of Life and his purpose with man and woman on his Way. YHWH Elohim does not withdraw but remains present with man and woman and assures the defeat of the Serpent through the Seed of the Woman (Genesis 3:15).

From that time the Holy Spirit reveals in this foundation book two main lines. There is the line of the Way of Life with the presence of YHWH in Bond with his chosen people. Opposite to the Way of YHWH runs the line of the way of the Serpent. He places idols of himself into the hearts of unbelievers leading the nations astray. Throughout history the Serpent is even partially successful in placing idols of himself into the hearts of YHWH's chosen people. This happened to such a great extent that only Noah and his family pleased the LORD God and were preserved in Bond with God on his Way of Life. This happened in the world-wide flood in which all rebels perished. After the flood the line of the Seed of the Woman in enmity with the Seed of the Serpent continued. The curse on Canaan and the blessing on Shem shows the continued presence of the LORD God able to bless and able to curse. God's Way of Life prevails over the Serpent's way of death. With chapters 10 and 11 we have come to the time after the flood.

In the chapters 10 and 11 we once more find the two foundation lines. In the line of Shem we find the LORD God continuing his Way of Life. In the line of Canaan and Nimrod we find the line of the Serpent rebelling against the LORD God as anti-god and luring man to his way of death. The line of Shem is found at the end of chapter ten and once more at the end of chapter eleven. In chapter ten the line of Shem looks back to Noah and his blessing. At the end of chapter eleven the line of Shem links forward to Genesis twelve and following chapters with the blessing of Abraham, *In your Seed shall all nations be blessed.*

In contrast to this, the line of Canaan and Nimrod in chapter ten links forward to the rebellion in the plain of Shinar with the building of the tower that would reach into heaven. In the person of Nimrod, the line of anti-god, in rebellion against the LORD God and his Way of Life becomes foundational for the coming of the Anti-Christ. (I Chron. 1:1:10; Micah 5:6)

DID THE LORD GOD NOT KNOW WHAT WAS GOING ON IN BABEL? WHY DID HE NEED TO COME DOWN TO SEE?

The key to the answer for this question is the foundation line of the presence of God. Since God sent Cain away from his presence the line of the presence of God became twofold. The LORD God remained present with the righteous, Seth, Noah, Shem, Abraham etc. The presence of the LORD God was not with the wicked who rebelled against God and considered themselves equal or above God. The presence of the LORD God was not with Nimrod who built the Tower in defiance against God. Neither was the presence of the LORD God with the Pharaohs who built the Pyramids. That the LORD God came down to see does not reveal his ignorance but reveals that the LORD God is not with the wicked who rebel against him. When the LORD God comes to see them and their wicked efforts against him then he comes in judgment and presence to destroy wickedness and rebellion.

THE DIVISION POINT IN THE "TABLE OF NATIONS" IN CHAPTER 10 "PELEG"

Genesis 10:25
"To Eber were born two sons: the name of the one was Peleg, for in his days the earth was divided".

Before Peleg, the population of the earth was centralized geographically and of one language. During the life of Peleg the rebellion in the plain of Shinar took place. However, the person instigating the rebellion is not Peleg from the line of Shem but Nimrod, son of Cush, of the line of Canaan.

NIMROD, AND THE ORIGIN OF THE REBELS WHO BUILT THE TOWER REACHING INTO HEAVEN

The way Nimrod is described as *a mighty hunter before the LORD* may sound favorable. Some authors, however, raise the possibility that the ending of the name **"Nimrod"** is from the verb *marad - to rebel*. [16] This leads me to doubt whether *"before (lifenë) the LORD"* is favorable. The Hebrew preposition *lifenë* may also be translated as an adversative (contrast).

Nehemiah 13:4 may serve as an example of 'before' (*lifenë*) as against the LORD
The verses 1-3 describe the LORD's prohibition against the presence of Ammonites in the assembly. Contrary **(lifenë)** to this prohibition the priest Eliashib had provided the Ammonite, Tobiah with a large room in the area of the storehouses for the temple service. The differ bible veresions read this as a preposition of time and translate "before". The context, however, clearly calls for the adversative "contrary": this is in harmony with the root meaning of *pnh*, to turn.

The rebels who begin to build the tower migrated from the East to the plain of Shinar and settled there (Genesis 11:2). The maps show the mountainous regions of the Zagroz to the East of the plain of Shinar. The Mount Ararat where the ark came to rest after the flood is marked as part of the North wing of the Zagroz. This plain is where Nimrod began his empire by first building Babel. Nimrod's rebellion against the LORD and the people building the tower with its top in the heavens must be seen in opposition to the LORD's punishing wickedness and corruption with the Flood.

---

[16] Walter Brueggemann, Genesis, p. 92, John Knox Press, Atlanta 1982. W.H. Gispen, Genesis, p. 327, Kampen, 1974.

A tower, with its top reaching into the heavens would defeat God's punishment. The people were building their safety-valve. Such a tower would be a refuge against the anger of the LORD and safely perpetuate the human race. This continuing of the human race would not be with the LORD on his Way of Life. It would be a continuing of the human race on the Serpents way of death. Nimrod, builder of Babel and rebel against God was part of the people who came from the East to the Plain of Shinar to build the tower.

Notice **first** of all that the nations listed in chapter 10 were known to Moses who had been educated as adopted son of Egypt's Daughter of Pharaoh. The **second** item we must notice is that the list of nations in chapter 10 shows the political and geographical map from both before and after the dispersion of the nations revealed in chapter 11. The **third** item we must note is that in the list of nations in chapter 10 the nation of Israel is missing. Israel was still in bondage to Egypt and its idolatry when Moses wrote this list.

CONCLUSION OF THE THREE BOUNDARIES MENTIONED ABOVE

The list of nations, given to Moses by the LORD, in chapter 10, gives us the political and international situation at the time of Israel's Exodus from Egypt and entrance into the Promised Land. **The list of nations in chapter 10 forms a message of YHWH to the enslaved descendants of Abraham in Egypt in the light of chapter 10.**

The nations listed in chapter 10 owe their geographical and political place to YHWH. The LORD God gives to each nation and people its place. The enslaved descendants of Abraham in Egypt have no land of their own. However, they have the assurance of a land of their own (Genesis 15). The LORD God sent Moses to set the Hebrew slaves free and bring them into a land of their own prepared for them by the God of Noah and his descendants, Shem, Abraham, Isaac and Jacob (See Dan. 7:27). Egypt and its idols have no power to prevent YHWH from allotting to Israel its promised inheritance where the Seed of Abraham would become the blessing to the nations. At the "beginning" God opened the Way of Life with power to complete his road at the last day. No tumult of nations can prevent him from doing so. This message is to wean people with idols in their hearts away from the Serpent's way of death to the true God in an Exodus to his Way of Life.

The LORD God armed Moses with the completed book of Genesis. This was the main tool for Moses in the mission from YHWH to wean Abraham's descendants from Egyptian idolatry and to bind them to YHWH and his truth. We are to approach chapter 10 with that insight in mind.

Verses to read with Genesis 10-11.
Deut.32:8-9
⁸When the Most High gave to the nations their inheritance,
when he divided mankind,
he fixed the borders of the peoples
according to the number of the sons of God.
⁹But the LORD's portion is his people,
Jacob his allotted heritage.

Isaiah 14:12-14
¹²"How you are fallen from heaven,
O Day Star, son of Dawn!

How you are cut down to the ground,
you who laid the nations low!
¹³You said in your heart,
'I will ascend to heaven;
above the stars of God
I will set my throne on high;
I will sit on the mount of assembly
in the far reaches of the north;
¹⁴I will ascend above the heights of the clouds;
I will make myself like the Most High.'

Daniel 7:24-27
²⁴As for the ten horns,
out of this kingdom ten kings shall arise,
and another shall arise after them;
he shall be different from the former ones,
and shall put down three kings.
²⁵He shall speak words against the Most High,
and shall wear out the saints of the Most High,
and shall think to change the times and the law;
and they shall be given into his hand
for a time, times, and half a time.
²⁶But the court shall sit in judgment,
and his dominion shall be taken away,
to be consumed and destroyed to the end.
²⁷And the kingdom and the dominion
and the greatness of the kingdoms under the whole heaven
shall be given to the people of the saints of the Most High;
their kingdom shall be an everlasting kingdom,
and all dominions shall serve and obey them.'

Genesis 11:6 (ESV)

⁶ And the LORD said, "Behold, they are one people, and they have all one language, and this is only the beginning of what they will do. And nothing that they propose to do will now be impossible for them".
¹⁷וַיֹּאמֶר יְהוָה הֵן עַם אֶחָד וְשָׂפָה אַחַת לְכֻלָּם וְזֶה הַחִלָּם לַעֲשׂוֹת וְעַתָּה לֹא־יִבָּצֵר מֵהֶם כֹּל אֲשֶׁר יָזְמוּ לַעֲשׂוֹת׃

Usually בָּצַר is translated with *gather / cutting off* as grapes. The translation *impossible* makes the builders of the Tower the subject. However, if we translate "prevented" as a sense of cutting off, then the LORD God is the subject. They cannot be prevented from doing anything. Their science and technological skill is limitless. That is because the LORD God has created man in his image. Here the veil that rests upon man's left-over abilities after the fall into sin is partly lifted. On the one hand it is tribute to the greatness

---
Biblia Hebraica Stuttgartensia: With Westminster Hebrew Morphology. 2001 (electronic ed.) (Ge 11:6). Stuttgart; Glenside PA: German Bible Society; Westminster Seminary.

of God creating man in his image. On the other hand it is evidence of the great threat the Serpent, and those who belong to him, are to the LORD's Way of Life and his purpose with his creation. There was, however, one way in which men could be prevented from accomplishing against God whatever he would. That is, by God the Creator taking back from mankind the gifts of understanding and knowledge. When God disturbed their language the impact was greater than merely not being able to talk together.

THE IMPACT OF THE LORD'S TAKING BACK HIS GIFTS

The impact of depriving them of being able to counsel together is tremendous. Not only do they speak differently, they are unable to pool their resources. Depriving them of the gift of language the LORD God robs them of the high level of science and technology they possessed. They used this level to rise up against God and his Way and create their own Way. The Nephilim spirit from before the flood is present in ever increasing power. The impact of the LORD's taking away their power reduces them to "primitive" men. Here is no evolution of the species but a devolution from the height of God's good creation. This was caused by the LORD God taking back his gifts.

The impact was not only felt in the Plain of Shinar. There is at least one area where the impact of the LORD's taking back his gifts is evident and that is Egypt.

The building of the Great Pyramids at about 2500 B.C. is still an enigma to all scientists. The level of scientific knowledge of measurement and design, as well as the technological skill needed to cut, transport and place up high blocks of tons of weight, cannot be understood against the background of primitive man. Added to the enigma is the fact that just as suddenly as the Great Pyramids were constructed, the Egyptians stopped building them. Only small pyramids appear. The pyramid afforded their dead god, Pharaoh, the opportunity to rise up to heaven and continue a life after life as god. What happened to rob the Egyptians of their great skill to provide a living place for their dead god, Pharaoh? The LORD God robbed them of their skill and reduced them to primitive men.

The height of Nimrod's rebellion and proud rising above the LORD God in Shinar was also found in Egypt. The Pyramid of Unas, the last recorded Pharaoh of the Fifth Dynasty had proud and cruel words written in his tomb. These words are copied among the so-called Pyramid Texts. Part of these is the so-called Cannibal Song. The Song shows how Unas expects to be in the after-life. Here are some excerpts:

"Unas is the bull of heaven
Who rages in his heart,
Who lives on the being of every god,
Who eats their entrails
When they come, their bodies full of magic
From the Isle of Flame".

"Unas eats their magic, swallows their spirits:
Their big ones are for his morning meal,
Their middle ones for his evening meal,
Their little ones for his night meal,
And the oldest males and females for his fuel.
The Great Ones in the northern sky light him fire

For the kettles' contents with the old ones' thighs,
For the sky-dwellers serve Unas,
And the pots are scraped for him with their women's legs.[18]

The language of this text shows the character of one who belongs to the Nephilim who were cruel among men and rebels against God, considering themselves almighty. After Unis the central power of the Pharaoh started to decline and the power of the rulers of the nomes (or city states) began to rise leading to a slide that ended in the First Intermediate Period.[19] This shows that the LORD God disturbed the unity of the rebels against God both in Shinar and in Egypt. Some scholars place Nimrod, Babel and the Great Pyramids, at about 2500 – 2300 years B.C.

The Hebrews entered Egypt about 1750 B.C. They observed the mighty Pyramids as evidence of Egypt's superior, even divine, power. They also could observe the end of the Great Pyramids and the appearance of smaller pyramids and more mastabas (more flat and rectangular tombs known as 'eternal house'). The LORD God sent Moses with his foundation book Genesis including the record of his action in the Plain of Shinar. Thereby, the LORD declared to the enslaved descendants of Abraham in Egypt, that it is not the idols of Egypt that have power to raise up and to bring down, but only YHWH. *"That they may know that I am the LORD"*.

The line of rebels against God who consider themselves God reaches far. It reaches Nebuchadnezzar and others in the O.T., Caesar Augustus, and others, in the New Testament. Finally, it reaches past the 'Withholder 'of Thessalonians, to 'Antichrist 'in Revelation ch. 20 and his defeat, the Glory of the LORD filling the earth in the recreation of heaven and earth.

APPENDIX ON PYRAMIDS

Jan Assmann, The Search for God p. 33 "They, too, were signs of the divine on earth and sprang from the desire to establish a relationship between the heavens and the earth – or, as it is stated in the Hermetic tractate to make the earth in to the image "imago - of heaven." Compare this to the Tower of Babel.

I.E.S. Edwards, The Pyramids of Egypt Penguin Books Ltd. Reprint 1976 pp. 293-4
"The Egyptians were not the only ancient people of the Middle East who believed that heaven and the gods might be reached by ascending a high building; a kindred trend of thought prevailed in Mesopotamia. At the centre of any city in Assyria or Babylonia lay a sacred area occupied by the temple complex and a royal palace. Within the temple complex was a high brick tower known as the Ziggurat. Describing the Ziggurat of Babylon - the supposed origin of the Biblical Tower of Babel - Herodotus states:
'In the middle of the precinct there was a tower of solid masonry, a furlong in length and breadth, upon which was raised a second tower, and on that a third, and so on up to eight. The ascent to the upper towers is made on the outside, round all the towers. ... On the topmost tower there is a spacious temple, and inside the temple stands a great bed covered with fine bedclothes, with a golden table by its side. There is no statue of any kind set up in the place, nor is the chamber

---

[18] *Miriam Lichtheim, Ancient Egyptian literature Vol. I, p.36-7 University of California Press, Berkely, 1976, 2006*

[19] See Appendix

occupied of nights by anyone but a single native woman who, as the Chaldeans, the priests of this god, affirm, is chosen for himself by the deity out of all the women of the land. They also declare - but I for my part do not credit it -that the god comes down in person into this chamber, and sleeps upon the couch.'

Ziggurats, like the Pyramids, were given individual names, the Ziggurat of Sippar, for example, was called the 'House of the Staircase of the bright Heaven' - a name which itself emphasizes that the building was considered as a link between heaven and earth. The resemblance between the two edifices does not, however, extend to sepulchral realms, for the Ziggurat was certainly not a tomb, whereas every Pyramid was intended for that purpose."

Cyril Aldred, The Egyptians, p. 107 (Fifth Dynasty)
"Four of the early kings of this dynasty moved the sites of their tombs to Abusir so as to avoid comparison with the mighty works of their predecessors at Giza, which indeed was never again used as a royal burial place. But six kings of the Fifth Dynasty also built special temples to the sun god in the Abusir area and these enterprises must have depleted their treasuries; so much so that from the reign of Isesi the practice was relinquished."

N. Grimal, A History of Ancient Egypt, pp. 75-80 (Dynasty V 2510-2460 Userkaf first kind of this Dynasty) p. 75

"The new order was also expressed through the Horus name chosen by Userkaf, which was Iry Maat (He who puts Maat into practice), Maat being the universal harmony that the creator had to maintain. By this means Userkaf was deliberately claiming responsibility for the (p.76) *maintenance of the whole of creation".*
(JVR: Note the similarity with Nimrod, Babel, and the Nephilim.)

P. 78 "Isesi … chose the name Djedkare – "The Ka of Ra is stable" – as his *nsw-bity* (king of Upper and Lower Egypt) title, thus placing himself under the protection of Ra; but he did not build a sun temple and he had himself buried at southern Saqqara, nearer to Memphis and in the vicinity of the modern village of Saqqara".

The Tecnicists of the Last Days. Egbert Schuurman, A Confrontation with Technicism As the Spiritual Climate of the West *Vol. 58: Westminster Theological Journal Volume 58.* 1996 (1) (71–84). Philadelphia: Westminster Theological Seminary.

In section 7 of Christian Faith and Culture, Schuurman writes:
"Now I come to an assessment of the position of Christians in the technological culture. Generally speaking, Christians have accepted the ongoing technological development uncritically. The main reason for this is that they have been spellbound by the positive effects of technology, such as the enrichment of material life, the enhancement of the duration of life, the turning of the tide in the struggle against poverty and illness, and so on. Are those things not all signs of the kingdom of God? Abraham Kuyper, founder of the Free University (as a Christian institution) in Amsterdam in 1880, stressed the need for technology. But he did not recognize the danger of technicism, the ideology of technology. Perhaps he was already a victim of it himself, when he wrote in his *Pro Rege* that the wonders of technology are greater than the miracles of Jesus. Although Simon Ridderbos has made clear that Kuyper's view of technology was rather more complex,[41] it cannot be denied that Kuyper

warns more against dance, theater, and card playing than he does against a technicistic trend in our culture.

The error of Kuyper—as a child of his time—was that he accepted technology as free of problems; in a certain sense he accepted technology as neutral with respect to values. Kuyper, and most Christians with him, forgot the biblical warning that since the Fall, technology in the sense of the craftsman's technique has been a power that leads astray—the more so as the ages roll by. Technology has more than once been a means to rival God, to make a name for oneself on the earth and to build a culture without God, that is, a Babel-culture. The origin is the Fall into sin: human autonomy with a main connection to (classical, small-scale) technicism.

At its core, technicism wants to save human life without God. The Bible teaches us about Cain, about Lamech, about the building of the Tower of Babel, about Nebuchadnezzar, and so on. The Renaissance, Descartes, and the Enlightenment have given a new impetus to the modern form of technicism, namely, absolutized scientific-technological control. The possibilities of modern technology have enhanced the ideology of technology. This ideology is mainly implicit. The gravity of this situation is often concealed by the numbing effects that emanate from a sweeping material prosperity. Most Christians have failed to give much attention to technicism."

JVR: It is noteworthy that Schuurman connects our age of technicists with the technicists of the Tower of Babel. I would like to venture an opinion about the "Babel spirit" of our age. It seems to me that mankind presently is finding a way around God's act of taking back his gifts. The disunity of nations is still there. However, scientists and technicists have developed means of being able to pool their resources and tools. This started with mathematics and developed into calculus. Presently the language of science and technology is not words but numbers and symbols. The International Space Station is evidence of the nations pooling their resources. The mapping of routes for space travel is not based on empirical proof but originates with the calculations of space and time working out the principles laid out since Einstein. I repeat that this is an opinion but I add that this is also a challenge to Christian scientists and technicists to pursue this line of thinking.

DISCUSSION POINTS GENESIS 10-11

1. Israel is not mentioned among the "table of nations" in chapter 10. What do you conclude from this?
2. Chapter 10:25 mentions that in Peleg's day the earth was divided. Was chapter ten written before or after the so-called Tower of Babel?
3. Which mountains are to the East of the Plain of Shinar?
4. Who built Babel as the beginning of his empire?
5. His name tells us that he was a rebel against God. Explain.
6. What does this rebel against God have in common with the Nephilim of chapter 6?
7. Were these rebels against God "sons of God" or "sons of god"?
8. What does the Tower of Babel have in common with the Pyramids of the "Old Kingdom" of Egypt?
9. Did the LORD God have to come down to see because of ignorance (Genesis 11:5)?
10. With whom is the LORD God present and with whom is the LORD God not present?
11. What difference does it make for you whether the LORD God is present with you or not present?

12. What was the level of intelligence before God disturbed the language of mankind?
13. What gifts did the LORD God take back from mankind when he disturbed their language?
14. How does this explain the mystery of building the Tower and the gigantic pyramids?
15. The LORD God sent Moses to the enslaved descendants of Abraham with the Rod of God to perform God's miracles. How do the Words of God in Genesis 10 and 11 reveal to the estranged Hebrews the power of the LORD God to deliver and to lead them out on his Way of Life?
16. Evolutionists speak of "primitive man". Was mankind before Babel primitive? Or did man become "primitive" because God took back his gifts? Was there evolution or devolution?
17. How could scientists and technicists overcome the disturbance of language? Could they find other means to communicate and pool resources?
18. Check 2 Thessalonians 2:1-4. How do these verses show us the progression of the rebels against God in the "last days" in which we live?
19. How do these verses reveal to us that the God of "bereshit, at the beginning" is in control and not antichrist?
20. How does Revelation 20:7 ff. relate to 2 Thess. 2:7?
21. Check Revelation 18 and see the end of the Babylonian spirit and practice.

The Book of Genesis Continued from Genesis 11:27

THE RELATION OF GENESIS 11:27-32 TO THE REST OF THE BOOK OF GENESIS

The genealogy of Shem in the last verses of chapter eleven forms the bridge to the next 39 chapters of the book of Genesis. In the chapters 12 to 50(ESV), the families of Abraham, Isaac and Jacob stand out. Interpreting these chapters we could easily fall into the trap of becoming so wrapped up with the events of these families that we forget what comes first when interpreting the Words of God. God and his road are first. God is placing Abram on his Way of Life and in the midst of idolatrous nations.

In the previous chapters we have met the nations of Ur/Babel and Egypt. From chapter 12 on Canaan is added. The LORD God draws Abram away from the idolatrous nations of Mesopotamia and places him and his descendants in the midst of Canaanites. Abram is also brought into contact with the idolatrous nation of Egypt. In the midst of all this the LORD God sets Abram apart for himself and calls Abram to trust and obey.

As we continue our studies of the book of Genesis we will keep in mind the first addressees, Abraham's descendants enslaved in Egypt. With the contents of this book the LORD God equips Moses to teach the enslaved Hebrews to trust the LORD God and to warn them away from trusting in Egyptian idols.

With the book of Genesis the LORD God addresses not only the Hebrews but also peoples of all times, including us. Christians must study the Scriptures as "Children of Abraham by faith" (Rom. 4 and Gal. 3). This applies also to us who presently are studying the book of Genesis. Our position in this fallen world unites us with the descendants of Abraham in the fallen world of ancient Egypt. The first chapter of our continued studies is chapter twelve. In this chapter the LORD God confronts the enslaved Hebrews, together with peoples of all times and places, with the call, "Come out of her". This call is first heard in Genesis twelve and rings loudly throughout the Scriptures and into our ears.

Chapter 12

1 *Now the* LORD *said to Abram, "Go from your country and your kindred and your father's house to the land that I will show you".*

The first word in chapter twelve, here translated as 'now', was usually translated with the copula 'and'. The copula 'and' shows that chapter twelve is progressing from what went before. With chapter twelve we enter a new phase in God's road of life but it is still the same road. This is further emphasized by the fact that it is the same LORD God who spoke to Noah who now is speaking to Abram. It is the first time we get to hear of Abram but it is not the first time we hear revelation of the LORD God.

THE LORD'S COMMAND TO ABRAM

"Go from your country". The Hebrew word for 'country' shows that Abram is to leave the very soil he has walked on, and he has worked with.
"Go from your kindred". The wording conveys to us the picture of Abram having to leave the people among whom he was born and with whom he grew up.
"Go from your father's house". The circle of people Abram has to separate himself from becomes even narrower. Abram is to become completely isolated and on his own.

PATRIARCHAL JOURNEYS TO AND FROM HARRAN

WHAT KIND OF SOCIETY WAS ABRAM TO SEPARATE HIMSELF FROM?

The geographical location the LORD God called Abram away from is Ur. (Genesis 11:28, 15:7; Josh. 24:2; Neh. 9:7; Acts 7:2,4,7; Heb. 11:8). Ur was originally built by Nimrod who also built Babel. Instead of repeating ourselves lets go back and find the societal information in **Discussion Points** on chapter 10. The LORD God called Abram out of the land of rebels who set themselves up against the LORD God. It was the land of the Ziqqurats with their "staircase to heaven".

DISCUSSION POINTS

1. What did we learn about Abram's environment in Ur?
2. In the Bible we find the LORD's call to come out of Babel repeated a number of times. It will be good for us to look those up using reference texts: Isaiah 48:20; Revelation 18:4.
3. How does that call come to us Christians today?
4. Are there similarities between the society Abram was called out of and our present day society?
5. Does the call "to come out" determine the way we bring the call of the Gospel to our neighbor and in mission?

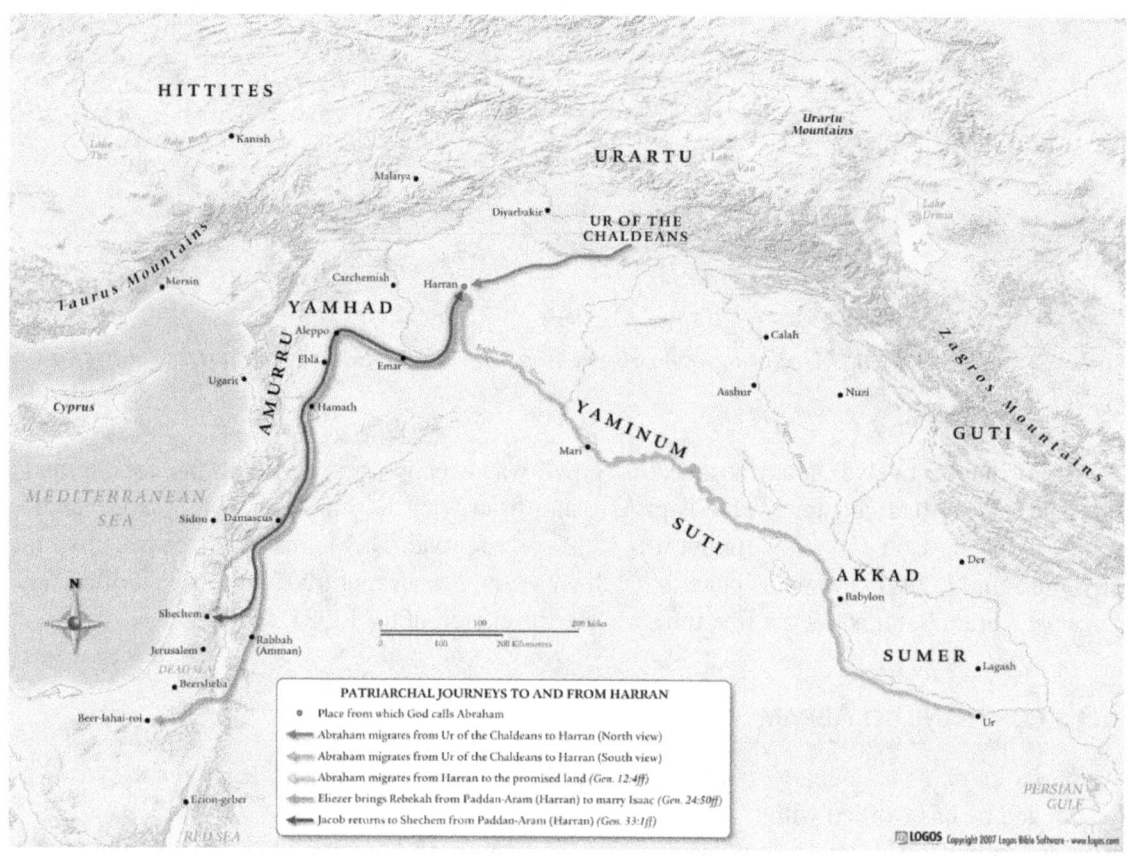

Page 72. Exported from Logos Bible Software 4, 11:27 AM October 4, 2013.

7. What does Joshua 24:14 tell us about whom the descendants of Shem served when living in Ur of the Chaldeans? *"Now therefore fear the LORD and serve him in sincerity and in faithfulness. Put away the gods that your fathers served beyond the River and in Egypt, and serve the LORD."*
8. Which river is meant by "the River"?
9. The LORD God promised Abram to show him the land to which he was ordered to go. What does this tell you about the presence of the LORD with Abram?

The LORD God gave the book of Genesis to Moses to convince the enslaved Hebrews of his presence to lead them out. As he showed their father Abram so he would show them where to go. The enslaved descendants of Abraham needed to trust the presence of the LORD for two reasons:

1. They were tainted with the idolatry of the Egyptians who did not know of a presence of their gods. The gods had left and were out of reach. (Please look back the section that discusses, *"The Truth that the LORD [YHWH] continues to be present"*)
2. By his presence the LORD God was going to lead them out of slavery into the freedom and inheritance of the land he would show them.

QUESTIONS

1. Christians are on their way to the New Earth. Who has promised to be with us all the way and through all times?
2. Where do you find this in the Gospels?
3. Is this the same as the presence of the LORD going with us?

Genesis 12:2

"And I will make of you a great nation, and I will bless you and make your name great, so that you will be a blessing."

QUICK QUESTION

Earlier the LORD God spoke words of promise to many individuals like Noah. What new word of promise do we find in this verse?

Never before did the LORD God reveal this Word until he spoke to Abram. The words "bless" and "blessing" in this verse remind us of the time that the LORD God created Adam and Eve. When God saw that what he had created was "good" he "blessed". God's blessing creates a "good" situation with "good" results.

QUESTIONS

1. In which place on earth would the LORD God make Abram into a great nation?
2. The LORD God said that Abram would be a blessing. How did the LORD God empower Abram to be a blessing?
3. The blessing of the LORD God would make Abram's name "great". What kind of "greatness" would this be?
4. What obligation did this lay upon Abram?
5. Christian believers are descendants of Abraham by faith. Are Christian believers empowered by God to be a blessing?
6. Does the LORD God have a great nation for Abraham today?
7. Where is this great nation to be found now?

Genesis 12:3

*3 I will bless those who bless you, and him who dishonors you I will curse, and in you all the families of the earth shall be blessed." (In Hebrew: "and him who **curses** you I will curse.")*

DISCUSSION POINT

What benefit does the presence of the LORD have for his travelling chosen people – then – and – now? Please show from the New Testament that all the families of the earth indeed have been blessed in Abraham.

Genesis 12:4-5 (ESV)

"4 So Abram went, as the LORD had told him, and Lot went with him. Abram was seventy-five years old when he departed from Haran. 5 And Abram took Sarai his wife, and Lot his brother's son, and all their possessions that they had gathered, and the people that they had acquired in Haran, and they set out to go to the land of Canaan, and they arrived there."

TO CONSIDER

1. Did Abram have a map to go by?
2. How did Abram know the way from Ur to Haran and from Haran to Canaan?
3. Our road through life is not the same as Abram's road. Yet there is an important similarity. Which one?
4. Did Lot belong to Abram's father's house or did Lot belong to Abram's house?
5. What obligation did Abram have toward Lot?

Genesis 12:6-7 (ESV)

"6 Abram passed through the land to the place at Shechem, to the oak of Moreh. At that time the Canaanites were in the land. 7 Then the LORD appeared to Abram and said, "To your offspring I will give this land." So he built there an altar to the LORD, who had appeared to him."

The map on page 58 is small but the blue line that bends off and ends at Shechem is visible. In the verses 6 and 7 we are told several facts.

1. At Shechem there was a great tree with the name of Moreh.
2. At the time of Abram's arrival the Canaanites were in the land.
3. The LORD appeared to Abram.
4. The LORD makes a promise.
5. Abram built an altar there to the LORD.

Central to these five points in verses 6 and 7 is number three: *"The LORD appeared to Abram"*. From the time that the LORD God had spoken to Abram in Ur and Haran the LORD God had not appeared to Abram. Now Abram has arrived in Canaan in the vicinity of the town of Shechem and there the LORD God *"appeared"* to Abram. This means that there is progression. The LORD God no longer only makes himself heard in words. He now also makes himself visible to Abram. We are not told in what form the LORD God appeared to Abram but there is a visible presence. Abram had trusted the LORD God to *"show"* him the land and the LORD God had shown himself true: Abram had arrived. Upon arrival Abram found the presence of the LORD there near a tree named *Moreh*. Linguistically the name *Moreh* is related to the words *"show,"* and *"appeared."*

The name of the tree kept the memory alive that the LORD God had **shown** Abram the land and had **appeared** to him there. **Moreh:** tree of seeing. Tree of making Abram see with the eye of faith a promised future: *"To your offspring I will give this land."* The tree is called *"great"* not because of its size. Terebinth trees are broad shade trees but not extra tall. The tree is called *"great"* because there the LORD God revealed himself in words as well as visibly. The LORD's visible presence guaranteed that the LORD's words revealing the future would become true.

It will be worth our effort when we keep track of the concept of "seeing" in the Bible. Throughout the Bible the LORD God continues to make his people see him in his Words and in his visible presence. God's visible presence will especially come true in the arrival of the promised seed of Abraham, Jesus Christ the Son of God.

*"So he built there an **altar** to the LORD, who had appeared to him."* He built the altar **while the Canaanites lived in the land.** Abram did not yet own a grain of soil in Canaan, **but the LORD God did!** Just like Noah built an altar, and sacrificed to the LORD God after being placed on God's earth immediately after the Flood, so Abram built an altar to the LORD immediately after arriving among the Canaanites of the land. He did so believing the words of promise spoken by the visible presence of the God of all the earth. The altar marked Shechem and Moreh as a place where the LORD God had appeared. From then on the places where the LORD God appeared to his people were places where the LORD God made his Name to be **remembered** (Exo. 20:24).

Many interpreters of Genesis 12 approach Shechem and the tree named Moreh from a background of idolatrous heathen oracles. God the Holy Spirit however, does not present Genesis 12 in that way. Central is the LORD God progressing on his Way of Life in a fallen world. In this world the LORD God took Abram and made him the father of the promised offspring. This promise was first given in Genesis 3:15, where the offspring was named the Seed of the Woman. Progressively, the Seed of the Woman is further revealed as the Seed of Abram.

QUESTIONS

1. The LORD God appeared to Abram. What was so special about that? What did Abram see?
2. What did the LORD God call the land where Abram was to go?
3. How did the name of the tree 'Moreh' keep the memory alive that the LORD God had appeared to Abram near that tree?
4. What promise did the LORD God give Abram as he appeared to him?
5. How could Abram "see" the future?
6. What do we know about the fulfillment of the promised *"offspring"* (Gal. 3:16)?
7. Do we need to research custom of heathen oracles in order to understand Genesis 12 and the tree called Moreh?
8. Can you find examples in Old and New Testament of *seeing, showing, and appearing* of the LORD God?
9. What did the Lord Jesus say to Thomas about seeing and believing?

10. Who spoke these words, *"When you have seen me you have seen the Father?"*
11. Are men able to live when seeing the *"face"* of God?
12. Abram arrived in a land he did not own. Who was the owner of the land?
13. Who is the owner of the land on which we work and raise our children?
14. How significant was it for Abram that he found the LORD God's presence in a foreign land?
15. How do we find God's presence in our "foreign" land today?
16. Noah built an altar to the LORD God at a time of new beginnings after having been preserved throughout the flood. Abram built an altar to the LORD God at a time of new beginnings after arriving in the land the LORD showed him. Do we know of more altars in the Bible built at a time of new beginnings (Genesis 12:8–9, ESV)?
17. Which supreme sacrifice ushered in the New Beginnings of the New Testament?
18. Are new beginnings new roads of God, or continuations of the same Road of Life?

Genesis 12:8,9

*⁸ From there he moved to the hill country on the east of Bethel and pitched his tent, with Bethel on the west and Ai on the east. And there he built an altar to the L*ORD *and called upon the name of the L*ORD*. ⁹ And Abram journeyed on, still going toward the Negeb.*

Near Shechem in Canaan the LORD God had appeared to Abram. In doing that the LORD God had fulfilled his word to Abram. He would show Abram the land he was to inherit and the LORD had done what he promised. Now Abram moves from Shechem to a place between Bethel and Ai and there is a continuation. A pattern develops. It is the pattern of the Bond of the Covenant. At Shechem, Abram had experienced the presence of the LORD God as the owner of this new and strange land. In that certainty Abram now moves on. Abram makes it publicly known that he is among the Canaanites as a servant of Yahweh, the LORD God, owner of the land. Abram does that by once again building an altar to the LORD God. That altar became a visible, and by public confession: The owner of the land is here and I am his servant.

Abram further calls publicly on the name of the LORD. We met this calling upon the name of the LORD for the first time with Seth. Let us consider the earlier notes on Seth in whose day men started *to call upon the Name of the LORD.* The LORD is Yahweh, that means, "HE IS". The LORD God was present with righteous Seth and in faith Seth exercised the bond of communion with the LORD God in prayer and worship. Now Abram does exactly the same thing. Abram lives in the presence of the God who IS. In the midst of a Amorite society where the gods are far away and no bond is possible Abram proclaims the presence of his LORD in sacrifice on the altar and in worship. He speaks to the LORD and knows that his LORD is there to hear and to act. We called this pattern: The Bond of the Covenant.

TO CONSIDER

1. This pattern of the Bond of the Covenant holds true for Christian believers today. We are to follow the pattern of Genesis 4 and 12. How shall we do that today?

2. Christians are children of Abraham by faith who worship publicly on the Sunday. We do that amid a decaying society. What does that tell you about the need to be faithful in Sunday public worship?
3. Does the fact that our worship is **public** have an effect on the world around us?
4. Does this make **public worship** a duty from God?

Abram does not stay between Bethel and Ai but continues to move southward into the Negev. Verse 9 forms the bridge to what follows in the second half of chapter twelve. The Negev brings Abram closer to the power sphere of Egypt.

Genesis 12:10-20

EGYPT COMES INTO THE PICTURE FROM VERSE TEN TO THE END OF CHAPTER TWELVE..

10 Now there was a famine in the land. So Abram went down to Egypt to sojourn there, for the famine was severe in the land. 11 When he was about to enter Egypt, he said to Sarai his wife, "I know that you are a woman beautiful in appearance, 12 and when the Egyptians see you, they will say, 'This is his wife.' Then they will kill me, but they will let you live. 13 Say you are my sister, that it may go well with me because of you, and that my life may be spared for your sake." 14 When Abram entered Egypt, the Egyptians saw that the woman was very beautiful. 15 And when the princes of Pharaoh saw her, they praised her to Pharaoh. And the woman was taken into Pharaoh's house. 16 And for her sake he dealt well with Abram; and he had sheep, oxen, male donkeys, male servants, female servants, female donkeys, and camels.
17 But the LORD afflicted Pharaoh and his house with great plagues because of Sarai, Abram's wife. 18 So Pharaoh called Abram and said, "What is this you have done to me? Why did you not tell me that she was your wife? 19 Why did you say, 'She is my sister,' so that I took her for my wife? Now then, here is your wife; take her, and go." 20 And Pharaoh gave men orders concerning him, and they sent him away with his wife and all that he had.

Abram was faced with famine and hunger so he made a decision. Apparently Abram made this decision without the LORD God appearing to him. This may lead us to look at Abram's decision as an act of unbelief or even disobedience. The LORD God had given his word to Abram that he would give the land of Canaan to him. There, the offspring of Abram would be born and take possession. However, God the Holy Spirit, does not record any rebuke toward Abram.

What clearly stands out in the rest of chapter twelve is that the LORD God is teaching Abram a lesson. The LORD God teaches his children not only by words but also by practical life situations. Through this episode, Abram is to learn that Egypt is not to be looked upon for safeguarding the future of Abram and his promised offspring. It is the LORD God who would safeguard Abram and his family in an emergency. It is the LORD God who would safeguard the fulfillment of his promise concerning the offspring in whom all nations would be blessed. Following the account in chapter twelve we find out this:
1) Abram knows that the fear of the LORD is not in Egypt.
2) Abram considers himself in Egypt without the LORD. Yet, the LORD God was present with him in a country like Egypt: Canaan.

3) Abram uses his own wisdom to protect himself. He tells his wife Sarai to let on that she is his sister. This will keep Abram alive.

The LORD God had bound Abram and Sarai together in his Word of Promise and in the Bond of the Covenant. The LORD's Way of Life will not run via Egypt or a divided Abram and Sarai. The promise of the LORD will be fulfilled through Abram and Sarai in the land of Canaan. Therefore, the LORD's wisdom overrides Abram's folly. The LORD acts to preserve his Way by terrifying the household of the king of Egypt.

Abram receives his wife Sarai back and together they are sent back to Canaan. With them they take to Canaan the people and goods received in compensation.
With these goods and people Egypt is made to support the chosen ones of the LORD.

DISCUSSION TIME

1. Was the LORD God the God of Egypt?
2. Was the LORD God present in Egypt?
3. Was the LORD God present in Egypt as the God of Abram?
4. What was Abram's folly?
5. How did the LORD's presence become evident?
6. Why did the LORD God rescue the situation?
7. With the slaves Sarai received and took into her household Abram's household became a mixed household with Egyptian elements. Was this a good thing or was it a consequence of his folly?
8. Can you think of a situation where we would foolishly protect ourselves?
9. What does it mean for us to "wait on the LORD"?

Yahweh sent Moses to his enslaved people in Egypt with the book of Genesis. Abraham's descendants in Egypt had become ignorant of the LORD God and his presence.

QUICK QUESTIONS

1. They heard from Moses of the LORD's presence with Abram in Canaan and in Egypt and of his protection. How should this hearing of the presence of the LORD affect them in their enslavement?
2. How should the same hearing of the presence of the LORD affect present-day Christians who are persecuted?

IN CHAPTER TWELVE THE LORD GOD TELLS THE ENSLAVED DESCENDANTS OF ABRAHAM OF HIS FIRST ENCOUNTER WITH EGYPT.

When the LORD God sent Moses to deliver Israel from bondage he told Moses to tell them, *"The LORD, the God of your fathers, the God of Abraham, the God of Isaac, and the God of Jacob, has sent me to you"*. (Exo. 3:13-17). How well known to them were the LORD's dealings with their father Abraham? After some four hundred years in Egypt they did not know much. You could say that they did not know their church-history. In a world that is estranged from God it is easy to forget that deliverance and help comes from the LORD God in the past and is to be trusted for the present.

When Moses arrives in Egypt with the content of the book of Genesis, the Hebrews are taught the history of God's powerful acts of deliverance. These acts of deliverance took place in Egypt, the land of their suffering. Abraham their father had schemed to save his life from Egypt's power at the cost of the purity of his wife Sarai. He failed to trust in the LORD God for deliverance. In spite of Abram's lack of faith the LORD God had sent deliverance. That was the first powerful encounter of YHWH with Egypt. The king was forced to give up Sarai and sent Abram on his way with rich compensation.

This is the message of Genesis 12 to Abraham's descendants, *"As I powerfully delivered your father Abraham from Egypt so I am going to deliver you from the power of Egypt. Trust me to deliver you"*.

QUESTIONS

1. What is the teaching of Church history about?
2. Where all should Church history be taught?
3. How far back should Church history be taught?
4. How does knowing the history of the Church relate to the glory of God?
5. What comfort does Genesis 12 bring to persecuted Christians today?

Genesis 13

Abram went up from Egypt to the Negev. The dictionaries tell us that Negev means parched or dry. Verse three tells us that Abram went from place to place. With the large herds of both Abram and Lot it was necessary to relocate frequently for soon they would run out of food and water. Relocation was a necessity. As they relocated, they once more arrived at Bethel where Abram had *"first built an altar. There Abram called on the Name of the LORD."*

In chapter thirteen, there is a further progression in the setting apart of Abram. The LORD God had brought Abram away from Ur of the Chaldeans and subsequently from Haran. Now a further separation takes place: Abram and Lot go their separate ways. Lot chooses the lush Jordan Valley near the city of Sodom, and Abram moves from place to place in the Negev and the hill country.

There is a key-word here and it is **city.** Cities provided defence and safety. Cities also provided permanence. **Permanence** is the second key-word. Lot chooses lush vegetation for his herds and the safety and permanence of the city.

In contrast to Lot's choice Abram chooses the uncertainty of the life of a Nomad. The dangers of the open country are his. Lack of vegetation or water forces him to move on. Lot chooses to live among the inhabitants of Sodom who were *"wicked and great sinners against the LORD."* Abram, however, lives apart but at home with the LORD God who promised Abram the whole land.

QUESTION PERIOD

1. How do the verses 14-17 show that the LORD God approved of Abram's decision?
2. How do these verses show also that Abram was not merely a Nomad?
3. What is the significance of Abram again building an altar and calling upon the Name of the LORD?
4. Abram did not choose for the permanence of the city. What kind of permanence did the LORD God promise to Abram?
5. Scripture later testifies that Abram did expect a future city. What kind of city is that (Use a concordance to look up "city".)?
6. Are we, Christians, Nomads?
7. Are we, Christians, expecting to receive a city?
8. Should Christians avoid living in a city?
9. What should a Christian know about life in the city?
10. What makes it possible for a Christian to live in a city?
11. How did the LORD God confirm Abram as the heir of Canaan?

In chapter fourteen we meet three parties.
1. There are the kings of the North even from as far as Babylon.
2. Then there are the kings of the South from the Valley of the Jordan River.
3. The third party is Abram with the three brothers who are Abram's allies.

The kings of the North are from the country that Abram had left as the LORD God commanded him. They do not have the LORD at their side. In 13:13, the kings of the South are called *"wicked, sinning greatly against the LORD"*. They do not have the LORD at their side either. There is only one party that has the LORD at his side and that is Abram.

The kings of the North rout the armies of the kings of the South. They carry away everything they own, men and women and children included. Also, Lot and his family with his possessions are carried away. When Abram is told about this he brings out his 318 trained men. Together with his allies from Mamre, Abram pursues the enemies, overtakes them and defeats them. He sets the prisoners free and takes back all the booty.

TO CONSIDER

1. Who gave Abram the authority and the power to act as ruler and protector of the inhabitants of the land?
2. Why does Abram not allow the king of Sodom to make Abram rich?
3. If Abram had accepted the possessions of the king of Sodom what would Abram's relation to Sodom be?
4. What does Abram's refusal teach us about our dependence upon those who *sin greatly against the LORD*?
5. What should Abram's refusal teach the people of our nation regarding the corruption scandals that lately have plagued our nation in government, trade, commerce and construction?

MELCHIZEDEK KING OF RIGHTEOUSNESS, KING OF PEACE, PRIEST OF THE MOST HIGH GOD.

In the verses 17-20, we find a meeting between Melchizedek and Abram. For our understanding of this meeting we need to take into account not only chapter 14:17-20 but also Psalm 110, plus the letter to the Hebrews chapters 6-7. Central to the verses 17-20, is the name of God. Melchizedek is priest of *God Most High* (לְאֵל עֶלְיוֹן / le ël Elyon) The interpretation of this name of God is crucial for the understanding of the position of Melchizedek as priest and the passage as a whole.

Many scholars of the critical schools tell us that Melchizedek was priest of a Canaanite deity. Most High would indicate the presence of other gods. This in turn would lead to a comparison of God (El) to other gods below him. Their conclusion is then that Melchizedek was not a priest of the LORD (YHWH) but of a Canaanite god.

Indeed, the Bible recognizes the existence of gods. These gods can be kings and rulers. These gods can also be the man-made gods of the nations. The LORD God is far above all these, not in comparison but as the only true God.

Below please find a small selection of Scripture verses where God the Holy Spirit himself places The LORD (YHWH) equally side by side with Most High (עֶלְיוֹן / Elyon). These verses clearly show that the LORD God is the Most High. Melchizedek met Abram as priest of the only true God.

Psalm 18:14 "The LORD also thundered in the heavens, and the Most High uttered his voice, hailstones and coals of fire."

Psalm 21:8 "for the king trusts in the LORD, and through the steadfast love of the Most High he shall not be moved."

Psalm 46:5 "There is a river whose streams make glad the city of God, the holy habitation of the Most High."

Psalm 95:3 (ESV) "For the LORD is a great God, and a great King above all gods."

Psalm 96:4 (ESV) "For great is the LORD, and greatly to be praised; he is to be feared above all gods."

Psalm 97:9 (ESV) "For you, O LORD, are most high over all the earth; you are exalted far above all gods."

1 Chronicles 16:25 (ESV) "For great is the LORD, and greatly to be praised, and he is to be feared above all gods."

QUICK QUESTIONS

1. In the Bible we meet the title *"Most High God"*. Why may this never be interpreted as a pagan god?
2. How do Abram's words to the king of Sodom in 14:12 help you to answer this?

MELCHIZEDEK WAS NOT A JEBUSITE

The Jebusites were Canaanites who did not serve the only true God. If Melchizedek were a Jebusite he could not have been priest of the Most High God. It is specifically revealed that Mechizedek was king of Salem which is to be distinguished from Jebus. Melchizedek's city of Salem is the city of peace. Melchizedek is also King of righteousness. "Righteous" here has two sides. He owes his kingship to God Most High who is the Righteous One. He must also perform righteous deeds in his service to God Most High.

Melchizedek comes out of his city of peace to meet with Abram who is returning from war. Abram has liberated righteous Lot and all other prisoners with him. The king of the wicked city of Sodom comes out of hiding and also arrives. Melchizedek arrives in time to witness a confrontation between Abram and the king of Sodom. The place where they all meet is the Valley of Shaveh. The name "Shaveh," is related to even, smooth. Before the king of righteousness and peace, the priest of the Most High God, Abram refuses to benefit from the king of the wicked city. In contrast to this Abram recognizes Melchizedek as a servant of God Most High. Abram offers a tithe of all he gained from the war and hands it to the priest Melchizedek. Melchizedek in turn blesses Abram :

19 And he blessed him and said, "Blessed be Abram by God Most High, Possessor of heaven and earth;
20 and blessed be God Most High, who has delivered your enemies into your hand!"

DISCUSSION TIME

1. What dispute was settled in the Valley of Shaveh? Or what was "evened out" in the Valley of Shaveh.?
2. Why would the Valley of Shaveh be called the Valley of the Kings? Which kings?
3. How did Absalom misuse the reputation of the Valley of Shaveh (2 Samuel 18:18)?
4. In whose presence was this dispute settled?
5. Whom did this person represent?
6. Did Melchizedek bring out bread and wine for Abram and his allies or for the king of Sodom and his allies?
7. On whose side was Melchizedek as King of Righteousness?

MELCHIZEDEK'S NAME IS NOT ABIMELECH

In the book of Genesis we several times find the name Abimelech as title of a king. Abimelech means *my father is king*. "My father is king" indicates that the king received his kingship from his father. Melchizedek as King of Righteousness did not inherit his kingship from his ancestor but received it from God Most High.

THE FURTHER TESTIMONY TO MELCHIZEDEK IN SCRIPTURE CONFIRMS WHAT WE HAVE FOUND

In Psalm 110, David speaks through the Spirit of God in verse one, *"The LORD says to my Lord ... (vs.4) You are a priest forever after the order of Melchizedek"*. "My Lord" is David's Lord who in essence is Jesus Christ the Son of God and Saviour of the world (Mark 12:35-37).

In the letter to the Hebrews 6:20 – 7, God the Holy Spirit provides us with continued revelation concerning the relation of king Melchizedek and the King of kings, Jesus Christ. Melchizedek and the Lord Jesus Christ are of a unique order. They do not owe their office to parental descent but directly from God. Chapter 7:3 testifies concerning Melchizedek, *"He is without father or mother or genealogy, having neither beginning of days nor end of life, but resembling the Son of God he continues a priest forever"*.

QUESTIONS

1. Which two priestly *"orders"* do Psalm 110 and Hebrews 6-7 speak of?

2. What is the difference between the two *"orders"*?
3. In Psalm 110 and Hebrews 6-7 we are given more information about Melchizedek than in chapter 14 in the book of Genesis. Where did this additional information come from?
4. Which similarities are there between Melchizedek and the Lord Jesus Christ?
5. Which similarity is there between Enoch (Genesis 5:24) and Melchizedek?
6. Melchizedek and the Lord Jesus live forever as Priests and Kings. Can they still be historical, real life, persons?
7. Was there ever another person who was both Priest and King?
8. Which king of Judah became leprous when he tried to be priest?
9. In H.C. Lord's Day 12, we confess that Christian believers are Prophet, Priest, and King. How was this made possible?

The LORD God firmly establishes Abram as the rightful heir to the land of Canaan. The LORD does this by granting Abram success in victory over the wicked kings of the North. The LORD God also does this by blessing Abram by means of his servant Melchizedek, King of Righteousness, King of Peace, and Priest of the Most High God. The blessing tells everyone that God's good Way of Life runs through the generations and offspring of Abram.

TO CONSIDER

1. How did the words of Melchizedek confirm the LORD's promises given to Abram?
2. When God blesses someone, what does God then say about this person – maybe even you?
3. Melchizedek blessed God. Some versions translate the Hebrew verb with *Praise* instead of *Bless*. To me "praise" does not properly translate the Hebrew verb, *"BARACH to Bless"*. When we bless God we say that God is ... (See our discussion points on 'bless' earlier. The verb "to praise" does not specifically say that God is ... for that verb is too broad in meaning.
4. How did the words of Melchizedek, "God Most High *Possessor* of Heaven and Earth, confirm the LORD's promises given to Abram?

ISRAEL IN EGYPT ENCOURAGED BY THE LORD'S JUSTICE AND PEACE REVEALED IN GENESIS 14

The sojourn of Israel in Egypt exposed them to a system of justice totally different from the justice and peace the LORD God revealed to them in Genesis 14. It is necessary for us to understand Egypt's pagan system of righteousness and peace if we are to understand the LORD's message of truth in Genesis 14 sent to enslaved Israel.

A quote from Theban literature outlines Egypt's system of righteousness and peace in a compact manner. [20]

> *"Re has installed the king*
> *on the earth of the living*
> *for ever and ever*
> *so that he may give justice to mankind,*

---

[20] I owe this quotation to Jan Assmann's Of God and gods : Egypt,Israel, and the Rise of Monotheism, 2008, The University of Wisconsin Press. P. 11. Also in his Religion and Cultural Memory, Stanford CA 2006 p. 34

and please the gods,
so that he may create maat *and drive out* isfet.
He (the king) brings divine sacrifices to the gods
And offerings to the dead."

Here the king owes his position and authority to Re, that is the Sun-god. The king's task is to give justice to mankind and please the gods – plural. One of the gods is the goddess of creation order and justice, Ma'at. The king is to create Ma'at's order and justice and drive out Ma'at's opposite which is Isfet. Isfet is violence, lies and chaos (Assmann p. 32). Israel is the victim of the murder of their little boys, and of slave labour, in Egypt for they are considered *isfet*. The Israelites are a threat to Ma'at, to Egypt's order and peace. Pharaoh by oppressing the Israelites is upholding Ma'at and destroying Isfet and satisfying the gods.

To these Israelites the LORD God sends Moses with his book of Genesis, including chapter fourteen. In chapter fourteen YAHWEH is holding before the oppressed descendants of Abram: His Man, His King of Righteousness and Peace; His Priest who "satisfies" YAHWEH. There is an amazing contrast here. Melchizedek, king of righteousness and priest of the God Most High forever, blesses Abram the forefather of Israel. The king of Egypt, who pretends to live forever, curses Abram's descendants by his gods.

In the New Testament era we find this contrast in larger measure. The New Testament Scriptures reveal to us the contrast between Christ and Antichrist. God put forth Jesus Christ, King of Righteousness and High priest in the order of Melchizedek, who blesses his people with peace and everlasting life. Satan, however, put forth Antichrist, who curses Christ and wages war against the Christian (Revelation 12). There is great comfort here. The God of Melchizedek and of Jesus Christ is the same today as he was and will be forever.

The LORD is going to lead the Israelites out from Egypt and into Canaan. The LORD is going to deliver them from the idolatrous injustice and disorder of Egypt and bring them to a land where the LORD God will establish his order, truth, justice, and peace. That is to be to Israel the miracle of the grace of the LORD. To convince the enslaved Israelites of the LORD's power to establish his righteousness and peace for them the LORD tells them of the miracle of his rule in Genesis fourteen. Melchizedek and Jesus Christ stand out in history as towers of God's power to save.

With that we are back to the history of God's Church. That is not only "the" history of God's Church. That is for us Christians "our" history. For the Church is the Israel of God (Eph. 2).

QUESTIONS

1. Explain what it means to belong to the Israel of God.
2. How can the history of Abram and Melchizedek be the history of Israel in Egypt?
3. How can that same history be "our" history? (Psalm 66:6)
4. Are there symptoms in our nation that the Christian is considered a threat to society?
5. What is the public order of justice and freedom of our nation based on?
6. What is the consequence of separating Genesis 14 from Psalm 110 and Heb. 6-7?
7. Whom do we "grieve" if we refuse to interpret Genesis 14 in the light of Psalm 110 and Heb. 6-7?

Vs. 1 "After these things". Seemingly these words are insignificant. The word "after" tells us that we leave what happened in chapter 14 behind and we now proceed. The word "things" comes across to us as a general term without much meaning. The phrase, *"After these things"*, connects the "things" of chapter 14 to the "things" of chapter 15. Let us take these "things" out of their seeming generality and make them very specific.

To our surprise we find that the word we translate with "thing" in the Hebrew text of the Old Testament is "word". When the LORD God speaks he creates, his Word makes things happen. [21] In 14:22 Abram swears by *"the LORD, God Most High, Possessor of heaven and earth"*. The Possessor of heaven and earth is the God by whose Word the heaven and the earth were created. He spoke and things materialized.

In the same way the *"things"* that happened in chapter 14 took place by the Word of the LORD. The migrating hordes of the five kings of the North were delivered to Abraham by the Word of the LORD. By the Word of the LORD Melchizedek was brought forth as an everlasting priest and king to establish the "Order of Melchizedek". By the Word of the LORD Abram was given the wisdom and faithfulness to accept his separation from the wicked king of Sodom. By the Word of the LORD Melchizedek, king of righteousness and peace, priest of God Most High, blessed Abram.

With the phrase *"after these things/words"* God the Holy Spirit takes us back to the mighty deeds the LORD God performed from the time of creation and forward into Abram's day. In chapter 15 God the Holy Spirit leads us further. Abram and his descendants are privileged to hear assurances in Words that are guaranteed to become mighty deeds.

THE POWER OF THE WORD OF THE ONLY TRUE GOD, A MESSAGE TO ENSLAVED HEBREWS IN EGYPT

The Egyptians of the Middle Kingdom (Eighteenth Dynasty) claimed that the words of their king had divine power. This power of the word was equal to magic. Pharaoh's word reached far to bring victory to his armies or punishment to the fugitive. This explains how in Hebrews 11:27 it can be said of Moses that he fled to Midian "not being afraid of the anger of the king." According to Egyptian idolatry the word of the king could effectively destroy Moses. Moses, however, endured as "seeing him who is invisible."
Here follow some quotes from Egyptologists about the power of the word in ancient Egyptian cults:

---

[21] *A good example of this is found in Psalm 145:5, "... on your wondrous works I will meditate". The Hebrew original reads, "... on your wondrous words I will meditate".*

Jan Assmann, The Search for God in Ancient Egypt, p. 165, *"The king rules as orator, as enjoined on him by the Instruction for Merikare: 'Be artful in speech that you may overcome, [for] the strong arm [of a king] is (his) tongue. Words are stronger than any fighting'."*

Dr. Ogden Goelet, The Egyptian Book of the Dead p. 147 col. 1a in commentary on *The Papyrus of Ani,*

"The very phrase 'the god's words', the most common word for their language, expressed the Egyptian's belief that the divine was implicit in words". [22]

p. 145 col. 2a *"According to the Coffin Texts, when the creator deity fashioned the universe, one of his first acts was to create magic, his eldest son, named Heka. Sometime after this he entrusted both gods and mankind with magic as one of his 'great deeds'.*

p. 145 col.2b *"Heka image is many things, but above all, it has a close association with speech and power of the word. In the realm of Egyptian magic action did not necessarily speak louder than words – they were often one and the same thing. Thought, deed, image and power are theoretically united in the concept of Heka. The Memphite Theology, which stated that the god Ptah Tatenen brought forth the universe through the spoken word, places the power of the word at the center of the Egyptian world view."*

QUESTIONS

1. From which two sources would Abram's descendants, enslaved in Egypt, have been able to understand that the "word" and "thing" is one action?
2. Would the Egyptian's understanding of "word" and "thing" have helped the Hebrews in their understanding or would it have confused them?
3. Show how the enslaved Hebrews in Egypt should have become convinced by the actions of the LORD, recorded in Genesis 14, that the LORD's Word had power to set them free and lead them out to the Promised Land.
4. The Egyptians attributed their power to kill and enslave the Hebrews to the divine power of the word of their king. Was the word of the king of Egypt divine or was it magic?
5. Can magic ever be divine?
6. Who is always the source of the power of magic?
7. By the Word of the LORD the heaven and the earth were created. Does, or did, the Word of the LORD create anything for you?
8. Where do we meet magic in the world today?
9. Please evaluate the magic in the Harry Potter books and movies.
10. Do the same with the magic in fairy tales. Are these suited for our young children?

Vs. 1. cont'd

"After these things the word of the LORD came to Abram in a vision: "Fear not, Abram, I am your shield; your reward shall be very great."

---

[22] Jan Assmann, The Search for God in Ancient Egypt, New York, 2001.

Vision

Once again we are told of the LORD God speaking. This time the word of the LORD came in a vision. From what we just learned about "word" and "thing" we may expect to find that in this vision there are words and actions of the LORD God. That's exactly what we will find.

Ears hear when the Word of the LORD comes. In this vision Abram does not only get to hear the Word of the LORD; Abram also gets to see the Word of the LORD. That is what the word *vision* tells us. This is the first time in the Bible that we hear of a person receiving the Word of the LORD in a vision. The earmark of a vision from God is that the vision is not conjured up by a human being. The vision is created by God and takes place in God's environment. The vision is a spiritual event even though the vision may contain elements from everyday life. In this vision the animals Abram is to bring are real, but are part of the vision from God.

The LORD's word in the vision addresses Abram in his contemporary situation. Abram lives in a foreign land. He was confronted with the onslaught of the hordes of the kings of the North. The impact of the hordes of the kings of the North should not be underestimated. The fact that Abram defeated them was nothing less than a miracle from God. In this foreign land Abram experienced the power of the Word of God, the 'Possessor' of the land, acting on his behalf. Abram's God showed himself as sovereign King, able to protect his servant Abram. All this the LORD God puts before Abram in one word, *"shield"*, *"I am your Shield I protect you and govern you."*

In the book of Psalms we find this word "shield" about fifteen times. When in Psalm 84 we read of God that he is a shield, then we are told that God is sovereign King over all he has made. He alone is able to protect his servants in all circumstances.

Discussion Time

1. What does it mean to us in the practice of life that the LORD is for us a sun and shield?
2. What do the Father, the Son, and the Holy Spirit mean for us as a Shield?
3. Consider how the LORD God in the baptism of believers and their seed promises to be their Shield.

To this the LORD God adds, *"I am your very great reward."* We may also translate, *"I am your exceedingly great reward."* Some versions have *"your reward shall be very great."* In this translation we lose the connection with the *"I"*. The sentence begins with an emphatic *"I"*. This *"I"* covers both parts of the sentence: "I am your shield; I am your reward." The person who speaks is guaranteeing the fulfillment of the Words.

With this part of the sentence the LORD God is once more addressing Abram in his contemporary situation. Abram is rich. He has many possessions but he owns no land and has no offspring. The LORD God has given him many Words. The LORD God told Abram to walk up and down the land that God would give him. In Abram's offspring, all families of the earth would be blessed (12:3; 13:16-17). Abram finds himself in an impossible situation. In this real life situation the LORD God points to himself as he begins by saying *"I"*. Here the LORD God is saying, "Abram! Look away from your impossibilities and look to ME the possessor of heaven and earth. Trust ME Abram. I am you shield, your exceedingly great reward."

Abram understood the emphatic *"I"*. That is clear from how Abram addresses God.

² But Abram said, "O Lord GOD, what will you give me, for I continue childless, and the heir of my house is Eliezer of Damascus?" ³ And Abram said, "Behold, you have given me no offspring, and a member of my household will be my heir."

Abram's question contains two parts. Accordingly the LORD dealt with Abram's question in two parts. The first part is about offspring (vs 3-6) and the second part is about the land (vs 7-21). From this we must conclude that the whole of chapter fifteen is one vision. Some commentators limit the vision to only the first six verses. The way the LORD God deals with Abram's question confirms our conviction that the whole chapter is one vision.

First part vs 3-6.

OFFSPRING

The NIV translates, *"O sovereign LORD"*. This is the better translation of the Hebrew. The Hebrew reads, *"Adonai Yahweh"*. Adonai is the title of Yahweh which reveals him as sovereign Master. By calling God *"Adonai"* Abram links up with verse one where the LORD called himself Abram's *"Shield"*, Abram's sovereign Protector. By addressing God "Adonai Yahweh" Abram honours God as his Master, Creator and Possessor of the heaven and earth from the beginning who is able to do as he spoke.

The question Abram directs at his sovereign LORD is not one of doubt or complaint. Abram accepts that Adonai Yahweh can do all things. Abram's realistic situation is that there is no future for him for he has no child.[23] There is no heir to inherit. All Abram has will go to the head-servant in his house, Eliezer of Damascus. Anything Adonai Yahweh can give him will go to Eliezer. The LORD's answer is that not Eliezer but a son "coming from your own body will be your heir". To assure Abram of the fulfillment of his Word the LORD takes Abram outside into a clear night and shows him a firmament full of stars. There the LORD challenges Abram to count them if he can. Then the LORD speaks more words, words that are assurances of divine actions: *"So shall your offspring be."*

We might expect Abram to voice doubts or more questions but we expect wrongly. Abram speaks words of trust that continue to ring through the Bible and through the history of God with his people: *"Abram believed and the LORD counted it to him as righteousness"*.[24]
Two aspects in these words need our attention: *believed* and *righteousness*.

BELIEVED

The best way to approach the word 'believed' is to remember what we confess about true faith in L.D. 7 of the Heidelberg Catechism. *"True faith is not only a sure knowledge ... but also a firm confidence."* **To**

---

[23] Literally Abram says that he continues naked, stripped. This is reflected in Rom. 4:19 "... when his body was as good as dead ...". W.H. Gispen quotes the Genesis Apokryphon on Genesis 15 :2 "Naked I will die and end up childless". De Knecht Van Abraham, in De Knecht, Studies rondom Deutero Jesaja aangeboden aan Prof. Dr. J. Koole, p. 53, Kampen 1978).

[24] See Rom. 4:3 and 9; Gal. 3:6; Jas. 2:23.

believe is to trust. Abram trusted Adonai Yahweh upon his Word! The Word of the LORD is trustworthy. Adonai Yahweh will make good on what he has spoken.

QUESTIONS

1. What is it that the LORD God had earlier spoken to Abram (see ch. 12:3)?
2. What is it that the LORD God spoke to Abram in ch. 15?
3. Consider that the Opening of the Way of Life runs via Abram and his Seed. How does the promise of a *"son of his own body"* fit into that?
4. Was Abram not too bold in the way he voiced his plight to the LORD God?
5. Consider what it takes for us to have the courage of faith to ask God for what he has promised?
6. In what attitude should we place our questions before God?
7. Did the LORD God reveal to Abram immediately that the promised son would be by Sarai?
8. Why did the LORD God make Abram wait?
9. Do we receive everything right away? Why does the LORD God make us wait?

ACCOUNTED IT TO HIM AS RIGHTEOUSNESS

W. Gispen writes that to be righteous is to be, and act, in complete harmony with the will of the LORD. [25] Adonai Yahweh approved of his servant Abram's attitude of complete trust.

Let us recall earlier commentary where we already dealt with 'righteousness'. Under the heading **But Noah found favor in the eyes of the LORD** we discussed Genesis 6:8-9, *"... Noah was a righteous man, blameless in his generation."* Here we found righteous and blameless in parallel position. Looking not only back, but also forward, we will have to come back to this topic when we deal with Genesis 17:1 *"Walk before me and be blameless."*

Second part vs. 7-21.

THE LAND

In verse seven the LORD reminds Abram of what he has done for Abram in the past and why he had done this. The LORD had commanded Abram to go to the land he would show him. The LORD had been faithful to his Word. His Word had become deed. Abram had arrived in Canaan and he had experienced the presence of the LORD there. The purpose of the action of the LORD was to give this land to Abram to take possession of it. The LORD is reminding Abram that he is as good as his Word.

In verse eight Abram once again addresses God as Adonai Yahweh, Abram's sovereign Master (Adonai), Possessor of heaven and earth (Yahweh). Abram trusts the LORD to do as he has spoken. Nevertheless he asks the LORD God for a sign. He does not ask *"How shall I know this"*, as most versions have it. He

---

[25] W.Gispen, COT Genesis, p. 106 Kampen 1979, "het gedrag, dat beantwoordt aan de goddelijke eis".

literally asks *"by what shall I know this?"*[26] The LORD accedes to Abram's request. Abram receives a sign.

QUICK QUESTION

What is the difference between asking questions of the LORD God and questioning him? (See John 16:29-30).

The verses 8-20 reveal to us the manner of the sign and the purpose of the sign. The manner and purpose of the sign can be summarized with the phrase *"cut a covenant"*, (כָּרַת בְּרִית karat berith). We find this in verse18 where the versions do not translate literally but render *"made a covenant."* At the end of this chapter we will pay broader attention to the matter of *Covenant*.

THE MANNER OF THE SIGN

The cutting of the covenant is made visible in a row of cut up animals. Three clean animals, three years old, are halved and the pieces are placed opposite each other. A bird is added but the bird is not cut in half. It is important for the understanding of the sign to maintain that there were six pieces and one bird making a total of seven. We are so used to reading the plural birds in the versions that no one seems to question the plural. However, the Hebrew in vs. 10 reads הַצִּפֹּר (hatsipor) which literally means **the bird.** The bird refers back to the command given in vs. 9. There the Versions render *"... a dove and a young pigeon"*. This contradicts the singular we found in vs. 10. I choose for the translation *"a turtledove, namely a young one"*.[27] This gives us the age of the bird and brings it in line with the other animals whose age were also specified, namely three years old. The six pieces and the one bird represent the number seven which is the number of the oath.

Practically all commentators recognize the ceremony as the cutting of a covenant oath. However, the number eight does not fit the oath. The number seven does fit. The Hebrew word for oath sounds like seven. It can be said that to swear an oath is "to say seven." Comparison with Genesis 21: 27-31 confirms this.

There Abraham and Abimelech come to terms about a disputed well of water. They swear an oath between them that Abraham has dug this well. As a sign of the oath Abraham points to seven ewe lambs he set apart from the animals he gives to Abimelech. Then they call the well *Beersheba* which means *"Well of the Oath"*.

THE IMPORTANCE OF ESTABLISHING THE PROPER SETTING OF THE CUTTING OF THE COVENANT OATH

Seven pieces, one oath. It was necessary to establish that for the understanding of what Adonai Yahweh is doing for Abram and his descendants. Going into the verses 10-20 we need to establish in this oath ceremony who is the subject and who is the object. Who swears the oath and who benefits from the oath?

---

[26] Idem, p.109, "… waardoor zal ik het weten ….". C.Westermann, Genesis, p. 121, "Abraham's request for a confirmatory sign ...". London 2004.

[27] I read the vau in וְתֹר וְגוֹזָל as an explanatory vau, namely a young one.

It is God who swears the oath and the beneficiaries are Abram and his offspring. Abram is allowed to bring and arrange the necessary animals. Then Abram is to wait for the LORD God to come and to act. Apparently Abram has to wait some time for he needs to drive the vultures away from the carcasses. The sun sets and a thick and dreadful darkness comes over Abram. That the darkness is deep and terrifying tells us that Abram was being prepared for the majestic arrival of the LORD God. The darkness is also connected to the heavy words the LORD God is going to speak about Abram's descendants.

In this darkness the LORD God arrives and speaks, *"Know for certain"*. These words are like a formula that fits the oath of the LORD God. The LORD is giving a visible oath but also puts it into words. The words are heavy for father Abram but in between the LORD God assures Abram that he will *"go to your fathers in peace and be buried at a good old age."* What is to happen will be well after Abram's time.

The LORD speaks, *13 Then the LORD said to Abram, "Know for certain that your offspring will be sojourners in a land that is not theirs and will be servants there, and they will be afflicted for four hundred years. 14 But I will bring judgment on the nation that they serve, and afterward they shall come out with great possessions.*
16 And they shall come back here in the fourth generation, for the iniquity of the Amorites is not yet complete."

In these verses the LORD explains to Abram why he cannot inherit the land now. Neither will his descendants inherit the land in the near future. The time is not ripe for *"the iniquity of the Amorites is not yet complete."* This tells us several things. It explains why Abram at that time could still find persons that feared God in Canaan. It also tells us that the time would come for full judgment upon the Amorites once their sin was full.

QUESTIONS

1. Did Moses bring the words of verses 13-16 to Abram's descendants enslaved in Egypt?
2. What were the enslaved descendants to do with the words of this oath?
3. What do the words of this oath tell us concerning the tribulations of the end times foretold in Matt. 24, 2 Thess. 2:1-4 and the book of Revelation?
4. Are Christians today waiting for the time of judgment to be ripe?
5. Is there for Christians of the end time a promise of deliverance?
6. What is that promise?
7. How and when will that promise be fulfilled?

At verse 17 the LORD God arrives in the fire of his Glory. In the vision, God becomes visible to Abram in the smoking fire pot and blazing torch going through the street of blood between the pieces of the animals. The cut up animals and the bird are roasted in the fire.

QUICK QUESTION

What is the significance of this act of God?

We could consider what researchers tell us about similar oath signs in the nations of the East in Abram's time. A faster route is to consider an instance in the Bible namely: Jeremiah 34.

The core of Jer. 34 is vs. *18 And the men who transgressed my covenant and did not keep the terms of the covenant that they made before me, I will make them like the calf that they cut in two and passed between its parts.*

The situation is this: The nobles of Judah had enslaved their own brother Israelites and refused to set them free. The LORD rebuked them and the nobles promised to set their brothers free. They confirmed this with a visible oath. They cut up a calf and passed through the pieces. This is generally called an *imprecatory oath* or *self-curse*. We can paraphrase what the nobles did by going through the cut up pieces. By it they said: "May we be cut up as this calf was killed by cutting if we do not keep our oath and set our brothers free." They did set their brothers free and then reneged on their oath. Then the LORD did to them according to the self-curse; they indeed would be like the calf.

This helps us to understand the significance of what the LORD God did by going through the pieces in the fire of his Glory. God signified the oath in such a way that we humans could understand him. That way was the way of the self-curse. The LORD God did put his truthfulness on the line. We hesitate to put it in our words but this is what our Adonai Yahweh actually assured Abram of: May I be as these animals if I do not keep my oath to Abram and his descendants.

DISCUSSION TIME

1. Consider how this awesome self-curse of the LORD God guarantees the Hebrew slaves their Exodus from Egypt.
2. Consider how this awesome self-curse guarantees us our Exodus from death to life.

THERE IS ONE OTHER BIG ITEM IN THE OATH-SIGN TO BE CONSIDERED AND THAT IS THE SIGNIFICANCE OF THE BIRD

The animals were cut up but not the bird. The bird was not just any kind of bird. The bird was a dove. The dove is domestic, belongs to the home's environment. In Psalm 74:19 God's oppressed people is called *"Your dove"*.

Psalm 74:18–20

18 Remember this, O LORD, how the enemy scoffs, and a foolish people reviles your name. 19 Do not deliver the soul of your dove to the wild beasts; do not forget the life of your poor forever. 20 Have regard for the covenant, for the dark places of the land are full of the habitations of violence.

What we find in Psalm 74 helps us to understand what the LORD God is telling us with the dove of the Covenant oath. The undivided dove in the covenant oath of the LORD God represents the soul of God's dove, Israel in bondage. In Egypt they will be as dead but the LORD will revive them (ch.15:13-14). The bird is not cut apart but remains undivided as a sign of future resurrection. Abram's offspring will go through death to life. Ultimately this oath of the LORD God foretells the death and guarantees the resurrection of the promised Offspring in whom all nations will be blessed, the great Son of Abraham, Jesus Christ.

The street of the cut up animals is the street of death. However, on this street of death we stumble over the bird. The street of death is not open. The street of death is not forever. There is the uncut bird. That uncut bird is the oath guarantee of the LORD God that his Open Way of Life will be realized through death. Abram's descendants in Egypt will go through the valley of death but the LORD God will lead them out on his Open Way of Life. As the bird of the cutting of the Covenant Bond was not broken, so Israel will go free after having eaten a lamb, roasted whole. Not one bone of that lamb was to be broken. As the bird that remained whole as the guarantee of the Open Way of Life, so would the Lamb of God be. The cutting of the oath of the Covenant Bond reaches far and wide.

The LORD God will send His only Son into the world to bring the Opening of the Way of Life through his death and resurrection. This good news from the LORD God tells us the importance of reading the manner of the oath cutting the right way. There was one bird and with that bird the LORD God guarantees Abram, his Offspring, and all of us, the opening and completion of God's Way of Life. The LORD God began this Way of Life at the head of his Way and preserves it throughout all history into eternity.

WE NOW MUST COME BACK TO WHAT WE EARLIER CALLED THE CORE OF THE CHAPTER, VS:18, THE CUTTING OF THE COVENANT OATH

COVENANT/BERITH

At this point, we must take a look at the translation of *Berith* in our English language Bibles.
Throughout chapter fifteen we are shown that the LORD God is subject and Abram object.
In other words, it is the LORD God who covenants. It is not Abram who covenants. It is the LORD God who swears the oath by going in between the pieces, not Abram. Abram and his offspring are the beneficiaries of the LORD's oath. Here, there is not a making of a covenant **'between'**. That is to say, there is here no making of a covenant between Abram and the LORD God. The process is totally one-sided from God.

This one-sidedness makes our translation of *Berith* with *Covenant* weak. Covenant comes from the verb to convene, to come together. However in the Bond of the Covenant we do not come together with God. We and God are not equal partners. There is no contract. There is our Sovereign, our LORD, who comes and one-sidedly binds himself to us who believe. The continental German and Dutch Versions have a better word, and actually so do we have a better word than Covenant. The German Versions have *Bund*. The Dutch have Bond or *Verbond*. In English we have the word *Bond*. In Ezekiel 20:37, the LORD God speaks to his people, *"I will bring you into the bond of the covenant."*[28] These three words have in common that they clearly represent what the *Berith* of Adonai Yahweh is. In his Bond the LORD God binds himself to Abram and his offspring to make his oath true. The whole of the Bible bears witness to the fact that the Word, Adonai Yahweh spoke, became action, fulfillment, truth (see Psalm 105 and Hebrews 6:13-20 for confirmation of the interpretation we have given of Genesis 15).

---

[28] וְהֵבֵאתִי אֶתְכֶם בְּמָסֹרֶת הַבְּרִית *Here we find that the essence of* הַבְּרִית *is to be bound to the will of the LORD God.*

Genesis 15:13–14 (ESV)

"But I will lead them out." The Exodus foretold

13 Then the LORD said to Abram, "Know for certain that your offspring will be sojourners in a land that is not theirs and will be servants there, and they will be afflicted for four hundred years. 14 But I will bring judgment on the nation that they serve, and afterward they shall come out with great possessions.

In these verses we receive a 'first'. This is the first time that the LORD God specifies future tribulation for the descendants of Abram and their way out into freedom. This will happen for the LORD will punish the oppressor and lead out his chosen people. We could call this the introduction of the Exodus theme.

This Exodus oath of God was of utmost importance for the enslaved Hebrews in Egypt. The LORD God had Moses record this and take it to Egypt. Thereby the LORD God provided the oppressed Hebrews with assurance of his plan for them. The LORD God is going to lead them out as surely as he once swore this to Abram, their father. As slaves of Egypt, the Hebrews are now experiencing the darkness Abram experienced in the vision, but the LORD God is going to bring them into the light of life.

I called this a 'first'. Yet this prophecy and the fulfillment thereof, is in line with what God the Holy Spirit foretold in Genesis 3:15, *"I put enmity between you and the woman, between your seed and her seed. He will bruise your head and you will bruise his heel."* Genesis 15 is further development of that prophecy. Throughout history the LORD God is dealing, and will deal, with his chosen people in the way of Exodus. In tribulation there may be the darkness of death but the LORD God will lead his own out in his Way of Life. By preparing the bird for death and resurrection, the LORD God takes it upon himself to pay the cost of setting the offspring of Abram free through the death and resurrection of the *Apple of His Eye*, Jesus Christ.

Questions

1. Where in Scripture do we read of more occasions and times where the LORD God made his people go through darkness to lead them out into freedom?
2. Where in the Gospels do we read of Moses and Elijah speaking with the Lord Jesus about his exodus?
3. What promise does Genesis 15:13-14 hold for the New Testament Church? Is there to be an Exodus for God's New Testament people?
4. How is this a comfort to us as we experience rapidly growing darkness and hostility in the world around us?

The Seed of Abraham and the Blessing to all nations will not come in the way of Egyptian error but in the Way of Yahweh, the Opener of the Way of Life. (Chapter 16 to 18:15)

THE LORD GOD EXPOSES AND CORRECTS THE ERRATIC EGYPTIAN WAY OF LIFE IN ABRAM'S TENT

The LORD God had assured Abram that a son from his own body would be his heir (ch. 15). It is important to note that the LORD had not told Abram that the heir would be born through Sarai. This might have been implied but was not expressly stated. For this reason we should not be hasty to qualify Abram's acts as unbelief and lack of trust. We must keep in mind that the LORD God himself does not voice such a judgment upon Abram. That does however, not mean that Abram and Sarai are acting wisely. Their choices are the wrong choices. They are choosing a way different from the Way of the LORD for with Hagar they are following the way of Egypt. The LORD needs to correct the situation and bring it in line with his Way. We will see this below.

To Abram and Sarai's household belongs an Egyptian woman named Hagar. She has arrived with Abram from Egypt as part payment for the wrong Pharaoh had done to Sarai (Ch. 12). Sarai owns Hagar. As personal servant to Sarai, Hagar is not just any servant. Hagar is an important person in Sarai's tent.

From vs. 3 we learn that *Abram had lived in the land of Canaan ten years.* That is ten years after the LORD God had for the first time given his Word to Abram that *in him all the nations of the earth shall be blessed* (ch. 12 repeated in ch. 15). Sarai speaks to Abram and says, *"Behold now the LORD has prevented me from having children."* Sarai then proposes to Abram a substitute to the Way of the LORD. She proposes to give her Egyptian servant to Abram so that there will be an heir. Hagar's children will be counted as belonging to Sarai. Abram listens to Sarai and conceives a child by Hagar.

Most interpreters see in this a substitute marriage and look for its origin to Babylonian customs and laws. However, Hagar is not from Ur of Mesopotamia but from Egypt. She comes from the harem of the king of Egypt. Hagar's actions are typical for an Egyptian servant of high position. Hagar despises Sarai. The word used can mean to make light of or even to curse. According to Hagar, Sarai is cursed by her god for she is barren. Hagar, however, is favoured by her Egyptian gods and is pregnant. Moreover, in Hagar's eyes Sarai is an Asiatic and therefore inferior to an Egyptian. Hagar elevates herself above Sarai as if she is Abram's princess and Sarai the servant. (The name Sarai means, *'princess'.*)

When Sarai complains to Abram about Hagar's insubordination, Abram reduces Hagar to the servant position. Abram tells Sarai, *"Behold, your servant is in your power; do to her as you please."* Abram does not support Hagar in her aspirations. Sarai then *"dealt harshly with her."* Literally, it says that Sarai *humiliated* Hagar. Hagar flees from Sarai into the wilderness of Shur. Shur means *wall*. Hagar the Egyptian, flees in the direction of the *Wall of Egypt*. She stops at a spring of water and there the Angel of the LORD finds her. To her surprise, Hagar finds that it is not her Egyptian gods who come to help her. To her amazement, it is the God of Abram and Sarai who comes to her. The Angel of the LORD confirms the decisions made by Abram and Sarai. The Angel orders her *"Return to you mistress and submit to her."*

Literally, it says *"humble yourself under her."* We could say that the Angel of the LORD put Hagar in her place. The Angel of the LORD restores the relations in Abram's household to the right order.

At this point it is necessary to state that the Angel of the LORD was not just one of the angels but Yahweh himself appearing in the form of the Angel. This is confirmed in verse thirteen where it is said of Hagar *"So she called the name of the LORD (YAHWEH) who spoke to her ...."*

To our surprise, the Angel of the LORD does not deal harshly with Hagar. The LORD God sympathizes with the misery, or humiliation, Hagar is experiencing. Hagar has not brought herself into Abram's household. Neither has she placed herself in Abram's arms. The child she is carrying is Abram's child. She is owed consideration from Abram and Sarai but is not getting it. Yahweh, Abram's Master, takes the consequences of Abram's actions. The Angel of the LORD assures Hagar that he will *"multiply her offspring so that they cannot be numbered for multitude."* She will bear a son and call his name *"Ishmael, because the LORD has listened to your affliction."* However, the Angel of the LORD does not use the word *"blessing."* On the contrary, Ishmael will not be a man of blessing but a wild man and a man of strife.

13 So she called the name of the LORD who spoke to her, "You are a God of seeing," for she said, "Truly here I have seen him who looks after me."

These are exceptional words for an Egyptian woman. What happened to Hagar at the spring of water is impossible to an Egyptian. Please consider earlier commentary on Genesis 3. There we found that to the Egyptians of Abram's day the gods had withdrawn from the earth because of man's rebellion. Because of the withdrawal of the gods there was no longer communication between the gods and mankind. They simply are not seen and the gods do not appear. Here, however, an Egyptian woman experiences that the only true God who is called *He Is – YAHWEH* is present wherever he wills. Abram's God appears, sees, and looks after whomever he wills. He even looks after the Egyptian woman Hagar and her offspring. *"Therefore the well was called Beer-lahai-roi."* That is "the well of the Living One who sees me." Hagar's son was born just as foretold by the Angel of the LORD and Abram called him Ishmael. At that time *"Abram was eighty-six years old."*

TO CONSIDER

1. How do you evaluate Sarai and Abram's decision to have Hagar as Abram's wife?
2. How do you evaluate Hagar's position as wife of Abram? Did she belong to the line of the Bond of the Covenant the LORD God made in chapter fifteen?
3. Hagar humiliated Sarai. How did the 'Egyptian' come out in Hagar in the way she humiliated Sarai?
4. How did Abram return Hagar to her old position in Abram and Sarai's house?
5. What was the impact of the humiliation Sarai inflicted on Hagar?
6. Why did Hagar flee in the direction of Shur?
7. How do we know who the Angel of the LORD was who appeared to her at the well?
8. How did the Angel of the LORD restore the right order in Abram's household?
9. What position did the Angel of the LORD give Hagar when he told her to go back?
10. How was Hagar's reaction to the appearance of the Angel of the LORD typically Egyptian?

11. Can you describe the similarity between the LORD's disapproval of the line of Egypt in Abram's arms and 2 Corinthians 6:14, *"Do not be unequally yoked with unbelievers, for what partnership has righteousness with lawlessness ...?*
12. The LORD's actions in chapter 16 carried a message to the enslaved Hebrews in Egypt. What message was that?

Chapter 17

THE TIMES AND SEASONS OF THE LORD OUR MASTER

(For Adonai Yahweh See notes at ch. 15:2)

In chapters sixteen and seventeen God the Holy Spirit carefully informs us of times in the life of Abram. Abram had lived ten years in the land of Canaan since the LORD God had first promised him offspring (Genesis 12). After ten years, Sarai had given Abram her servant Hagar as wife. Chapter 16 ends with telling us that Abram was 86 years old at the birth of Ishmael.
Chapter 17 begins with the information that Abram was 99 years old when the LORD appeared to Abram. That adds up to 23 years of waiting since the LORD God had first given Abram his Word that *"in his offspring all nations would be blessed"* (ch. 12). The inheritance of the land by Abram's offspring in the fourth generation (ch. 15) is not only remote but seems impossible.

The word *waiting* in the previous sentence presses itself upon our mind. For twenty three years Abram and Sarai were waiting for the LORD God to fulfill his Word.
When you read through the Bible you meet numerous persons who are waiting. Today Christians are still waiting. The crucial point is whether we are waiting in faith and trust or whether we are giving up on the LORD.
Abram, Israel in Egypt, Christians in the End-times, all need to trust that the LORD God is going to act at his time and on time. "Wait" and "time" are the keywords here.

DISCUSSION POINT

1. What do the terms *"times and seasons of the LORD"* mean to you?
2. Discuss the crucial point mentioned in the precious paragraph.

At this point we do well to remember the words our Lord Jesus Christ spoke to his disciples before he ascended into heaven. In the book of Acts, chapter one, we read of the disciples asking the Lord a question. *"So when they had come together, they asked him, "Lord, will you at this time restore the kingdom to Israel?" He said to them, "It is not for you to know times or seasons that the Father has fixed by his own authority."* (Acts 1:6-7)
Let's add to this Deut. 29:29, *"The secret things belong to the LORD our God, but the things that are revealed belong to us and to our children forever, that we may do all the words of this law."*

QUICK QUESTIONS

1. What are the secret things that belong to the LORD our God?

2. What are the things revealed to us and to our children?

This is what Abram, Israel in Egypt; Christians in the End-times have to accept in faith and trust: The LORD God has his eternal plan and time schedule and he will act on time. He gave his Oath-Word in the Bond which he cut before Abram. For Abram and Sarai this means that the LORD God will make his Word true: There will be a son and there will be the inheritance of the land, but according to the LORD's schedule. This means for Israel in Egypt that the LORD God will lead them out and bring them to this land in the fourth generation, and that there will be an end to oppression in Egypt, but only according to the schedule of the LORD God. The LORD will do this at his time and on time. That is the message Moses brings them with the contents of the book of Genesis. For Christians, who are living in the End-times, this means that we look back on the time and season of the LORD when he cut off his Son on the cross, and look forward to the time of the fullness of the Kingdom of God which the Father has set in his own counsel.

QUESTIONS

1. What did God reveal to Israel in Egypt through his Word to Abram?
2. What time and season do Christian believers look back on?
3. How do Christian believers look ahead in these troubled times?

Genesis 17: *"When Abram was ninety-nine years old the LORD appeared to Abram and said to him, "I am God Almighty; walk before me, and be blameless, ² that I may make my covenant between me and you, and may multiply you greatly." ³ Then Abram fell on his face. And God said to him, ⁴ "Behold, my covenant is with you, and you shall be the father of a multitude of nations. ⁵ No longer shall your name be called Abram, but your name shall be Abraham, for I have made you the father of a multitude of nations. ⁶ I will make you exceedingly fruitful, and I will make you into nations, and kings shall come from you. ⁷ And I will establish my covenant between me and you and your offspring after you throughout their generations for an everlasting covenant, to be God to you and to your offspring after you. ⁸ And I will give to you and to your offspring after you the land of your sojournings, all the land of Canaan, for an everlasting possession, and I will be their God."* [29]

"When Abram was ninety-nine years old." At this time of Abram's life it is thirteen years since Abram had appealed to his Master, Adonai Yahweh, saying that he would die childless (*naked*). God the Holy Spirit reveals to us in Romans 4:19 that at age ninety nine Abram's *"body was as good as dead ...."* According to human timing there was no hope for Abram to have offspring at age 99. The mentioning of Abram's age seems poor but actually it is rich. It brings out the poverty of man's timing, and the riches of the timing of the LORD God. It is time for Yahweh to act and do what only he can do. At age 99, Yahweh is going to bring this dead Abram to life and make him from Abram into Abraham, the father of many nations.

QUICK QUESTION

1. What does the timing of Abram's age bring out in two ways?

---

[29] *The Holy Bible: English Standard Version.* 2001 (Ge 17:1–8). Wheaton: Standard Bible Society.

"The LORD appeared to Abram and said 'I am God Almighty (El Shaddai)'." For the right understanding of the times and seasons of the LORD God we must translate this sentence as literally as possible. *"HE IS showed Himself to Abram and said 'I am God the Judge of all the earth'."*

First of all: This sentence shows that Yahweh is progressing. There is progression in the manner Yahweh shows himself to Abram. This time Yahweh does not come to Abram in a vision. The LORD God shows himself in person and in an awe inspiring manner. We are not told what Abram saw but in the verses three and seventeen we are told that Abram fell on his face before Yahweh. The appearance is so clearly divine that Abram prostrates himself before the LORD God and in his presence.

This progression is also noticeable from what Yahweh reveals about himself. Yahweh reveals that he is *El Shaddai*.

Discussion Point

4. Show the progression in the manner in which Yahweh shows himself to Abram.

El Shaddai

To translate the Hebrew words, *El Shaddai*, into English seems difficult. Many suggestions are made but in the end we get nowhere if we look for a clear dictionary meaning. The better way is to explain *Shaddai* from how God the Holy Spirit uses this word throughout the Old Testament Scriptures.[30] We find that *Shaddai* is used in the context of God as Judge. A good example of this is the book of Job where Job frequently presents his just cause to *Shaddai*. In the larger context of Genesis 17 we find how in Genesis 18:27 Abraham speaks, *"...shall not the Judge of all the earth do right?"* Yahweh is on his way as *El Shaddai* to judge wicked Sodom and the other cities. Yahweh does this as the judge of all the earth. This gives us the best meaning of *El Shaddai: Judge of all the earth.*

Questions

1. The Versions translate both *El Shaddai* and *Yahweh Tsavaoth* with God, or LORD *Almighty*. Where, on the page, do the Versions tell you which Hebrew title of God is behind their translation?
2. Would you agree that it is better to translate *"God the Judge"* and *"LORD of Hosts"*?

Yahweh is on his way to judge Sodom. We can easily accept that. However, it becomes harder to accept that Yahweh comes to Abram as Judge. Reading the whole of 17:1 will help us. Yahweh commands Abram as El Shaddai to *"walk before Him and be blameless."* Of Enoch and Noah we read that they *"walked with God"* (Genesis 5:24; 6:9), but Abram is commanded to walk *before* God. Yahweh is bringing Abram into a special relationship to himself. "Walking before," means that Abram is given the very special position of herald and representative of Yahweh, the judge of all the earth. In this official position Abram is to be *blameless*. The command to be blameless comes to Abram from the judge of all the earth. In his position of walking before Yahweh, Abram has the watchful eye of his Master upon him to see whether Abram acquits himself of his task blamelessly.

---

[30] We are given a good overview of the use and meaning of Shaddai in Scripture in the unpublished Master's Thesis of Revelation M.H. VanLuik, (EL) SHADDAI: A FOCUSSED EXEGETICAL STUDY 1980. His excellent study corresponds well with my own limited research of this topic.

1) How do Christian believers *walk before the Lord* today?
2) What does it mean to have the *watchful eye* of our God upon us?

BLAMELESS

Often the word *blameless* in the Bible is taken to mean perfect. If blameless were to mean perfect, then Abram and all his descendants would be unable to walk before the Judge of all the earth blamelessly. The only exception would be the Lord Jesus Christ who alone walked before his Father blamelessly. However, following the word blameless through the Bible we find that the biblical meaning is wholehearted, with an undivided heart.

DISCUSSION POINT

1. Blameless cannot mean perfect. Can you reason that out?
2. Which Man alone is perfect?
3. How can we be perfect before God?

Many good examples of the scope of being blameless are found in the book of Psalms. Here are two examples: First, Psalm 101,

> *I will ponder the way that is blameless.*
> *Oh when will you come to me?*
> *I will walk with integrity of heart*
> *within my house;*
> *³ I will not set before my eyes*
> *anything that is worthless.*
> *I hate the work of those who fall away;*
> *it shall not cling to me.*
> *⁴ A perverse heart shall be far from me;*
> *I will know nothing of evil.* [31]

In these verses blameless runs parallel with integrity of heart. Blameless is contrasted with worthless, with falling away, with a perverse heart.

The second example is **Psalm 19:13**:

"Keep your servant also from wilful sins; may they not rule over me. Then will I be blameless, innocent of great transgression."

It is important to note that the psalmist does not pray that the LORD will keep him from sinning. He prays that the LORD will keep him from wilful sins so that he may be innocent of great transgressions.

Here God the Holy Spirit is providing great comfort to all who follow our God and Saviour Jesus Christ with an undivided heart. A true Christian does not rebel against God. The heart of a true Christian is not divided between God and Satan. In all his or her weaknesses the true Christian is blameless before God because God himself says so in his Word, **and our God does not lie.**

---

[31] *The Holy Bible: English Standard Version. 2001 (Ps 101:2–4). Wheaton: Standard Bible Society.*

QUICK QUESTION

1. What great comfort does a true Christian receive in his or her weakness before God?

17:2 *"... that I may make my covenant between me and you, and may multiply you greatly"*. Literally it says *"that I may give my covenant,"* or even, *"that I may continue to give my covenant."*

Several remarks need to be made concerning verse two. Let's begin with discussing the tremendous new revelation we receive here. After the cutting of the Bond of the Covenant in chapter 15 there is progression. In chapter 15, Yahweh bound himself by oath to make Abram into a great nation, to redeem his descendants from slavery, to bring them back in the fourth generation. At that time we did not meet the word *"between"*. At that time the LORD God did not make this Bond between himself and Abram. The Bond was one-sided. Although Abram and his offspring were the beneficiaries of the Words of Yahweh, Abram was not yet given a place within the Bond of the Covenant with Yahweh.

QUICK QUESTION

1. What progression is there with respect to the Bond of the Covenant from ch. 15 to ch. 17?

In Genesis 17:2 the LORD God brings a new thing into this fallen world. That new thing is a word, and that is the word: **"between"**. With the word 'between', our strong God establishes a breakthrough. Yahweh, El Shaddai, the Judge of all the earth, binds himself to a man, namely, to Abram and to his offspring. The LORD God brings Abram and his offspring alongside himself. In 2 Chr. 20:7, Isaiah 41:8, and Jas. 2:23 we are informed that in this new relation, which the LORD God created between himself and Abram, the man Abram became the *"friend of God."* Nevertheless, in the Bond of the Covenant the LORD God always remains Abram's Master, our Master, and our Judge. Our God always continues to speak of *"My Bond, My Covenant"*. Abram and his offspring never have become equal partners with the LORD God. Even when the Son of God became the man Jesus of Nazareth, he made himself a subject of his Father within the Bond of the Covenant doing his Father's will *"taking the form of a servant"* (Phil. 2). [32]

We find here the miracle of God's grace to undeserving people. The LORD God is at work restoring his good creation and the crown of what he made. God is restoring his image: man. Since Adam, our forefather, sinned there had never been a man walking before the Living God in the intimate Bond of the Covenant. What Yahweh did for Abram he did to his Glory and for our benefit. All creation, and all mankind, still benefits from the breakthrough Yahweh accomplished when he made Abram to walk before him as the friend of God.

QUESTIONS

1. How does the word **"between"** show that God brought progression in the life of his Covenant Bond with Abram?

---

[32] Genesis 17:2 (ESV) that I may make my covenant between me and you, and may multiply you greatly." The ESV seems to be the only Version that literally translates the cohortative וְאֶתְּנָה literally and in line with the second cohortative וְאַרְבֶּה.

2. What honorable mention does Scripture give to Abraham?
3. What would that mean in the practice of Abraham's life with God?
4. Does the Bond of God's Covenant ever become "*our*" Covenant?
5. What does the LORD God himself always say about the Bond of the Covenant?
6. Do we ever become equal partners with God in the Bond of the Covenant?
7. Who subjected himself to his Father's will within the Bond of the Covenant?
8. Can you substantiate that from Scripture?

THE LORD GOD CONTINUES HIS BOND WITH ABRAM AND HIS OFFSPRING ONLY WHEN WE REMAIN BLAMELESS, WHOLEHEARTED, WITH UNDIVIDED HEART AS SERVANTS OF THE LORD GOD

*"Be blameless **that** I may give My Bond with you and your offspring."* This has the sense of that I may *continue* to give. There is a warning to Abram and all his offspring in these words. We may not rebel against the sovereign LORD of the Covenant Bond. If we do, we break the Bond and suffer the consequences. To this present day mankind is experiencing the consequences of rebellion against the LORD God. The LORD God never is present to bless those who rebel against him. The LORD God is only present to bless those who serve him with an undivided heart. Compare this with what our Saviour teaches us in the Gospel of John chapter fifteen. *"I am the vine; you are the branches. ... If anyone does not abide in Me he is thrown away like a branch and withers."* (see also Hebrews 10:26-32).

QUICK QUESTION

1. Do we remain within the Bond of the Covenant between the LORD God and us no matter how unfaithful we become?

THE LORD GOD CHANGES ABRAM'S NAME INTO ABRAHAM.

The name Abram means *exalted father*. The name Abraham is explained by the LORD God himself in 17:4-8, *"Your name shall be Abraham, for I have made you the father of a multitude of nations. ... and kings shall come from you ... and I will establish my covenant between me and you and your offspring after you throughout their generations for an everlasting covenant ...."*

Yahweh continues to speak of new things he will do for Abraham. The Bond of the Covenant between God and Abraham and his offspring will have an ongoing, even everlasting history. It will be a history of nations and of kings who all will have their origin in God who made Abraham fruitful. By the will of the LORD God this history will be an Abrahamic history. All peoples who know the Bible, and believe the Words of God, are familiar with this Abrahamic history. It spans the centuries.

The nation of Israel, with her kings, was the fruit of Yahweh and his everlasting Bond with Abraham and his offspring. In the everlasting Bond of the Covenant our God and Saviour Jesus Christ has become King of kings and Lord of lords. This is in fulfillment of the everlasting Bond given to Abraham and his offspring. All who believe on the only Saviour Jesus Christ are declared to be children of Abraham since they share the faith of Abraham. See Gal. 3:29, *"And if you are Christ's, then you are Abraham's offspring, heirs according to promise."*

The *times and seasons* of the LORD God shape and govern all of history. All his Words (devarim) become deeds true and sure. Nothing happens outside his control. He still establishes his everlasting Bond today with his believers, and has made his Son the Judge of all the nations. Since Genesis 17 the world is not the same.

QUESTIONS

1. How long does the LORD says that the Bond of the Covenant will endure?
2. Explain what *"everlasting history"* means.
3. Explain the term *"Abrahamic history"*.
4. How does the Abrahamic history *"span the centuries"*?
5. What kind of *"children"* are Christian believers called in Gal. 3:29? What does that mean for us?
6. Show God's *"times and seasons"* in the history of the world during the fifteenth century.
7. When Moses brought Yahweh's Words to the Hebrews in Egypt did they believe the times and seasons of Yahweh?
8. The times and seasons of the LORD shape history in an ongoing divine course with a definite future. We call this linear. Pagan nature religions experience history in a circular pattern. As long as nothing changed, as long as there was stability, Egyptians were satisfied. How did this circular thinking affect the Hebrew sojourners in Egypt? Think of their frequent murmuring in the desert.
9. Is the emphasis on the economic welfare of our population linear or circular? In other words: Are we governed by the Christian faith and trust in the times and seasons of God and his Christ? Or are we just content to have a stable economy and welfare state?
10. Are there similarities between the Egyptian aim at stability and our Canadian and world society?
11. Is it enough to claim Christianity but exclude God from our planning?

17:9-11

⁹ And God said to Abraham, "As for you, you shall keep my covenant, you and your offspring after you throughout their generations. ¹⁰ This is my covenant, which you shall keep, between me and you and your offspring after you: Every male among you shall be circumcised. ¹¹ You shall be circumcised in the flesh of your foreskins, and it shall be a sign of the covenant between me and you. ¹² He who is eight days old among you shall be circumcised. Every male throughout your generations, whether born in your house or bought with your money from any foreigner who is not of your offspring, ¹³ both he who is born in your house and he who is bought with your money, shall surely be circumcised. So shall my covenant be in your flesh an everlasting covenant. ¹⁴ Any uncircumcised male who is not circumcised in the flesh of his foreskin shall be cut off from his people; he has broken my covenant."

In this section of chapter seventeen the LORD adds new things. Central among these is **circumcision.** We tend to make the new element of circumcision so central that the other elements in these verses recede to the background. We must make an effort to understand this passage in the context of the whole chapter. There is continuation and there is progression.

The LORD God continues to use the new word *between*. No longer is the Bond where he bound himself one-sided. By divine, sovereign act, Yahweh has made the Bond of the Covenant two-sided. However, there is not only continuation. There is also progression. In the oath cutting ceremony of chapter fifteen Yahweh had bound himself to make his Words to Abraham true. By that oath the LORD God had laid his Name, his reputation, on the line. Now pay attention to the words of the LORD in the beginning of verse nine, *"as for you"*. These words tell us that the LORD God is switching from his duties within the Bond to the duties of Abraham and his offspring after him.

DISCUSSION TIME

1. Why was the word *between* a new word?
2. How do we benefit from the fact that the LORD made the Bond of the Covenant two sided?
3. In the two sided Bond is our position that of servants and/or sons and daughters?
4. What task is the LORD laying upon us by saying *"as for you"*?

To keep. In the *between* of the Bond of the Covenant the LORD God demands from Abraham and his offspring to *keep* their side of the Bond. Often the word *keep* has the value *"to guard"*. In this command to *keep the Bond,* the LORD God continues to demand of Abraham to be *blameless* before El Shaddai (17:1). The Bond must be kept *wholeheartedly*.

QUICK QUESTION

1. What does keeping the 'bond of the covenant' mean for us?

TO KEEP THE BOND IS TO BE CIRCUMCISED

The LORD God lays upon Abraham and his offspring a command. We might expect the LORD God to present Abraham with a set of rules. To our surprise there is only one rule, *every male among you shall be circumcised*. Keeping the Bond of the Covenant means to be circumcised. *"This is my covenant, which you shall keep, between me and you and your offspring after you: Every male among you shall be circumcised in the flesh of your foreskins, and it shall be a sign of the covenant between me and you."*

DISCUSSION TIME

1. Could you compare the circumcision in the flesh with the grafting of a tattoo into the skin of a person?
2. Are tattoos just innocent fancies?

A SIGN SPEAKS

This is the second time that the LORD God gives a *sign of the covenant*. After the flood (Genesis 9), the LORD God gave the sign of the rainbow. From that we learn how a sign speaks. God said to Noah when I see the sign of the rainbow in the sky *"I will remember my covenant that is between me and you and every living creature of all flesh."* The function of the sign is **to make us remember**. God gives us the sign of the Bond of the Covenant so that we should remember to what the LORD God has bound himself, and what he binds us to.

It is of great comfort to the believer to know that our strong God is the first one to see the sign and remember how he bound himself to our father Abraham and to us his offspring. The LORD God is not only the first one to see the rainbow. The LORD God is also the first one to see the sign of circumcision and remember his Bond of the Covenant. The second to see circumcision in their flesh are Abraham and his offspring after him. Seeing circumcision in their flesh Abraham and his offspring are to remember their obligation to love the LORD wholeheartedly in the Bond of the Covenant.

In the New Testament the same applies to baptized believers and their offspring. When the LORD God sees our baptism he remembers the blood of his Son who washed sinners clean. When we and our children remember our baptism we are to remember to walk with God wholeheartedly and in love.

QUESTIONS

1. Compare the sign of circumcision with the sign of the rainbow. What have these two signs in common?
2. Who is the first one to see the sign of the rainbow, the sign of circumcision, and the sign of baptism?
3. What does God remember when he sees the sign of the rainbow, of circumcision and of baptism?
4. What are we to remember when we see the sign of baptism on our forehead?
5. What does *blameless* mean for us?
6. The Lord Jesus was circumcised at the eighth day. What did the Lord Jesus remember when he saw the sign of circumcision in his flesh?

CIRCUMCISION WAS ALREADY KNOWN

In a number of books we meet the claim that Abraham and his descendants learned circumcision from neighboring countries, especially Egypt. It is true that circumcision was practiced in Egypt. Pictures of circumcising men and teenage boys exist dating back as far as 4000. [33] The person to be circumcised was in a standing position while the person performing the cutting squatted in front. In Egypt it was not a general rule that all males were circumcised. The purpose had to do with the coming of age.

There is a misunderstanding as to whether other nations around Abraham practiced circumcision of boys and men. Gerald A. Larue in his paper, *Religious Traditions and Circumcision*, writes: *"Circumcision was practiced by some Semitic groups. Jeremiah, in the seventh century, included Edomites, Ammonites and Moabites as among the circumcised (9:25). Assyrians and Babylonians were not circumcised. Nor were the Philistines who are derogatively defined in the Bible as "the uncircumcised" (Jug. 14:3; 15:18; 1 Sam 14:6, etc.). An eleventh century B. C. E. ivory from Megiddo, portrays a ruler seated on his throne between cherubim (Figure 5). Among those in the approaching procession is a soldier leading two nude captives, presumably Semites, both of whom are circumcised."*

Abraham originated from Mesopotamia, where, according to Larue, circumcision was not practiced. The Edomites, Ammonites, and Moabites were either descendants of Abraham, or of Lot, Abraham's nephew.

---

[33] Wilson, John (1950): Circumcision in Egypt, in James F Pritchard, edit, Ancient Near Eastern Texts Relating to the Old Testament, Princeton University Press, p. 326. Gerald A. Larue , Religious Traditions and Circumcision Presented at The Second International Symposium on Circumcision, San Francisco, California, April 30-May 3, 1991.

CIRCUMCISION WAS NOT COPIED FROM OTHER CULTURES. GOD'S COMMAND TO CIRCUMCISE WAS UNIQUE, ONE OF A KIND

In God's command to circumcise there are distinct differences. This is evident from what the LORD God says in Genesis 17. **First**: The living LORD gave circumcision as a sign of the Bond between him and Abraham and his offspring. In Egypt of Abraham's day such communication of the living LORD and a man was unknown, even considered impossible. In Egypt there was no presence of the god nor was there a command to circumcise. Neither was circumcision in Egypt a sign.

Second: In Egypt circumcision of infants at the eighth day was not practiced. To circumcise a baby boy would have caused the baby to bleed to death. Only in modern times it became known that at the eighth day the body would produce vitamin K, which is needed for the blood to coagulate. The Creator of heaven and earth created the human body and he alone knew that at the eighth day it was safe to circumcise a baby boy. In his Bond with Abraham Yahweh gave a unique and safe command, the cutting of the sign of circumcision in the flesh of a boy at eight days of age.

QUICK QUESTION

What in God's sign of circumcision was different from the act of circumcision in Egypt?

THE BLOOD OF THE SIGN OF CIRCUMCISION SPEAKS

In the act of circumcision blood is poured out, caused by the cutting off of the foreskin. The action of **cutting off** is important. There is a relation between Yahweh cutting the Bond of the Covenant in an oath sign (Ch. 15) and Abraham cutting off the foreskin. In both cases blood flows and in both cases we are presented with the sign of the oath. In Genesis 15, the LORD God does an awesome thing when he calls himself to witness his Words of Promise. "May I be as these dead animals if I do not keep my oath." In the blood of circumcision Yahweh holds his servant responsible to trust and obey his Master and walk before him blamelessly.

If Abraham, or his descendants, would become disobedient, their blood would be demanded from them. For us, New Covenant people of God, despising our baptism would be the same as despising the blood of Christ by which he established the New Bond of the Covenant. When we despise God's baptism we break the Bond of the Covenant God has established with his people.

As in the oath sign of Genesis 15, the bird remained whole, foretelling the death and resurrection of Jesus, the Lamb of God. So too, the blood of circumcision foretold of the blood of the Lamb of God who would take away the sin of the world.

Discussion Point

1. Compare God's oath cutting sign in Genesis 15 with the oath cutting sign of circumcision of Genesis 17. What is different and what is similar?
2. The letter to the Hebrews speaks of the blood of the Lord Jesus as the *blood of the covenant*. How was the blood of circumcision foreshadowing the blood of the Lord Jesus?
3. Compare the consequence of despising the blood of the Covenant in circumcision with despising the sign of Christ's blood in holy baptism?

The Sign of Circumcision and the Righteousness that is by Faith.

(See Rom. 4:3 and 9; Gal. 3:6; Jas. 2:23.)

The New Testament reveals that Abraham received circumcision as a sign of the righteousness that is by faith. This is not a quote from the book of Genesis. God the Holy Spirit however confirms in the New Testament what we already find in Genesis seventeen. There the LORD God spoke to Abraham of circumcision as *"a sign of my Bond in your flesh."* This tells us that the life giving God signed and sealed his gracious presence with believing Abraham. To trust and obey wholeheartedly is crucial for having God's seal of righteousness upon us in grace and in mercy.

Discussion Point

1. May a baptized person who rebels against the LORD count on being righteous in his sight?

Circumcision on the Eighth Day and Infant Baptism

Infant baptism is often rejected on the basis that a baby cannot confess the faith. This is in connection with the conviction that baptism is the confession of faith of the believer. However, the LORD God commanded that babies at eight days of age were to receive the same oath sign of the Bond of the Covenant as their father Abraham. Our human logic says that this was impossible for Isaac could not believe and confess. Sorry, but the logic of our heavenly God and Father supersedes our human logic. Infant baptism is warranted because the LORD God commanded that Isaac would receive the sign or seal of the righteousness that is by faith.

Questions

1. Could eight day old Isaac already be righteous by faith?
2. Why was Isaac circumcised?
3. Did circumcision mean something to Isaac or did it mean nothing?
4. What does baptism of a baby of believing parents mean to the parents?
5. What does the baptism of a baby mean to him or her while growing up?
6. Who is the first one in the act of circumcision?
7. Who is the first one in the act of baptism? Is it the believing person or is it God?
8. Whose logic must we follow in administering the sign and seal of baptism to infant children of believers?

Every male in Abraham's house was to receive circumcision vs 10-14

The LORD God extended his Bond to Abraham and his household. Every male person in Abraham's household was to carry the sign of the Bond of the Covenant in his flesh. Thereby even slaves, bought by Abraham, were charged to be bound to Yahweh and serve him wholeheartedly. In the New Bond of the Covenant there may not be any one who is not baptized. The same applies to a Christian family. The whole family of believing parents is holy to the LORD.

Discussion Point

1. Do believing parents with their children form only a social unit or do they form a Christian family unit in the Bond of the Covenant that God has with them as a family?
2. How should growing sons and daughters evaluate themselves as members of a Christian family within the Bond of the Covenant?

Refusing to be circumcised is breaking the Bond with the LORD God

Acceptance of circumcision in faith and trust is maintaining the Bond with Yahweh. Refusing to be circumcised is breaking the Bond with Yahweh. Within the Bond of the Covenant the LORD God remains El Shaddai, the Judge of all the earth. By accepting circumcision righteous Abraham committed himself to keep the Bond with the LORD wholeheartedly. Circumcision was for Abraham the sign of his oath of allegiance to Yahweh.

Quick Question

1. If refusing to be circumcised is breaking the Bond of God how must we view refusal to be baptized into the name of God the Father, God the Son and God the Holy Spirit?

Genesis 17:15-24

15 And God said to Abraham, "As for Sarai your wife, you shall not call her name Sarai, but Sarah shall be her name. 16 I will bless her, and moreover, I will give you a son by her. I will bless her, and she shall become nations; kings of peoples shall come from her." 17 Then Abraham fell on his face and laughed and said to himself, "Shall a child be born to a man who is a hundred years old? Shall Sarah, who is ninety years old, bear a child?" 18 And Abraham said to God, "Oh that Ishmael might live before you!" 19 God said, "No, but Sarah your wife shall bear you a son, and you shall call his name Isaac. I will establish my covenant with him as an everlasting covenant for his offspring after him. 20 As for Ishmael, I have heard you; behold, I have blessed him and will make him fruitful and multiply him greatly. He shall father twelve princes, and I will make him into a great nation. 21 But I will establish my covenant with Isaac, whom Sarah shall bear to you at this time next year." [34]

---

[34] *The Holy Bible: English Standard Version.* 2001 (Ge 17:15–21). Wheaton: Standard Bible Society.

From "My Princess" to Princess

Sarai means "my" princess. That is how Abraham called his wife. The LORD tells Abraham to no longer call his wife "my princess" but Princess. Capitalizing *Princess* brings home to us the fact that Sarah from now on has an office and an official title. The LORD God is taking her into his service. The LORD God is going to open her womb. The LORD God is going to give Abraham a son through Sarah. Sarah will become nations; kings of peoples shall come from her.

This is too much for Abraham to believe. He falls on his face, laughs, and speaks inside himself. He and Sarah are just too old to have a child born to them. Abraham then voices his doubts to the LORD God and asks a question: *"Oh that Ishmael might live before you!"*

Questions

1. Why was Abraham wrong in his desire that Ishmael might live before the LORD God?
2. Ishmael received the sign and seal of circumcision. What was Ishmael's position in the Bond of the Covenant?
3. A baptized child of Christian believers may in later life rebel against God similar to Ishmael. What is the position of such a baptized person under the Bond of the New Covenant?
4. What is the difference between Abram and Abraham and Sarai and Sarah?

Yahweh is opening the Way of Life

We have seen earlier that the Way of the Opener of the Way of Life could only run via Abraham and his offspring. The Way of Life could not continue via the mixed Egyptian line of Abraham's son Ishmael. In this chapter the LORD God makes that clear by his answer to Abraham's exclamation, *"Oh that Ishmael might live before you!"*

The LORD answers Abraham with an emphatic *"on the contrary!"* Not the son of Hagar, but a son whom Sarah will give birth to is the promised offspring. His name is to be Isaac for there will be laughter in Abraham's tent and among all nations. The LORD God is opening the power of procreation in Abraham as sure as circumcision opened Abraham's foreskin. Similarly the LORD God will open Sarah's womb to give birth to the son whose name is to be laughter. The LORD God, who is from the beginning the Opener of the Way of Life, has chosen to push forward his Way through Isaac. The Bond of his Covenant will continue through Isaac and not through Ishmael. Natural descent does not determine who God's firstborn son is, but God's sovereign decision determines that. The LORD God passed over Hagar and chose Sarah. Likewise the LORD God passed over Ishmael and chose Isaac.

Questions

1. Do you know from Scripture other times that the LORD God opened the womb in his sovereign way?
2. Do you know from Scripture other cases where the LORD God passed over the first son and chose another son as the firstborn?
3. Why could God's Open Way of Life not continue through Ishmael?
4. Was Isaac better than Ishmael?
5. Why Isaac?
6. In whose conception and birth was this pattern of the firstborn made full?

7. Why would we rejoice in Jesus Christ as the Opener of the Way of Life?
8. God the Holy Spirit speaks of the "Church of the Firstborn" (Heb. 12:23). What does that tell you about where the route of the Open Way of Life is found?
9. Is that because of "good" Christians as members of the church?
10. What does that tell you of the need to belong to the Church identified as the Body of Christ and the Church of the Firstborn?

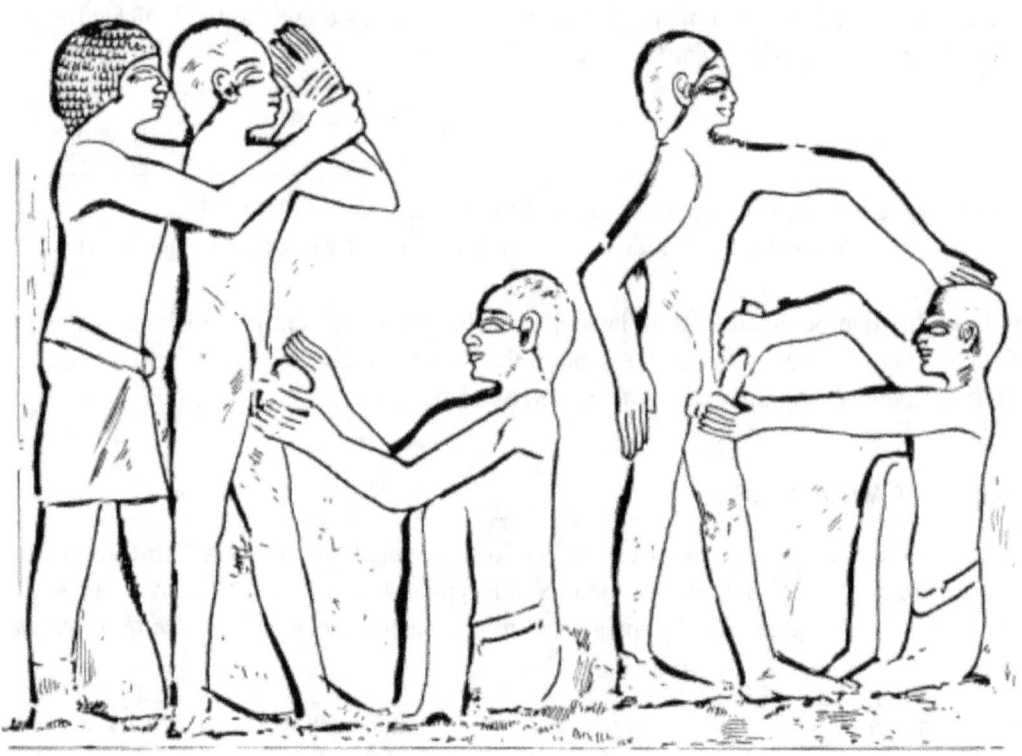

An ancient Egypt illustration of the circumcision of two young men by two squatting persons. This is how the men, recorded in Joshua chapter five, were circumcised at Gilgal.

GOD WENT UP

We read in verse 22, *"And when He finished talking with him, God went up from Abraham"*. We could easily take this as self-explanatory information. If we do so then we miss out on the magnificence of what is happening here. We must read 17:22 in conjunction with verse one of the chapter. The LORD appeared to Abram in person. In v.22 the LORD went up in person. That means that the LORD went back to where he came from, namely, to heaven. The person Abram saw was a heavenly person. The person who came to Abram was the God of heaven. The person who gave to Abram an everlasting Bond of offspring and inheritance especially came to Abram from heaven and returned to heaven. In this action Yahweh practiced the Bond of the Covenant personally in love and truth. Awesome! This is the Bond all Christians may have with the God of heaven through faith in Jesus Christ. The God of Genesis seventeen has not changed. He practices a living Bond with all who live by faith in Jesus Christ and in communion with his Spirit (Matt. 28:20; John 14:15-21).

God's Wonderful Works bringing life to Sarah's dead womb vs. 1-15.
God's Wonderful Works bringing final judgment on Sodom vs. 16-33.

Genesis 18:1-15

OVERVIEW

- Links of chapter eighteen to chapter seventeen.
- A visit with a purpose.
- The centre of the verses 9-15.
- The need for the LORD God to act **wonderfully.**
- The way in which the LORD God acted wonderfully.
- The relation of "year" in 17:21 to Genesis 18: 10 and 14 (a critique).
- The message of Genesis 18:1-15 to Abraham's descendants.

LINKS OF CHAPTER EIGHTEEN TO CHAPTER SEVENTEEN

Chapter 18 continues the contents of chapter 17. The two belong together. This is noticeable from four things. First of all the chapter begins with the conjunctive *And.* Most newer translations ignore this little word but the ESV gives us the connector and translates, *"And the LORD appeared to him."*

The second item that shows us continuation is this: Abraham's name is not mentioned. We simply are told that the LORD appeared to *him.* Who is the *him?* For the answer we must go back to chapter seventeen. It is Abraham.

The third item that connects chapter eighteen to chapter seventeen is the *LORD.* The same Person who appeared to Abraham in chapter seventeen appears to Abraham at the oaks of Mamre as recorded in chapter eighteen.

The fourth item that binds these two chapters together is *the purpose of the LORD's appearance*, namely the birth of the promised son Isaac.

This is not a technical matter, unimportant for the understanding of chapter eighteen. The four items mentioned above help us to understand who one of the three men is that came to Abraham's tent. It is clearly stated in 18:1 that one of the men is *the LORD.* This is the LORD of whom we read in chapter 17:1 that he appeared to Abraham. The connector *and* in 18:1 tells us that the LORD **continued** to appear to Abraham. There is now no great time lapse between appearances as we noticed in the transition of chapter 16 to chapter 17. [35]In chapter 17:21 the LORD had given Abraham assurance that Sarah would bear a son to Abraham *at this time next year*. The LORD's continued appearance falls within that promised time span. Before the year is over the LORD appears to repeat the promise of the birth of the son, conceived by Abraham, and born from Sarah. Sarah's womb had been closed but the LORD God is going to open Sarah's womb.

DISCUSSION POINT

1. What does the conjunction *"and"* at the beginning of a new chapter tell us?
2. One of the visiting three men evidently is the LORD (YAHWEH). Does this mean that he is God the Son?

A VISIT WITH A PURPOSE

The vs:2-8 record what at first seems to be the description of a case of Eastern hospitality to passing travelers. In verse two, however, there is an indication that Abraham's tent was the purpose of their journey. The three men were not merely walking by but stopped and *"placed themselves before Abraham."* [36] The tent of Abraham and Sarah was their target.

What at first appeared to be a social visit changes when the guests ask a social but unusual question. *"They said to him, 'Where is Sarah your wife?'"* (vs. 9). They knew Sarah was in the tent preparing the food but still they ask where she is. This is because both Abraham and Sarah are going to be addressed. The three men ask the question but only one is going to address Abraham in the hearing of Sarah his wife. Sarah needs to hear what the LORD is revealing to her husband.

DISCUSSION POINT

1. Was the visit of the three men just a chance visit?
2. Why did the men ask "Where is Sarah your wife?" while they knew all along where she was?

The centre of the verses 9-15

This passage needs to be interpreted from its centre. Why this is so will become clear as we go on. The centre is found in verse fourteen where the LORD says, *"Is anything too wonderful for the LORD?"* The word *wonderful* refers to an act of YAHWEH *"who alone does wonderful works."* (Psalm 72:18; 136:4). We need to take a moment to focus on the word *wonderful* which in the Hebrew language is a form of *fala (fl')*. [37]
There is no one equal to the LORD God. The LORD God stands apart and by himself. The word *wonderful (fala (fl')* reflects this. The basic meaning of *fala (fl')* is *to stand apart*. The LORD God stands

---

[35] Remember the "times and seasons" of the LORD.

[36] HAL s.v. נצב

[37] For an extensive treatment see my Essay, "His Name is Wonderful", soon to be available on my website, the LORD willing.

apart, his works stand apart. The LORD God and his works are unequalled, unique, one of a kind. When Abraham's ability fails then the LORD God acts in his unique, unequalled power, he acts *wonderfully*. From this centre we are going to interpret what is revealed to us in the verses 9-15.

QUESTIONS

1. Explain why the word *wonderful leads us to the centre of this section*,
2. The basic meaning of *wonderful* is to stand apart. Apply this to God. What does it mean that God "stands apart"?
3. What does the LORD God mean when he says "Is anything too wonderful for the LORD?"
4. Who all are able to do *wonderful works*?
5. Does the LORD God have equals?
6. What do Psalm 72:18 and Psalm 136:4 tell you about the LORD God and his works?

THE NEED FOR THE LORD GOD TO ACT "WONDERFULLY"

We must ask ourselves the question why the LORD God needs to act in his unique power, *wonderfully*. The answer is that the LORD God has made the continuation of the *Opening of the Way of Life* dependent on Abraham and Sarah. [38] In the Offspring of Abraham all nations will be blessed (Genesis 12:3). However, the LORD God is confronted with the barrenness of Sarah. Abraham is to conceive the promised son Isaac by Sarah, but *the way of women had ceased to be with Sarah (vs. 11)*. This plainly means that Sarah's body no longer produced the egg cell needed for ovulation. This made it impossible for Abraham to conceive a son by his wife Sarah. It was too wonderful for Sarah to reverse her age and experience ovulation, so she laughs. The way to the blessing for all nations is blocked. Essentially, this means that the way to the birth of Jesus, the Saviour of all nations is blocked.

THE WAY IN WHICH THE LORD GOD ACTED WONDERFULLY

At that moment the LORD God reveals his unique power. The LORD God is going to act *wonderfully*. Have the seasonal ovulations ceased for Sarah? Is there no regular *time of life* within her? Here is clear evidence that mankind has no power to create from nothing (see Heb. 11:3). The LORD God is coming to Sarah to create an appointed season for her. Before the year, mentioned in chapter 17:21, is finished, Sarah will conceive the promised son Isaac. In order to make his promise true, the God of the "times and seasons" is acting wonderfully.

Is no one in the whole wide world able to release in Sarah an *ovum* to be fruitful for conception of the son Isaac? The LORD God, creator of the *Path of Life (Genesis 1)*, he alone is able to *wonderfully* create in Sarah *"the way of women"*. Even in our technological advanced time no one is able to create in an old, barren woman her own living egg and ovulation. No one is able to copy the works of the LORD God. He alone does wondrous works.

---

[38] For the Opening of the Way of Life see Notes on Genesis 1 and 3:15.

QUESTIONS

1. The LORD God told them that Sarah would bear a son. Was this the first time that the LORD did this? When else did the LORD make the same promise?
2. Why did Sarah laugh?
3. What was humanly impossible in Sarah that is even impossible for modern science today?
4. How did the LORD God overcome the impediment in Sarah so that she could conceive a child?
5. Why is the LORD's action *"wonderful"*?
6. By acting wonderfully the LORD God made his promise come true. What promise was that?
7. What did the angel Gabriel say to Mary to overcome her objection *"I know no man."*?
8. How does that make you think of what the LORD God said, and did, to Sarah?
9. Compare the conception and birth of Isaac and the Lord Jesus. What similarity and what difference do you find?

THE RELATION OF "YEAR" IN 17:21 TO GENESIS 18: 10 AND 14. (A CRITIQUE)

Regarding the translation of Genesis 18:10 and 14 a decision has to be made. Are we going to translate literally or are we going to translate taking our cue from ch. 17:21 or a neighbouring language that is somewhat related to the Hebrew language of the O.T.? Versions like the NIV and the ESV have inserted the word "year" in Genesis 18:10 and 14. Even though the Akkadian language has an idiom "ana balat" (which only has limited similarity) we would do well to return to the literal reading of these verses. The Hebrew says, "according to the time of life." Kronholm makes this point:

Kronholm in ThDOT Botterweck et. al. P.441 writes about the translation of Genesis 18:10,14, *"The meaning of the expression* כָּעֵת חַיָּה *(Genesis 18:10,14; 2 K. 4:16,17) is disputed. Departing from earlier explanations, Yaron cites the analogous Akkadian expression ana balat, "at this time next year". The phrase occurs only in Genesis 18:10,14; and 2 Kings 4:16,17, in the same context; this is a certain sign that the phrase, otherwise unknown, was passed on in this particular narrative of the birth of a child (it is there in Genesis 17:21, in the same context, but somewhat altered)."*

Two reasons show us the error of inserting the word "year" in 18:10,14.
1. Simple arithmetic shows us that the LORD's return to Sarah falls within the year foretold in 17:21. Within that year Sarah will conceive the child in her womb and after nine months the child will be born. All this happens within the year spoken of by the LORD in 17:21. There simply is not another "year".
2. Inserting the word "year" does not fit the situation. Rather, it takes away the riches of the Wonders of the LORD God revealed in 18:10 and 14. Within the year foretold in 17:21, the LORD is coming to Sarah to wonderfully create for her "the time of life." There will be ovulation. There will be conception. There will be a nine month pregnancy. There will be the birth of Isaac. There will be continuation of the "Way of Life" and the blessing to all nations is secured.

Genesis 18:1-15 is a jewel in the crown of the LORD God, the Author of all creation and recreation. The KJV, the NKJ, the RSV, the Dutch SVV, the Vulgate, and the Portuguese Bible, give a literal translation. With some variation, these all agree that the LORD is going to return to Sarah *according to the time of life.* All other Versions who now follow the Acadian link should return to what Kronholm called *the earlier interpretations.*

THE MESSAGE OF GENESIS 18:1-15 TO ABRAHAM'S DESCENDANTS

ABRAHAM'S DESCENDANTS IN EGYPT

The LORD God sent Moses to Egypt to free Abraham's enslaved descendants. He said that he had heard their cry and remembered his Covenant with Abraham. (Exo. 2:25 etc). After four generations of sojourn in Egypt, where they served the idols of Egypt, most of them no longer remembered what the LORD had promised to Abraham. Neither did they remember how the LORD God had shown his wonderful works. In their plight they needed to know and believe that nothing is too *wonderful* for the LORD God. Israel considered it impossible to be set free from the power of Egypt. Egypt at that time was the mightiest of the nations.

Israel needed to know and trust the God of Abraham, Isaac and Jacob as their God who would wonderfully do what no army could do. The LORD God alone would perform the wonder of leading enslaved Israel out of the road closed by Egypt into his open road of the *Way of Life*. In Genesis 18 it was the first time that the LORD God used the word *wonderful* for himself: *fala (fl')*. It was necessary for Israel in Egypt to know how the LORD God dealt wonderfully with their forefather Abraham because of what Moses was to do for them. For the LORD God sent Moses to them to perform his *wonders* against Egypt with the *Rod of God* (nifleotim). In Egypt, Israel should be reminded of the LORD's assurance, *"Is anything too wonderful for the LORD?"*

DISCUSSION POINT

1. Why was it important for Israel in Egypt to know what the LORD God did for Abraham and Sarah?
2. Who informed Israel in Egypt of what the LORD God said to Sarah when she laughed?

ABRAHAM'S DESCENDANTS AT ALL TIMES

Throughout the Old and New Testament Scriptures the LORD God makes known to us that he alone does wonderful works. The climax of this is revealed in Luke 1:37. Mary, who is a virgin and "knows no man", is to conceive a holy one, the Son of God, for nothing is impossible (too wonderful) for God. The wonderful work of God is still being revealed each time a person is made alive, from death through sin, by God the Holy Spirit. Everyone who lives by faith in Jesus Christ must praise God for this miracle. It still must be said, *"He alone does wonderful works."* In Galatians 4:28, God the Holy Spirit reminds the Christian believer of this miracle in terms that remind us of Genesis 18. *"Now you, brothers, like Isaac, are children of promise."* The promise is the Word of the LORD. He gave his word (promise) to Abraham. By his Word the LORD God wonderfully created Isaac in Sarah's womb. By his Word of Promise the LORD God kept his Covenant (Psalm 112). Today's Christian believers are descendants of Abraham because by his Spirit and Word God created them to be his children. Indeed, Christians came to be God's children by the same Word of Wonders, just like Isaac.

QUESTIONS

1. Would it be correct for us to pray for God to work wonders for us?
2. Can you think of a situation that we would pray like that?
3. Would this help *"Now to Him who is able to do above prayer and expectation"* Eph. 3:20?
4. Has God ever worked *wonderfully* for you?

5. In what way are Christians *like Isaac*?

Genesis 18:16-33

GOD'S WONDERFUL WORKS BRINGING FINAL JUDGMENT ON SODOM

OVERVIEW

- The centre of this passage is not Sodom. The centre of this passage is Yahweh, the Opener and the Closer of the Way of Life.
- The LORD God does not place Sodom first but Abraham and his offspring.
- The LORD God needs to close the Way of Life for Sodom but he first deals with the future of the Way of Life and the promised offspring.
- The LORD God reveals his plan to Abraham according to the Bond of the Covenant.
- The LORD God needed to go down and see.
- Sodom's wickedness revealed in later books of the Bible.
- Abraham pleaded with God because the LORD God made Abraham *walk before him*.
- Abraham pleaded with God because he is El Shaddai, *the Judge of all the earth*.
- Abraham pleaded with God because of who God is.
- Christians must learn from their forefather Abraham how to plead with God for our world.
- The destruction of Sodom was not because of a natural phenomenon.
- The destruction of Sodom was a unique *wonder* worked by the Creator of Heaven and earth who alone does wondrous things.
- Israel, faced with idolatry and oppression in Egypt, was reminded of the wonders the LORD God worked in the unique destruction of wicked Sodom; Just like he did in the judgment of the world-wide flood.

THE CENTRE OF THIS PASSAGE IS NOT SODOM

In most commentaries the heading above 16:33 is simply "Sodom". Such a heading indicates that the author considers the destruction of Sodom to be the centre of the passage. In Genesis 18, from verse 16 to chapter 19:38, it seems to be all about Sodom. What happened to Sodom is memorable. To the present day, the name of Sodom and its fate is known worldwide. Sodom, however, is not first in view. We will first see that in Genesis 18:16-33.

THE CENTRE OF THIS PASSAGE IS YAHWEH, THE OPENER AND THE CLOSER OF THE WAY OF LIFE

From the time that the LORD God placed our first parents on his Open Way of Life the Devil has attempted to close God's Open Way of Life. By listening to the Devil, we and our first parents, have become unworthy to live in the life-giving presence of God. The Devil did not succeed to snatch man away from God's presence. The LORD God in grace chose our first parents to remain in his presence on

His Open Way of Life. That gracious action of the LORD God is again in evidence here. In his dealing with Abraham the LORD God is busy preserving a people for himself to live on his Open Way of Life.

TO CONSIDER

1. Are we of ourselves worthy to be in God's presence?
2. What is so special about the presence of God to make us unworthy?
3. What does it mean that we need "grace" to be in God's presence?

THE LORD GOD DOES NOT PLACE SODOM FIRST BUT ABRAHAM AND HIS OFFSPRING

The LORD God needs to close the Way of Life for Sodom but he first deals with the future of the Way of Life and the promised offspring. The LORD God himself makes this clear in the verses seventeen and eighteen. In these verses the LORD God verbalizes his thoughts. That in itself is big; very big. The LORD verbalized his thoughts so that future generations would know and believe, starting with Abraham. The end purpose here is the promised Offspring, Jesus Christ.

17 The LORD said, "Shall I hide from Abraham what I am about to do, 18 seeing that Abraham shall surely become a great and mighty nation, and all the nations of the earth shall be blessed in him? 19 For I have chosen him, that he may command his children and his household after him to keep the way of the LORD by doing righteousness and justice, so that the LORD may bring to Abraham what he has promised him." (vs. 19, a literal translation is: *For I have known him*)

THE LORD GOD REVEALS HIS PLAN TO ABRAHAM ACCORDING TO THE BOND OF THE COVENANT

The Bond of the Covenant always originates with the LORD God. This is also in evidence here. The Bond of God's Covenant with Abraham and his offspring did not originate with Abraham. We hear the LORD say *"for I have known him"*. When the LORD God knows someone then he forges an intimate bond between himself and that person. Because of this bond with Abraham the LORD God reveals his plan to Abraham.

QUESTIONS

1. In John 10:14 we read these words of the Lord Jesus, *"I am the good shepherd; I know my sheep and my sheep know me."* How does this help you to understand what God means when he says that he has known Abraham?
2. By what means does God know us, Christian believers, today?
3. What is the difference between being chosen and being known?
4. Does the one exclude the other or do they belong together?

Typical for the Bond the LORD God had with believing Abraham is that God treats Abraham as a believing father in his household. God lets Abraham know about his righteous judgment of the wicked. With that knowledge of God's righteous judgment Abraham is to command his children. Believing Abraham was not merely to teach his children. He was to do this with authority. Children of believing Abraham must know God's righteous judgment of the wicked. The way of wicked Sodom may never be the way of the children of Abraham. Children of believing Abraham must *keep the way of the* LORD *by doing righteousness and justice.*

In verse nineteen there is a further element that belongs to the Bond of God's Covenant. The LORD God has promised Abraham offspring in whom all nations will be blessed. This promise also includes the land, even the whole world (Genesis 18:18 and Romans 4:14). Children of believing Abraham will receive what is promised if they believe what their father commanded them and walk the path of righteousness and justice faithful to the LORD God. When children of believing Abraham leave the path of the LORD God and choose to live like wicked Sodom they will not share in the fulfillment of the promises.

DISCUSSION TIME

1. Who today are true children of believing Abraham?
2. Many reject baptism of the infants of believers because they maintain that their children are born as strangers to the Bond of the Covenant. Show from Genesis 18 that this teaching is false.
3. From Genesis 18 show what the task of believing parents is today.
4. What is the distinction between commanding and teaching?
5. How would you in practice command and teach your children?
6. Which helps are available to believing parents as they command and teach their children?

THE LORD GOD NEEDED TO GO DOWN AND SEE

God did not need to go down because he could not see. God said this because he came as the Judge of all the Earth. The LORD God spoke as Judge. No judge may pronounce a verdict unless he has made sure of the facts and the charge. The LORD God wants it to be known that he is a righteous Judge (Psalm 7:11).

1. How are the persecuted and oppressed Christians of our time comforted when they read in the Bible that the LORD God is a righteous Judge?

SODOM'S WICKEDNESS IS REVEALED IN LATER BOOKS OF THE BIBLE

Sodom's wickedness specified
2 Peter 2:6-10. Sensual conduct; lawless deeds; defiling passion; despising authority.
Jude:7. Indulged in sexual immorality; pursued unnatural desire.
Luke 17:28-30. They were eating and drinking, buying and selling, planting and building irregardless of the pending judgment.

The effect of Sodom's wickedness on the righteous
The wickedness of Sodom caused righteous Lot grief, tormented his soul.

Sodom's wickedness held up as an example
Matt. 11:23; Luke 17:28-30; 2 Peter 2:6-10; Jude:7.
Luke 17:28-30 *"Likewise, just as it was in the days of Lot—they were eating and drinking, buying and selling, planting and building,* ²⁹ *but on the day when Lot went out from Sodom, fire and sulfur rained from heaven and destroyed them all—* ³⁰ ***so will it be on the day when the Son of Man is revealed."***

QUESTIONS

1. What is wrong with *eating and drinking, buying and selling, planting and building* in the context of Sodom?
2. How and why will it be *so on the day when the Son of Man is revealed."*?
3. In Isaiah's day the LORD God compared the inhabitants of Jerusalem to Sodom. How does our society and Western world compare to Sodom?
4. Is God's anger to be feared today?
5. Compare God's judgment of Sodom to God's judgment of the world when Christ returns. What similarities do you find?

PLEADING ON THE RIGHTEOUSNESS OF GOD

Shall God sweep away the righteous with the wicked? Abraham pleaded with God because the LORD God made Abraham *walk before him*, El Shaddai, *the Judge of all the earth*. Abraham pleaded with God because of who God is. Christians must learn from their forefather Abraham how to plead with God for our world.

DISCUSSION TIME

1. Discuss the patience of God with the prayer of the righteous.

SHALL GOD SWEEP AWAY THE RIGHTEOUS WITH THE WICKED?

The verses of Genesis 18:22-32 contain the awesome pleading of Abraham on the righteousness of the LORD God and the answer of the LORD to Abraham. Being awestruck may not cause us to forget the connection of these verses to what went before. This is still part of the LORD's instruction to Abraham how to command his children. Believers of all ages need to have the right answer when their children ask, *"Is God just?"* At times grown-up believers need to learn to trust their God so that they can answer, *"Yes, God is just. God will not punish the righteous and God will not let the wicked go unpunished."* See Psalm 73 from vs. 13-28; Jer. 12:1-3.

ABRAHAM PLEADED WITH GOD, BECAUSE THE LORD GOD MADE ABRAHAM WALK BEFORE EL SHADDAI, THE JUDGE OF ALL THE EARTH

"Shall not the Judge of all the earth do what is just?" vs 25. In ch. 17:1 Abraham had been commanded to be blameless and walk before El Shaddai, the Judge of all the earth. Abraham was to be a righteous servant to the righteous God. Abraham speaks to God as a servant to his Master but he does so boldly. He speaks boldly for the LORD God himself appointed Abraham to be his personal messenger. In this close relationship Abraham does not demand but begs humbly.

Abrahams pleads for the righteous on the basis of who God is

God is holy and there is no unrighteousness in him (Psalm 92:15). Abraham knows God as the *Judge of all the earth.*

Christians must learn from their forefather Abraham how to plead with God for our world

1. Did Abraham pray for the wicked not to be punished?
2. Whom did Abraham pray for? Where do you find them?
3. Describe how we should pray for this world as believing children of Abraham.
4. Discuss the patience of God with the prayer of the righteous.

Genesis 19: Introduction

THE DESTRUCTION OF SODOM WAS NOT BECAUSE OF A NATURAL PHENOMENON

The destruction of Sodom was a unique *wonder* worked by the Creator of Heaven and earth who alone does wondrous things. Israel, faced with idolatry and oppression in Egypt, was reminded of the wonders the LORD God worked in the unique destruction of wicked Sodom, like he did in the judgment of the world-wide flood.

19:1-3. In chapter 18:22 we read that *men* went toward Sodom. From their presence with the LORD God at Abraham's tent we could already conclude that the two were angels. Now we are informed that the two indeed were angels. When the two angels arrive at Sodom they appear to Lot as men (see indented section on the next page).

They find Lot seated in the city gate. The fact that Lot is sitting in the city gate tells us about Lot's status in the city of Sodom.

Lot is no longer a wealthy nomad living in tents. Lot has moved into the city where he has a house. He is settled. Though a sojourner, he apparently is accepted as a citizen who counts. We may conclude this from the fact that he is sitting in the gate of the city. The gate of a city was the place where the men of the city conducted their official business. Because of his wealth Lot would be involved therein.

QUESTIONS

1. What are the differences between living in rural areas and living in a city?
2. Is it wrong for a Christian to live in the city?
3. Is it guaranteed that it is better to raise a Christian family in an agrarian culture?
4. How do we as Christians remain faithful to the Lord Christ in this wicked world?
5. Are we sheltering our children too much within the family, the church and the Christian school?

Lot differs in attitude from among the men sitting in the gate. Lot does not lounge back lazily with a hostile attitude. Lot rises up to meet the angels and addresses them politely. He respectfully bows with his face down and offers them his home. Knowing the dangers of spending the night in the town square, Lot insists. The angels eat and will stay the night. In this Lot conducts himself as a righteous man.

In the following, however, Lot again makes wrong decisions. All the male residents of the city surround Lot's house. They demand Lot to bring out his guests so they might sexually abuse them. To appease them Lot makes a foolish offer. He offers to bring his two virgin daughters out to the abusers. The men of Sodom were not after sexual abuse of female, but specifically after sexual abuse of men. They threaten Lot the sojourner and try to break down the door.

It is at that critical moment that the men who came to Lot reveal that they are angels. They pull Lot into the house and strike the men of Sodom with blindness.

So far we have not concerned ourselves with the problem of angels appearing to Abraham and Lot as men. We may find help from the book of Judges. In Judges 13 a man appears to announce the birth of Samson. He appears first to Manoah's wife and later to Manoah. The wife tells her husband of a *"man of God whose appearance was like the appearance of the angel of God very awesome."* Manoah prayed to the LORD for the *man of God* to come again. When the angel appears again Manoah asks of him, *"are you the man who spoke to the woman?"* Again the angel appears as a man. However, there is something about the man that makes him recognizable as a heavenly being for they call him a *man of God*.

From this we conclude that the men appearing to Abraham and Lot were indeed visible as men and yet recognizable as heavenly beings.

QUICK QUESTIONS

1. Could it be that in our day and age we would show hospitality to angels?
2. Does God in our day protect his own by sending out his angels?
3. What are angels?

Lot's sojourning among the wicked citizens of Sodom had led to more foolish decisions. Lot's daughters had become engaged to be married to men of Sodom. These men refused the offer of the angels to be saved from the destruction that is to come.
Lot himself hesitates to follow the angels to safety. The angels have to seize him and his family. In verse sixteen we are told that in the forceful action of the angels the LORD was *"being merciful to him."* The same mercy is evident when the angels grant Lot his request to flee, not into the mountains, but into a small city, called Zoar.

DISCUSSION TIME

1. Note the persistent foolishness of Lot. Nevertheless the LORD God shows mercy. Is it right for an unwise Christian to point to Lot and say that the LORD God will be merciful anyway?

There are those who claim that Sodom and satellite cities were destroyed by a natural disaster caused by the tar pits in that area (Genesis 14:10). By calling this a natural disaster we would exclude the Creator of heaven and earth. The LORD God determined the time, place and extent of the rain of sulfur and fire that destroyed Sodom and Gomorrah.

While at Lot's house the angels had impressed upon him and his family the need to flee and not look back As they came near Zoar, Lot's wife did look back and immediately she became a *"pillar of salt."* Apparently her looking back reflected her state of mind. She wanted to be back.

The state of mind of Lot's wife reminds us of the instructions our Lord gives us regarding his return on the clouds of heaven. We read his words in Luke 17:26-33.

*"²⁶ Just as it was in the days of Noah, so will it be in the days of the Son of Man. ²⁷ They were eating and drinking and marrying and being given in marriage, until the day when Noah entered the ark, and the flood came and destroyed them all. ²⁸ Likewise, just as it was in the days of Lot—they were eating and drinking, buying and selling, planting and building, ²⁹ but on the day when Lot went out from Sodom, fire and sulfur rained from heaven and destroyed them all— ³⁰ so will it be on the day when the Son of Man is revealed. ³¹ On that day, let the one who is on the housetop, with his goods in the house, not come down to take them away, and likewise let the one who is in the field not turn back. ³² **Remember Lot's wife."***

DISCUSSION TIME

1. What does it mean to "Remember Lot's wife"?
2. What impact does this command have on our daily life before God?

Verse 29

GOD REMEMBERED ABRAHAM

The LORD God had promised Abraham that he would not destroy the righteous with the wicked. God remembered his promise and stood by it. Lot and his daughters did not perish.

In 2 Peter 2:6-10 the Spirit of God once again assures the godly that he rescues them from the destruction that comes upon the wicked:

⁶"if by turning the cities of Sodom and Gomorrah to ashes he condemned them to extinction, making them an example of what is going to happen to the ungodly; ⁷ and if he rescued righteous Lot, greatly distressed by the sensual conduct of the wicked ⁸ (for as that righteous man lived among them day after day, he was tormenting his righteous soul over their lawless deeds that he saw and heard); ⁹ then the Lord knows how to rescue the godly from trials, and to keep the unrighteous under punishment until the day of judgment, ¹⁰ and especially those who indulge in the lust of defiling passion and despise authority."

QUESTIONS

1. Why did the LORD, "remember Abraham"?
2. How did the LORD demonstrate His grace in the life of Lot?
3. Discuss whether the promise of God to not destroy the righteous with the wicked is still valid today and in the future.
4. What comfort do Christians receive from God's dealings with Lot?

Genesis 19:30-38

The two daughters of Lot fear that their family will die out. After the LORD destroyed Sodom and Gomorrah they were stranded in a cave in the mountains. The two of them make their father drunk to have intercourse with him. In this manner offspring in their family was born. Each gave birth to a son whom they called Moab and Ben-Ammi. The names of the boys show the purpose of their birth. Moab sounds like "From father", and Ben-Ammi means "Son of my people". From these grandsons of Lot came the clans of the Moabites and Ammonites.

TO CONSIDER

1. Lot was not conscious when his daughters conceived their sons by him. Does that excuse him?
2. What are we to make of the fact that we do not read of the LORD rebuking Lot and his daughters?
3. No Ammonite or Moabite was allowed to enter into the assembly of the LORD, even to the tenth generation. Was that because of the way their forefathers had been conceived?

Annihilationism is the theory that nothing is left of the wicked after the LORD God destroys them. This theory is a denial of eternal punishment of the wicked. The argument against eternal punishment and the fire of hell is based on the goodness of God. Some consider it impossible that God would do this. They favor total annihilation.

DISCUSSION TIME

1. Discuss the right or wrong of annihilationism using the two passages quoted below. You may know of other passages in the Scriptures that can help our understanding.

2 Peter 2:6
⁶ if by turning the cities of Sodom and Gomorrah to ashes he condemned them to extinction, making them an example of what is going to happen to the ungodly;

Jude: 7
"just as Sodom and Gomorrah and the surrounding cities, which likewise indulged in sexual immorality and pursued unnatural desire, serve as an example by undergoing a punishment of eternal fire."

QUICK QUESTION

1. How should the command "Remember Sodom" resonate in the preaching of the Church?

The present leader of the Jehovah Witness apparently has done away their "annihilation of the wicked" doctrine to be replaced by a second chance upon resurrection.[39]

---

[39] I thank our editor Mrs. Liz DeWit for passing this information on to me.

20:1 Abraham is still a stranger in a strange land. From Hebron he moves south into the Negev. In the Negev he roams in an area between Kadesh and Shur. To the south-west of Shur is the Wall of Egypt (Genesis 16:7; 25:18). To the North of Kadesh is the city of Gerar. The ruler of the small city-state of Gerar is called Abimelech. The area where Abraham feeds his many cattle is under the government of Abimelech the city-king of Gerar. This explains why Abraham can be in the area toward the South and Egypt, and yet also toward the North and Gerar.

20:2 Abraham apparently has not yet learned to fully trust the LORD who brought him from Ur of the Chaldeans to this strange land. In Gerar he once again fears for his life because of Sarah. For the second time Abraham let it be known that Sarah is his sister. The result is that Abimelech takes Sarah into his house.

The ruler of a small city state apparently intends to forge a family relationship with the rich nomadic sheik Abraham. This view is confirmed by what we learn of what Abimelech does after Abraham's deceit has become known. Instead of sending Abraham away in anger Abimelech offers Abraham the protected position of a sojourner. With Abraham and his servants Abimelech has gained a powerful ally. There is strength in numbers (compare Genesis 14:13-14).

QUICK QUESTION

1. Sarah was about ninety years of age. Why would Abimelech desire an old woman as his wife?

What happens between Abraham and Abimelech reminds us of what we learned from Genesis 12:10-20. Also then Abraham roamed in the Negev but went into Egypt because of a famine. There Pharaoh took Sarai into his harem for Abram had let it be known that she was his sister. The LORD "struck Pharaoh and his house with great plagues because of Sarai, Abram's wife." In anger, Pharaoh sent Abram away. What happens at Gerar is similar to what happened in Egypt. The main difference, however, is how the LORD deals with Abimelech and the attitude of Abimelech toward the LORD.

20:3 In Egypt the LORD had not appeared to Pharaoh but immediately struck him with a plague. This was because Pharaoh considered himself to be god. The LORD does speak to Abimelech. Apparently Abimelech has no such claim as Pharaoh had, for the LORD speaks with Abimelech. The LORD communicates with Abimelech in a dream. This dream is not an ordinary dream like we experience when we sleep. The dream does not originate in the mind of Abimelech. The dream originates with the LORD. In the dream the LORD God is really speaking to Abimelech but Abimelech does not see the LORD. The word dream is used but it is not the sort of dream psychiatrists are eager to analyze.

Compare this with the way the LORD communicated with the boy Samuel. Samuel is lying down at night and the LORD *"came and stood and called."* Samuel did not see the LORD but he answered, *"Speak for your servant is listening."* I Sa.2:1-14.

The LORD spoke and Abimelech listened. The LORD reveals to Abimelech that he is a dead man for he took another man's wife.

QUESTIONS

1. What is the basic difference between Pharaoh and Abimelech?
2. How did Abimelech conduct himself before the LORD?
3. Explain why the LORD God would communicate with Abimelech.
4. Explain the difference between us having a dream and the dream in which the LORD God spoke to Abimelech.
5. Does the LORD God still communicate with people?
6. Explain how the LORD God would communicate with you who are a Christian.
7. Explain how the LORD God in Genesis 20 is protecting the line of the Holy Seed.
8. Explain that the LORD is acting *"wonderfully"* in ch. 20. (cp. Ch. 18:14).

20:4-6 Abimelech appeals to the righteousness of God: "Lord, will you kill an innocent people?" Abimelech addresses God as Adonai, Lord, Master. He does not address God with the name YAHWEH, as Abraham would. However, it is remarkable how much like Abraham, Abimelech pleads with God for his life and the life of his people. His pleading reminds us of Abraham pleading for the righteous that might be found in Sodom (Genesis 18:16 ff.).

QUICK QUESTION

1. Explain how Abimelech's pleading with the LORD is similar to the pleading of Abraham who spoke to the LORD in behalf of the righteous in Sodom.

Noteworthy is how the LORD God takes time to explain his actions to Abimelech.
"Then God said to him in the dream, "Yes, I know that you have done this in the integrity of your heart, and it was I who kept you from sinning against me. Therefore I did not let you touch her".

Several items need our attention here:
a. The LORD makes Abimelech aware of the power of God to act in the life of a man. The credit for not touching Sarah belongs to the LORD God. He kept Abimelech from sinning. Because of Abraham's lack of trust in the LORD's protection Abimelech experiences the power of the LORD God.
b. What is recorded here is to be accepted and believed by all who read this, starting with the descendants of Abimelech and Abraham right through our day and age. All who read this must take into account that God powerfully directs our lives. Abimelech did not resist God's powerful direction. He did not touch Sarah. We may not resist God's powerful direction of our lives either.

QUICK QUESTIONS

1. Explain why we should pray to God to direct our lives.

2. What good is it to pray to God to powerfully interfere in the lives of the people in power?
3. Explain how Moses in Egypt encouraged captive Israel with the example of Abimelech and God's power?

20:7 God had been gracious to Abimelech; God had prevented him from sinning against God. Now let us listen and learn from what follows.

"Now then, return the man's wife, for he is a prophet, so that he will pray for you, and you shall live. But if you do not return her, know that you shall surely die, you and all who are yours."

Abimelech is pardoned. God has shown grace, but that is not the end of the matter. A person who received God's pardon is under obligation to show obedience to God's will (compare John 8:11). For Abimelech this means that he immediately has to return Sarah to her rightful husband. Abimelech will forfeit the pardon if he fails to obey God's command. Disobedience will nullify the pardon: Abimelech and all who are his will surely die. God will not heal him and his people if Sarah is not returned to Abraham.

QUICK QUESTION

1. Explain what happens to a forgiven sinner who refuses to obey God?

Abraham also receives a task from the LORD. After Abimelech has restored Sarah to him Abraham is to pray for Abimelech so that he and his people might be healed. Abraham is to pray, not first of all as Sarah's husband, but **as a prophet**. It is remarkable that the LORD God gives unwise Abraham the title **prophet**. The LORD God does not mean this as a general title. Abraham is his prophet, a prophet in the service of YAHWEH.

To understand the magnitude of the fact that the LORD God calls Abraham his prophet, we must go back to chapter 17:1. There the LORD God appointed Abraham as his servant with the words, *"I am God Almighty; walk before me, and be blameless"*. There the LORD God officially took Abraham into his service.

In our notes on that passage we saw that *blameless* does not mean perfect but wholehearted. A man who serves the LORD with his whole heart may act in an unwise manner but the LORD will consider him blameless, righteous, if he wholeheartedly repents. Abraham was such a man before God. His task as prophet of the LORD goes back to Genesis seventeen.

QUICK QUESTIONS

1. Explain from 17:1 how God could call Abraham his prophet?
2. Compare Abraham's intercession on behalf of Abimelech with James 5:16 and explain.

This was not the first time that Abraham pleaded with the LORD for the life of the righteous. In chapter eighteen Abraham pleaded with the LORD for the life of the righteous in Sodom, *"Shall not the Judge of all the earth do right?"* Abimelech did the right thing before the LORD. He returned

Sarah to her husband. The prophet Abraham prayed to the LORD and the LORD heard. Abimelech and his people lived. They did not die.

Genesis 21

Genesis 21:1 (*Then*) *the* LORD *visited Sarah as he had said, and the* LORD *did to Sarah as he had promised.* [40]

To understand, and benefit, from the weight of this first verse in Genesis 21 we must remember what we have learned earlier, beginning from chapter 12. The phrases, *"as He had said,"* and *"as He had promised,"* force us to look back.

SO LET'S LOOK BACK

The LORD promised Abraham that he would have offspring and that in his offspring all nations would be blessed (12:2, 3; 18:18, 19).
The LORD stipulated that the offspring would be via Sarah and not via Hagar (Genesis 17: 18,19).
The LORD even set the time when he would return so that he would cause the son of Sarah to be born (Genesis 18:14).

CONTINUITY

The Hebrew text of verse 1 begins with a little letter that indicates progression (see note on p. 101). This little letter can be translated with *and* or also with *then*. It is good to know this even though most Bible Versions do not translate this little letter.

QUICK QUESTION

1. Show that in the Book of Genesis there is a forward thrust beginning from Genesis One.

It was the appointed time.
It was not because of a menstrual cycle that is was time for Sarah to conceive. Neither was it finally in the power of Abraham to conceive a son by Sarah. It was time in the power of God. The LORD God came at the time he had appointed. Sarah was ready to conceive the promised son by Abraham because the LORD God *visited* her at the time appointed.

Visit
The word visit here means more than paying a social visit. The Hebrew word used, tells us that this is a visitation by the Master to his servant. Like the commander of an army musters and commands his

---

[40] 21¹ וַיהוָה פָּקַד אֶת־שָׂרָה כַּאֲשֶׁר אָמָר וַיַּעַשׂ יְהוָה לְשָׂרָה כַּאֲשֶׁר דִּבֵּר׃ (Note the vau consecutive, or copula. JVR)

troops, so the LORD God musters, commands, his people, even his creation. [41] This helps us to understand what kind of visitation the LORD God made to Sarah. The LORD God personally came to Sarah and recruited her as one under his command. The LORD God came as the One who had created the first woman from a rib of the first man, Adam. As the Creator of woman, God is able to change a barren woman into a mother of children. As promised in Genesis 18:14 the LORD God *"wonderfully" created* in Sarah's barren womb the wonder of ovulation. The LORD God himself made Sarah's body ready to receive the conception of a son by Abraham.

Discussion Time

1. Explain what kind of visit the LORD made to Sarah.
2. Explain why it is not surprising that the LORD God could prepare Sarah's body for conception of Abraham's seed.
3. Show how the creative action of the LORD within Sarah can be of comfort to a "barren" woman.

Visiting in Scripture

The LORD *"visiting"* plays an important role throughout the Scriptures. The LORD God might visit *"the sin of the father upon the children to the third and fourth generation."* Or the LORD God might visit to *"show mercy unto thousands that love Me and keep my commandments."* (Exodus 20). When the LORD God *visits* his people then he comes according to the Bond of the Covenant, either with blessing or with curse. That is how the LORD God came to Sarah. He came according to the Bond of the Covenant of which we read in previous chapters of Genesis. In chapter fifteen we have read that the LORD in a Covenantal oath ceremony swore to Abraham that his offspring would inherit the land. In chapter seventeen we have read that the LORD confirmed the Bond of the Covenant with Abraham and gave his word to him that he would return at the appointed time and Sarah would bear a son named Isaac.

Questions

1. Explain the two kinds of visit the LORD makes.
2. Show examples in Scripture where the LORD God visits his people in judgment.
3. Does the LORD God visit people and nations today? Give examples.
4. Explain how God visits Christian believers in our personal lives.

Looking forward

Genesis 21:1 also makes us look forward. The fact that the LORD visited Sarah *"as He had said and as He had promised"* opened a rich future. Throughout our treatment on the Book of Genesis we have followed the progression of God who is *"The Opener of the Way of Life"*. The future of the Way of Life is in the power of our strong God. When the LORD God *visited* Sarah, he was not only opening her womb but he continued to open the Way of Life. Abraham's offspring surely is to be the blessing to the nations. Speaking of a future!

---

[41] In modern Ivrit to muster, to command, are the first English equivalents to פָּקַד. (Ben-Yehuda's pocket Hebrew-English, English-Hebrew dictionary. 10th pr. New York 1968)

DISCUSSION TIME

1. Describe the rich future the LORD God opened by visiting Sarah as He did.
2. Show how far that future extends forward and finally reaches the goal.

Promise

The LORD God guarantees the future of the Way of Life for his people by acting according to his promise. For the strengthening of our faith in the God who includes us in the Bond of His Covenant, we need to know more about the use of the word *promise*.

In the Hebrew language of the Old Testament there is no separate word for promise. The word we translate with *promise* is simply *word*. When we apply this to Genesis 21:1 we get this: "*(Then) the LORD visited Sarah as he had said, and the LORD did to Sarah as he had spoken.*" So here we have "*as He had spoken*" instead of "*as He had promised.*" The *promise* of the LORD God is his *word*. This is not a human word but his divine word, or Word.

When God gave his Word that he would open Sarah's womb he did not merely promise in the human sense of the word. He gave his word. The Word of the LORD is sure. When the LORD gives his Word it is done! No ifs or buts. Wherever in the Old Testament you read that the LORD gives his promise, you actually read that the LORD gave his word. You can rest assured that the LORD in his promise is giving his divine Word. The Word of the LORD is always effective. The LORD **does as he has spoken.**

Sometimes an employee is given a task to perform. The employee answers the employer with: "*Consider it done!*" The employee is only human and cannot guarantee that he or she will be able to do as promised.

NOT SO OUR GOD. When our God promises us eternal life by faith in Jesus Christ, **THEN CONSIDER IT DONE!** When God gives you his word, then this is the same word by which he created the heaven and the earth and our first parents Adam and Eve.

The Hebrew word is *debar*. As a noun it means both *word* and *thing*. As a verb it means both the sound of speaking and action. God speaks with creative power.

A good example of the LORD and his Word are these verses from Psalm 33:6-9
  6. By the word of the LORD the heavens were made,
  and by the breath of his mouth all their host.
  7. He gathers the waters of the sea as a heap;
  he puts the deeps in storehouses.
  8. Let all the earth fear the LORD;
  let all the inhabitants of the world stand in awe of him!
  9. For he spoke, and it came to be;
  he commanded, and it stood firm.

In the Form for Baptism, *Book of Praise* we read that:

"God the Father promises,
 God the Son promises,
 God the Holy Spirit promises."

Let us now read it this way:
"God the Father gives his Word,
 God the Son gives his Word,
 God the Holy Spirit gives his Word."

DISCUSSION TIME

1. Explain that it is legitimate to read *word* instead of *promise*.
2. Show what comfort we receive from reading *word* in the Form for Baptism.

"Now you, brothers, like Isaac, are children of promise." Galatians 4:28.
The LORD God had made Abraham the father of many nations. The LORD God had given his word that the birth of Isaac would be *wonderful*. Isaac indeed was a child of the *promise/word* of the LORD God. Today all who share the faith of Abraham are spiritual children of Abraham.

DISCUSSION TIME

1. Explain how Christians today can be called *children of promise/word* like Isaac.
2. What wonderful birth does God promise to Christian believers?
3. What *wonderful act of God makes our new birth possible?*
4. Explain what comfort we receive from being called children of promise?

The LORD God kept his Word

² *And Sarah conceived and bore Abraham a son in his old age at the time of which God had spoken to him.*

In this verse the ESV renders the clear translation *spoken* instead of *promised*. God had given his solemn word and the LORD God had made good. He had shown himself true.

QUESTIONS

1. Show from Genesis 15 how the LORD God had given his word that he would deliver Abraham's oppressed descendants from a cruel nation.
2. The LORD God had made his word to Abraham and Sarah true. Exactly at the time foretold by God, Genesis 21, Isaac was born. Show how Israel in Egypt should have been encouraged by that fact.
3. Before the Lord Jesus ascended into heaven he spoke, "I am with you till the end of the age." He spoke, that is: He gave his solemn word. Explain how the Lord Jesus is making these solemn words true for us today.
4. Apply this to God's people who are persecuted because of faith in Jesus Christ, the Son of God.

5. "At the time of which God had spoken to him." How does this remind you of the times and seasons of which the Lord Jesus spoke in Acts 1:6-7? (If you need a reminder then flip back to page 87.)

Genesis 21:3-5

FATHER ABRAHAM DID TO HIS SON AS THE LORD HAD COMMANDED HIM. HE NAMED HIM ISAAC AND HE CIRCUMCISED HIM

Isaac means Laughter

The LORD God had instructed Abraham to call his son Isaac, which means Laughter. The choice of name was not left to Abraham and Sarah. When the LORD God named the son of his wonderful action 'laughter', he erected a sign that would speak of the God for whom nothing is too wonderful. This sign of God has been preserved through all ages as a testimony of his faithfulness to his given Word.

QUICK QUESTION

1. Throughout the Bible we read that the LORD is the God of "Abraham, Isaac and Jacob". Explain how the LORD God makes that a reason for *Laughter* for us in our day.

Gen 21:4. *"And Abraham circumcised his son Isaac when he was eight days old, as God had commanded him."*

When we started with the first verse of this chapter we looked back and we looked forward. The phrase, **"As God had commanded him,"** also makes us look back and look forward.

Look back.
To understand the command God gave Abraham regarding the circumcision of Isaac on the eighth day we must go back to our notes on Genesis 17.

Look forward.
After having reviewed the notes on chapter 17 we now look forward.

DISCUSSION TIME

1. Re-reading these notes what do we know about the position of Isaac in the Bond of God's Covenant?
2. Re-reading these notes what did you learn about the relation of circumcision to infant baptism?

Genesis 21:5-7 *"Abraham was a hundred years old when his son Isaac was born to him. 6 And Sarah said, "God has made laughter for me; everyone who hears will laugh over me." 7 And she said, "Who would have said to Abraham that Sarah would nurse children? Yet I have borne him a son in his old age."*

GOD MAKES LAUGHTER

In these verses we find how Sarah has progressed from the laughter of disbelief to the laughter of giving praise to God who acted wonderfully. Note that she professes, *"God has made laughter for me."*
Then Sarah makes a far reaching statement, *"everyone who hears will laugh over me."* Good news travels fast. The good news of God making laughter for Sarah will cause neighbours to laugh and bring glory to God.

QUESTIONS

1. Explain how we can belong to the people Sarah refers to even so many years after God made laughter for Sarah.
2. How are we still laughing?

Genesis 21:8-21.

THE WORLD MUST SUBMIT TO GOD'S SOVEREIGN WAY OF LIFE

After Cain murdered righteous Abel, God sent Cain away from his presence. With this sovereign act the LORD God made a separation between the people of his chosen Way of Life and the people whom he sends away from his presence. In Ur of the Chaldeans, Abraham and Sarah lived away from the life-giving presence of God. The LORD God called Abraham and Sarah away from the way of death onto the life-giving Way of the LORD. Once the LORD God had placed Abraham on his Way of Life, he gave Abraham his solemn oath-word that in Abraham's offspring all nations of the earth would be blessed. Good would come to all nations through the offspring of Abraham. From that time on, all peoples of the earth were to join Abraham and his offspring on God's Way of life.

QUESTIONS

1. Explain why this is so.
2. Explain how Israel in bondage in Egypt should receive the decision of the LORD to send Hagar, the Egyptian and her son away.
3. Explain how the same applies to mission work today.
4. Explain why the separation of believers from unbelievers does not prevent us from showing charity to our neighbour.

ISHMAEL'S EGYPTIAN LAUGHTER THAT PERSECUTES

Isaac was weaned. Since children in the East were nursed at mother's breast till they were about three years old, Isaac was not a baby anymore. Abraham organized a great feast to celebrate the occasion. At the feast Ishmael laughed and this is Sarah's reaction:
"But Sarah saw the son of Hagar the Egyptian, whom she had borne to Abraham, laughing."
In this verse the laughter of Ishmael is not qualified. How will we be able to determine whether Ishmael laughed **with** God's Way or **deriding** God's Way? Looking at how Sarah reacted to Ishmael's laughter

may help us. Ishmael's laughter draws Sarah's attention to the matter of inheritance. Sarah speaks, *"Cast out this slave woman with her son, for the son of this slave woman shall not be heir with my son Isaac."*

From Sarah's words we may conclude that she understood Ishmael's intentions. Ishmael laughed because he was convinced that he, and not Isaac, was to be Abraham's heir. Ishmael's laughter was one of derision. Based on pagan and Egyptian custom Ishmael had a claim. He was Abraham's firstborn son and in the eyes of men, the heir. However, based on the revelation of the LORD God to Abraham and Sarah, Ishmael was not the heir. The sovereign, divine, decision of the LORD God overrules human customs and decisions.

QUICK QUESTIONS

1. Explain why Ishmael should have accepted that he could not be the heir of Abraham.
2. What position could Ishmael have had if he had obeyed the LORD and his Way?

God the Holy Spirit sheds light on this matter by inspiring the apostle Paul to write in **Galatians 4:28-31,** *"Now you, brothers, like Isaac, are children of promise. ²⁹ But just as at that time he who was born according to the flesh persecuted him who was born according to the Spirit, so also it is now. ³⁰ But what does the Scripture say? "Cast out the slave woman and her son, for the son of the slave woman shall not inherit with the son of the free woman." ³¹ So, brothers, we are not children of the slave but of the free woman."*

DISCUSSION POINT

1. Explain why it is legitimate to use Galatians 4 as help in explaining Genesis 21.

The issue, however, is not first of all being heir to riches and possessions. The main issue is the line of offspring that the LORD God will grant to Abraham as he promised, *"In you shall all the families of the earth be blessed."* The LORD God himself makes this clear in verse twelve, *"But God said to Abraham, 'Be not displeased because of the boy and because of your slave woman. Whatever Sarah says to you, do as she tells you, for through Isaac shall your offspring be named.'"*

The line of Abraham and Isaac has been fulfilled in the coming of the great son of Abraham, Jesus Christ. All who believe and confess that salvation is only through Jesus Christ will understand that the fulfillment of the promise could not be through Ishmael but had to be through Isaac.

DISCUSSION POINT

1. Show how, in the matter of sending Ishmael away, the forward line towards the Christ is preserved.

Hagar and her son were sent away and they wandered in the Wilderness of Beersheba to the South of the camp of Abraham. There the LORD God kept his word given to Abraham that he would make Ishmael into a great nation (Ch. 17). When their provisions ran out and death was near the angel of God called from heaven and showed Hagar a well of water which saved the lives of mother and son. For future history of Ishmael and Ishmaelites it is important to note that Ishmael dwelt in the

Wilderness of Paran towards Egypt in the West and Assyria in the North-East and married an Egyptian woman. This territory is what we now call: the whole of the Arabian Peninsula.

Genesis 21:22-34

PROTECTION FOR ABRAHAM AND USE OF THE OATH

At this time Abraham is still a stranger in a strange land and dependent on the good will of the owner of the land, Abimelech of Gerar. Abimelech is eager to safeguard his position and proposes to Abraham a treaty of mutual protection based on fidelity and truth. This is to be made official by means of the swearing of an oath. Abraham consents to swear but tells Abimelech that they first must remove a matter of distrust between them. Abraham *"reproved Abimelech about a well of water that the servants of Abimelech had seized."* The matter of the well is rectified and now the way is open to ratify their relationship in a treaty sealed in an oath swearing ceremony.

THE NUMBER SEVEN

27. So Abraham took sheep and oxen and gave them to Abimelech and the two of them made a covenant 28 Abraham set seven ewe lambs of the flock apart. 29 And Abimelech said to Abraham, "What is the meaning of these seven ewe lambs that you have set apart?" 30 He said, "These seven ewe lambs you will take from my hand, that this may be a witness for me that I dug this well." 31 Therefore that place was called Beersheba, because there both of them swore an oath."

Abraham honours Abimelech as the owner of the land by giving him large gifts. To protect his own position in the treaty Abraham sets aside seven ewe lambs.

Abimelech understands Abraham's intention and asks an official question that belongs to the ceremony, *"What is the meaning of these seven ewe lambs that you have set apart?"*

In verse 27, the making of the covenant between them literally reads in the Hebrew, *"... and the two of them cut a covenant."* This leads us back to the LORD God cutting a covenant with Abraham in Genesis 15. There, the cutting in half of the three animals and the whole of the one dove was the visible oath of the LORD with the use of the number seven.

From these verses we learn that the swearing of the oath had to do with the number seven. That is also clear from verse 31, *"Therefore that place was called Beersheba, because there both of them swore an oath"*. The name they gave to this place is significant. Beersheba means, "Well of the Oath", or, "Well of Seven".

DISCUSSION TIME

1. Explain how the LORD blessing the seventh day in Genesis 2 sanctified the number seven.
2. Explain from Genesis 15 that the LORD God himself set his stamp on the use of the number seven in the swearing of an oath.

ABRAHAM SOJOURNS

A sojourner had a more secure position than a nomad. This secure position was thanks to the LORD God who directed Abimelech to protect Abraham. Abraham first of all was a sojourner with God (cf. Psalm 39:12 *"... For I am a sojourner with you, a guest, like all my fathers"*). Abraham *"walked before the LORD"* in his service. The LORD God takes care of his chosen ones.

In his secure position of sojourner Abraham counted on staying in the area for he planted a Tamarisk tree. This tree is also called a Salt Cedar. The shape of this tree is low and broad. The leaves of this tree are a source of salt for cattle. Abraham had many cattle and needed this tree to provide the necessary salt for his herds and flocks.

QUICK QUESTION

1. We, Christian believers, are sojourners with God like Abraham. Explain what this means for us in the practice of life today.

Genesis 22

22:1 *After these things God tested Abraham and said to him, "Abraham!" And he said, "Here am I."* 2 *He said, "Take your son, your only son Isaac, whom you love, and go to the land of Moriah, and offer him there as a burnt offering on one of the mountains of which I shall tell you."*

To Consider

1. What is the difference between tempting and testing. Does God tempt? Find the answer in the Bible.

God the Holy Spirit knows our tendency to question. Questioning is different from asking questions. When we question we show reluctance to accept the answer as God's truth. By asking questions, however, we show readiness to be taught by God.

Quick Question

1. Compare John 16:19 and 29-31 to explain the difference between asking questions and questioning.

In Genesis 22 we are told that the LORD God demanded from Abraham to sacrifice the promised son Isaac. The first question that comes to mind is whether the LORD God is acting like the gods of the pagans. Pagans sacrifice children to their gods. If the LORD God is not like the pagan gods is there any indication in this chapter, or in the Bible, that God is not demanding this from Abraham as a pagan god? The answer to this is: "Yes, God is not like the pagan gods." God the Holy Spirit, as the first interpreter of his own written Word, gives us the answer in Genesis 22, and confirms this in Hebrews 11: 17-19 and Romans 4:20-21.

11:17 "By faith Abraham, when he was tested, offered up Isaac, and he who had received the promises was in the act of offering up his only son, 18 of whom it was said, "Through Isaac shall your offspring be named." 19 He considered that God was able even to raise him from the dead, from which, figuratively speaking, he did receive him back."
4:20 "No distrust made him waver concerning the promise of God, but he grew strong in his faith as he gave glory to God, 21 fully convinced that God was able to do what he had promised."

Discussion Time

1. Discuss how God was acting differently from a pagan god when He demanded from Abraham to offer Isaac?

As we make the effort to understand Genesis 22 we must first accept what God the Holy Spirit tells us in these scripture passages. Abraham knew that the LORD God was not asking him to sacrifice his son as if he were a pagan god. Abraham was convinced that God would act in accordance with his sworn Word, *"Through Isaac shall your offspring be named."* Isaac would live even if he would die. In our discussion of Genesis 22 we must start with accepting the interpretation God the Holy Spirit gives us in Hebrews 11. We may not question the testimony of God the Holy Spirit. We may, however, ask legitimate questions and do so in faith.

Questions

1. Discuss how Abraham could be so convinced that Isaac would live even though he died.
2. Discuss what we as New Testament Christians know about life after death.
3. Explain what it means for a Christian to *"be with Christ"?* Phil. 1:23.

A necessary question to ask is how this testimony of God the Holy Spirit in Rom. 4:20 and Heb.11:17 is already present in Genesis 22:1-18. In other words, did the LORD God give Abraham any indication that he would not deviate from the Path of Life which he had followed with Abraham and Isaac, and even from the beginning of the world?

The key to answering the above question is a line that runs through Genesis 22:1-18. We can trace this line by following the frequent use of the verb *to see* and verbs of the same stem, *to show, to provide, and to appear.*[42]

Discussion Time

1. Discuss how the words, the verb *to see* and verbs of the same stem, *to show, to provide, and to appear,* tell us of the LORD's presence with Abraham during this trial.
2. Discuss how important it is for us to firmly believe that our God and Saviour is present with us and sees us when we are being tested.

This line of the LORD being present with Abraham in his trial did not start in chapter 22, but started already in chapter 12:1. "Now *the LORD said to Abram, 'Go from your country and your kindred and your father's house to the land that I will show you.'"*

There is a remarkable similarity between chapter 12:1 and 22:2. In both cases, the LORD God knows the exact place where he is sending Abraham. All Abraham knows is that he is to trust the LORD God to be his guide. From experience Abraham knows that the LORD God is to be trusted. The LORD God did show Abraham the land where he now sojourns. Once again, the LORD God demands from Abraham to go sight unseen. Knowing the LORD God as trustworthy, Abraham also now goes as commanded. This time he goes to an unknown mountain as he is told by God.

This mountain is located in an area that the LORD God calls *"the land of Moriah."* In our chapter the line of *to see, to show, to provide, to appear,* begins here in verse 2.

---

[42] רָאָה See the dictionaries

There is much discussion about the word *Moriah*. Is it a land known by that name?
There is no record of a land named Moriah. It is the LORD God who gives the land where Abraham is to go the name "Moriah". With this name the LORD God gives Abraham a similar message as he gave Abraham when he was to leave Ur of the Chaldeans *"go to the land I will show you"* (12:1). This time the LORD God packs the same message in the word Moriah. In Moriah we find a form of the verb *"to see"* combined with the name of God *Yahweh*. The message to Abraham is to go to a land and a mountain unknown to him but with the assurance that the LORD God will provide. Yahweh will be present wherever he sends Abraham. Abraham will not be on his own when tested. He will obediently sacrifice his son Isaac, trusting the LORD God and his Way.

QUESTIONS

1. Explain how the LORD God packed in the name *Moriah* the same message as in ch. 12:1, *go to the land I will show you*. In this case *"go to the mountain I will show you."*
2. "So we are always of good courage. We know that while we are at home in the body we are away from the Lord, 7 for we walk by faith, not by sight" (2 Corinthians 5:6-7). From these verses explain how the verb "to see" functions in our life of faith.

We find confirmation of our interpretation of the name Moriah in 2 Chronicles 3:1. *"Then Solomon began to build the house of the LORD in Jerusalem on Mount Moriah, where the LORD had appeared to David his father, at the place that David his father had appointed, on the threshing floor of Ornan the Jebusite."*

Here we find the name Moriah connected to the LORD appearing.[43] In the Hebrew language "to appear" is a verb form of the verb "to see". Because of David's sin in numbering the people, the Angel of the LORD became the angel of death. The LORD God saw David's sacrifice at the threshing floor of Ornan and stopped the angel of death. The LORD God saw and gave life. By naming the place, where the LORD God stopped the angel of death, Moriah, David saw the connection with Genesis 22. The LORD God was present to bring life in the midst of death.

It helps us to know that Moriah was the LORD's message to Abraham that he would be present to provide. The meaning of Moriah helps us to see that the LORD God was not endangering his integrity. It also helps us to understand how Abraham could truthfully tell his servants that he and his son would come back to them (vs. 5). Abraham was also truthful when he told his son Isaac that the LORD would provide himself a lamb for a burnt offering (vs. 8).

From the time that God had commanded Abraham to leave Ur of the Chaldeans the LORD God had been powerfully present with Abraham. Also, at this mountain the LORD God was powerfully present with Abraham whom he had *"known/chosen"* (Ch. 18:19). The following verses clearly show that the LORD God was there just as Abraham had trusted that he would be. As Abraham lifted up the knife to sacrifice his only son whom he loved, the LORD God interfered.
11 But the angel of the Lord called to him from heaven and said, "Abraham, Abraham!" And he said, "Here am I." 12 He said, "Do not lay your hand on the boy or do anything to him, for now I know that you fear God, seeing you have not withheld your son, your only son, from me."

---

[43] נִרְאָה

Questions

1. Show how the LORD God was powerfully present with Abraham at the mountain.
2. How would you comfort a brother or sister who is being tested by God using Genesis 22?
3. Before his ascension the Lord Jesus spoke these words, *"I am with you till the end of the age"*. Explain how His words give us the same assurance as the LORD God gave to Abraham in Genesis 22.

The LORD God did indeed provide

Once again we are presented with the verb *to see* and its derivative *to provide*.

13 And Abraham lifted up his eyes and looked, and behold, behind him was a ram, caught in a thicket by his horns. And Abraham went and took the ram and offered it up as a burnt offering instead of his son.
14 So Abraham called the name of that place, "The Lord will provide"; as it is said to this day, "On the mount of the Lord it shall be provided."

Note on *to this day* in verse 14. [44]

The formula *to this day* (עַד הַיּוֹם הַזֶּה) is found frequently in the Old Testament. Most Bible Versions translate Genesis 22:14 as if in the Hebrew text it says עַד הַיּוֹם הַזֶּה and render *to this day*. The Hebrew, however, simply has הַיּוֹם which means *today*.

The translation *to this day* is not a literal translation of what the Hebrew text says. The translation *to this day* could be interpreted as meaning "this day and no further". The literal translation *as it is said today* emphasizes that these words have become a proverb among God's people. The origin of the sentence, *"On the mount of the Lord it shall be provided,"* is Genesis 22, but in later time God's people were not looking for a mountain. They did not expect the LORD God to provide for them in their need on a mountain either. The sentence *"On the mount of the Lord it shall be provided"* had become a proverb of faith. This proverb of faith was an everyday comfort. The LORD God was still the same, whatever the time or place. As he was present to see to the need of their father Abraham so he was present to see to the need of Abraham's children. His powerful presence was to be trusted at all times and in all circumstances.

Quick Question

1. Show how we can use the words,*" On the mount of the Lord it shall be provided"*, as a proverb of faith today.

There is more to this proverb, and that is a *prophetic aspect*. No sacrifice, not even the sacrifice of Isaac, could suffice to take away the sin of the world. The proverb *"On the mount of the Lord it shall be provided"* had to await its fullness until the Lamb of God, Jesus Christ, was crucified on the hill of Golgotha. He took away the sin of the world.

---

[44] See for the phrase 'to this day' B.S.Childs, A Study of the Formula, 'Until this Day', JBL .82 1963. On page 282 Childs refers to Genesis 22:14 הַיּוֹם as "frequentative".

2. Compare: Psalm 40:6-8
   "In sacrifice and offering you have not delighted,
   but you have given me an open ear.
   Burnt offering and sin offering
   you have not required.
   Then I said, "Behold, I have come;
   in the scroll of the book it is written of me:
   I delight to do your will, O my God;
   your law is within my heart."

From *"Behold, I have come"*, show how in his willingness to obey, the Lord Jesus exceeded the willingness of his father Abraham.

THE LORD GOD SWEARS BY HIMSELF

¹⁵ And the angel of the LORD called to Abraham a second time from heaven ¹⁶ and said," By myself I have sworn, declares the LORD, because you have done this and have not withheld your son, your only son, ¹⁷ I will surely bless you, and I will surely multiply your offspring as the stars of heaven and as the sand that is on the seashore. And your offspring shall possess the gate of his enemies, ¹⁸ and in your offspring shall all the nations of the earth be blessed, because you have obeyed my voice".

This is the second time that the LORD God swears an oath to Abraham. The first time is found in Genesis 15. There the LORD God presents Abraham with a visible oath. The second time is found in chapter 22. This time the oath is not given in a visible ceremony but orally. The LORD God assures Abraham that he has sworn by himself. The weight of this oath *by himself* is for us hard to understand in its fullness. Once again God the Holy Spirit, who is the author of the whole of the Scriptures, comes to help us in the letter to the Hebrews chapter 6:13-14,
"For when God made a promise to Abraham, since he had no one greater by whom to swear, he swore by himself, saying, "Surely I will bless you and multiply you."

QUICK QUESTION

1. For whose benefit did the LORD God swear by himself?

BOTH THE LORD GOD AND ABRAHAM SHOWED THEMSELVES FAITHFUL TO THE BINDING OF THE BOND REVEALED IN GENESIS CHAPTER SEVENTEEN

From Genesis 17 we learn that the LORD God had made Abraham his bonded servant by saying *"Walk before me and be blameless."* At that time the LORD God had bound himself to Abraham and his offspring saying, *"I will make you exceedingly fruitful, and I will make you into nations, and kings shall come from you. And I will establish my covenant between me and you and your offspring after you throughout their generations for an everlasting covenant, to be God to you and to your offspring after you."* (Genesis 17:1 and 6-7).
Then the LORD God bound Abraham to himself with the seal of the Covenant Bond of circumcision.

QUICK QUESTION

1. Explain from this how the Bond of the Covenant is one-sided in origin and by God's gracious provision becomes two-sided.

The LORD God tested Abraham within the Bond of this Covenant. The LORD God showed himself faithful to his sworn Covenant Bond by keeping open the Way of Life through Isaac. The LORD God found his servant Abraham blameless saying, *"you have obeyed my voice."*

QUESTIONS

1. Show from the above the two parts of the Bond of the Covenant: God's promise and our obligation of obedient love.
2. Show from the above how the LORD God kept his Word (promise) and how Abraham responded in obedient love.
3. Christians are Abraham's children by faith (Rom. 4; Gal. 3:29). What are we, Christians, to learn from Genesis 22 about our life within the Bond of God's Covenant?

THE ANGEL OF THE LORD

When looking at **Genesis 16,** we made a brief remark on the Angel of the LORD appearing to Hagar. We noted:

"At this point it is necessary to state that the Angel of the LORD was not just one of the angels but Yahweh himself appearing in the form of the Angel. This is confirmed in verse thirteen where it is said of Hagar *"So she called the name of the LORD (YAHWEH) who spoke to her ..."*

We are now working with chapter 22 where the Angel of the LORD twice speaks to Abraham from heaven. This is a good time to take a closer look at the person of the Angel of the LORD. In the commentaries the explanations vary from "the" Angel, to "an" angel of the LORD. Of the Bible Versions, the previous editions of NIV and ESV print "angel". The newer editions of these two Versions now print "Angel". From the note at Genesis 16 our choice clearly is for "the" Angel of the LORD.

Who is the Angel of the LORD? The first point to take note of is that this not an angel *from* Yahweh but the Angel *of* Yahweh. [45] Yahweh is present in the form of an angel.
Hagar called the Angel of the LORD *"Yahweh"*. In Genesis 22:1 it is God who tested Abraham. In Genesis 22:12 the Angel of Yahweh speaks on behalf of God and yet says *"you have not withheld your son from me."* These two verses show that the Angel of Yahweh is one with God (Elohim) and yet is to be distinguished from God (Elohim). Since the Angel of Yahweh is Yahweh himself in the appearance of the Angel we need to answer a further question. Why does Yahweh speak as God, command as God, give promises as God, and yet appear as an angel?

---

[45] For the genitive construction see, John H.Choi, RESHEPH AND YHWH SEBA'OT, VT liv.1 Leiden 2004 accessed on line.

For the answer we must go back to Genesis 2. There God (Elohim) for the first time appears as the LORD God (Yahweh Elohim). We use the verb *appears* on purpose. God appeared to Adam means that he is seen by Adam. God's visible presence with Adam is expressed in the name Yahweh. Yahweh literally means *He Is*. Adam sees a form, visible to the human eye, *walking in the garden* (Genesis 3:8). Moreover, "*Yahweh God made for Adam and for his wife garments of skins and He clothed them.*" (Genesis 3:21). From all this we conclude that Yahweh is God appearing in observable form to whomever he chooses.

Let us now apply this to Genesis 22. In Genesis 22 Yahweh is God appearing to Abraham in the observable form of the Angel of the LORD. The appearance of Yahweh in the form of the Angel of the LORD has ended with the appearance of the Son of God on earth who was named Jesus. The name Jesus means Yahweh saves. This is clear from the words God spoke to Joseph, "*She will bear a son, and you shall call his name Jesus, for he will save his people from their sins.*" Since the appearance of the Son of God as the man Jesus there no longer is a need for him to appear as the Angel of the LORD.

> **1Timothy 3:16**,
> *Great indeed, we confess, is the mystery of godliness:*
> *He was manifested in the flesh,*
> *vindicated by the Spirit,*
> *seen by angels,*
> *proclaimed among the nations,*
> *believed on in the world,*
> *taken up in glory.*

DISCUSSION TIME

1. How is Yahweh who saves present among us today?
2. How do Christians see him today?

Genesis 23

BURIAL OF SARAH IN HOPE

Sarah has died and Abraham weeps. There is reason to mourn when a loved one dies. However, Abraham rises and sets out to buy a burial place for Sarah. The way Abraham goes about this shows that Abraham wept but not as one who has no hope. Sarah has died at Hebron in the hill country north east from Beersheba. There Abraham looks for a permanent family grave.

Hittites were the people in power at Hebron. Abraham approaches them and ends up negotiating with Efron, the Hittite for a cave together with the field in which the cave is situated. In the negotiations, Abraham insists on buying the whole parcel of land. Abraham wants full ownership. The Hittites agree to sell the field and cave, even though Abraham is a sojourner with no property rights. Abraham becomes owner of what becomes known to future generations as the Cave of Machpelah.

ABRAHAM'S HOPE

Abraham was not satisfied with just any burial place for Sarah. Abraham looks ahead.
At the end of the first and second paragraph in this section we call the grave Abraham seeks to buy *a permanent family grave* and a grave for *future generations.*
This is because of the following: Abraham bases his strategy of a permanent burial place on the LORD. God had given Abraham his solemn Word that his descendants would inherit the land. Abraham's descendants would be oppressed in a foreign country for four hundred years but the LORD would bring them back to Canaan to possess the land (Genesis 15). Abraham wants a permanent grave in Canaan for future generations for the LORD will make them into a nation there.

Jacob's words in Genesis 49:29-33 give proof of Abraham's trust in the sure promise of the LORD God. Jacob commanded them and said to them, *"I am to be gathered to my people; bury me with my fathers in the cave that is in the field of Ephron the Hittite, 30 in the cave that is in the field at Machpelah, to the east of Mamre, in the land of Canaan, which Abraham bought with the field from Ephron the Hittite to possess as a burying place. 31 There they buried Abraham and Sarah his wife. There they buried Isaac and Rebekah his wife, and there I buried Leah— 32 the field and the cave that is in it were bought from the Hittites."*

QUESTIONS

1. On what does Abraham base his hope?
2. Explain how Abraham acts in hope.

3. Christians bury their dead and weep but not as those who have no hope. How is our hope and burial method similar to Abraham's hope and burial method?
4. Use the Biblical method of burying our loved ones in hope to disprove the method of cremating people who have died.

THE LORD GOD PROVIDES ISAAC WITH A WIFE WHO LEAVES HER KINDRED AND HER FATHER'S HOUSE TO JOIN THE WAY OF YAHWEH

Read as just a story, or even as a story of faith, then the main persons in the story are Abraham, Eliezer and Rebekah. Abraham observes the need for Isaac to be married. A wife for Isaac would fill the place Sarah left empty upon her death. A wife for Isaac would also bring further descendants of Abraham as Yahweh had promised. The line of the Way of the LORD must continue. Abraham calls the Head Servant in his house to him and gives him instructions to seek out a wife for Isaac.

Ever since he had left his kindred and his father's house Abraham has learned from the LORD God to trust the LORD to provide. In faith, therefore, Abraham makes Eliezer swear that he will take a wife for Isaac not from *"among the Canaanites among whom I dwell but* go to *his country and his father's kindred and take a wife for my son Isaac."*

Abraham knows that by marrying a Canaanite woman Isaac would become one with the Canaanites. No longer would Isaac be a sojourner. By marrying into a Canaanite family Isaac would become owner of the land prematurely. Abraham believes the word of the LORD spoken in Genesis 15. Ownership of the land would come only in the Way of Yahweh! The wife of Isaac must come and join Abraham's house as stranger in a strange land but at home with Yahweh.

Eliezer raises the possibility that the woman might not be willing to come. If that were the case what should Eliezer then do? Should he take Isaac back to Paddan Aram? Abraham replies that Eliezer is not to take Isaac back there.

At this point verse seven in the story shows us that the main person who provides a wife for Isaac is not Abraham, neither Eliezer, nor Rebekah. The one who provides a wife for Isaac is Yahweh, the LORD God.

Abraham knows that neither he, nor his servant Eliezer, will be able to guarantee a favourable outcome in the search for a wife for Isaac. Abraham shows Eliezer the One, the only one, who can provide a wife for Isaac namely, the LORD God.
Abraham speaks:
" 7 The LORD, the God of heaven, who took me from my father's house and from the land of my kindred, and who spoke to me and swore to me, 'To your offspring I will give this land,' he will send his angel before you, and you shall take a wife for my son from there. 8 but if the woman is not willing to follow you, then you will be free from this oath of mine; only you must not take my son back there."

From these words of Abraham we must learn not to read this chapter of Genesis as a story, or even a story of faith, but as revelation of the work that the LORD God was doing in Abraham's day as The Opener of the Way of Life.

DISCUSSION TIME

1. Explain why it is important not to read biblical accounts as just stories.
2. Show how we should read so-called historical passages in the Bible.
3. Explain from whom Abraham has learned to plan for Isaac's wedding as he did.
4. Show to whom we as Christians must look to guide us in planning for our children's future.
5. Explain how we can learn from Abraham and Eliezer how to guide our children toward a Christian marriage *in the LORD*.
6. Explain the consequences of making wrong choices for our children's marriages.

Eliezer leaves for the city of Nahor with ten of his master's camels and choice gifts. He arrives there and *"makes the camels kneel down outside the city by the well of water at the time of evening."* The servant of Abraham shares the faith of his master and speaks,
"O LORD, God of my master Abraham, please grant me success today and show steadfast love to my master Abraham. 13 Behold, I am standing by the spring of water, and the daughters of the men of the city are coming out to draw water. 14 Let the young woman to whom I shall say, 'Please let down your jar that I may drink,' and who shall say, 'Drink, and I will water your camels'—let her be the one whom you have appointed for your servant Isaac. By this I shall know that you have shown steadfast love to my master."

If we still were not convinced that the LORD God is the first one in this story, then Eliezer puts us to shame. Eliezer accepts that only the LORD God can provide a wife for Abraham's heir Isaac. Yahweh himself chooses the wife who will be pleasing to Yahweh and his Way. Moreover, Eliezer believes that the LORD God is present. He does not pray as if the LORD God was only present far away at home with Abraham. He believes that the LORD God is present where he has arrived and Eliezer counts on Yahweh to provide. And that is exactly what the LORD God did. He provided for.
"Before he had finished speaking, behold, Rebekah, who was born to Bethuel the son of Milcah, the wife of Nahor, Abraham's brother, came out with her water jar on her shoulder. 16 The young woman was very attractive in appearance, a maiden whom no man had known. She went down to the spring and filled her jar and came up. 17 Then the servant ran to meet her and said, "Please give me a little water to drink from your jar." 18 She said, "Drink, my lord." And she quickly let down her jar upon her hand and gave him a drink. 19 When she had finished giving him a drink, she said, "I will draw water for your camels also, until they have finished drinking." 20 So she quickly emptied her jar into the trough and ran again to the well to draw water, and she drew for all his camels. 21 The man gazed at her in silence to learn whether the LORD had prospered his journey or not.

QUICK QUESTION

1. Explain that Eliezer in his prayer is not telling the LORD what to do.

Eliezer gazed at her in silence for he does not yet know who the maiden is. He wishes to learn whether the LORD had prospered his journey or not. To find that out he does not ask the LORD for a sign. Eliezer rather uses the tools Abraham has taught him to use. He asks questions to see whether this unknown girl fits the qualifications of the Way of the LORD outlined to him by Abraham.

22 When the camels had finished drinking, the man took a gold ring weighing a half shekel, and two bracelets for her arms weighing ten gold shekels, 23 and said, "Please tell me whose daughter you are. Is there room in your father's house for us to spend the night?" 24 She said to him, "I am the daughter of Bethuel the son of Milcah, whom she bore to Nahor." 25 She added, "We have plenty of both straw and fodder, and room to spend the night." 26 The man bowed his head and worshiped the LORD 27 and said, "Blessed be the LORD, the God of my master Abraham, who has not forsaken his steadfast love and his faithfulness toward my master. As for me, the LORD HAS led me in the way to the house of my master's kinsmen." 28 Then the young woman ran and told her mother's household about these things.

Rebekah answers in a manner that convinces Eliezer that the LORD God has prospered his way. This is the maiden who is a fitting wife for Isaac and Eliezer credits Yahweh for providing. The LORD God remains in the centre: "blessed *be the LORD God."*

DISCUSSION TIME

1. Explain what we can learn from Eliezer when choosing a marriage partner who is to be pleasing to God.

It is good to take note of the words Eliezer, and Bethuel and Laban use. In their words and actions, they all submit to will of Yahweh and do so in typical covenantal language: *faithfulness and steadfast love.* Eliezer praises Yahweh for showing faithfulness and steadfast love. He pleads with Rebekah's family to show faithfulness and steadfast love to his master Abraham.

The action has shifted to *"her mother's household."* There, Eliezer continues to rely on the LORD God and in his words he continues to put Yahweh in the centre. Even Laban, brother to Rebekah, and Bethuel her father, do the same; *50 Then Laban and Bethuel answered and said, "The thing has come from the LORD; we cannot speak to you bad or good. 51 Behold, Rebekah is before you; take her and go, and let her be the wife of your master's son, as the LORD has spoken."* Their words *"as the LORD has spoken"* show how the words of Yahweh have authority among them. The will of the LORD is obeyed by all.

ELIEZER AND REBEKAH LEAVE AND ARRIVE AT A PLACE WHERE THEY MEET ISAAC

In the last verses of this chapter, the verses 62 to 67 we find several elements.
The first element is that Rebekah through her marriage to Isaac, fills the place in the family that Sarah had. There is continuation, a continuation provided by Yahweh. Isaac acknowledges this for, *"Isaac brings her into his mother's tent,"* and, *"So Isaac was comforted after his mother's death."*

DISCUSSION TIME

1. Explain what here is meant by "continuation".

The second element is that Isaac is now the head of the family and acts accordingly. It is Isaac who *"had returned from Beer-lahai-roi and was dwelling in the Negeb."* Abraham has faded to the background.

QUICK QUESTION

1. Abraham is fading into the background. Explain how this fits into the concept of "continuation".

This leads us to the third element. The verses 62-67 form a transition to what follows in chapter 25. Chapter 25 will show us the death of Abraham. The fading away of Abraham in the last verses of chapter 24 leads into the account of Abraham's death and burial. In these last verses, God the Holy Spirit mentions that Isaac returned from *Beer-lahai-roi*. The mention of Isaac returning from *Beer-lahai-roi* is significant for that is the name of the well where the Angel of the LORD spoke to Hagar while she was pregnant with Ishmael. *Beer-lahai-roi* is in the wilderness of Shur where Ishmael roams. This leads us from chapter 24 to chapter 25. In chapter 25 Ishmael is present at the burial of Abraham. In chapter 25 there is also a listing of the descendants of Ishmael.

QUICK QUESTIONS

1. Explain how the mention of *Beer-lahai-roi* is leading us from chapter 24 to chapter 25.
2. Explain that God the Holy Spirit is the author of the art of writing and style.

Abraham "went on"

1 Abraham took another wife, whose name was Keturah.

Was Keturah Abraham's concubine or wife? Did he marry her while Sarah was still alive or after her death? Genesis 25:1 tells us that Abraham took Keturah as his wife, not as his concubine. I Chron. 1:32 however speaks of Keturah as Abraham's concubine.

Scanning the different commentaries on the book of Genesis one comes across different interpretations. Many take it that Abraham took Keturah as a concubine while his wife Sarah was still alive. A minority among the commentaries consider that Abraham married Keturah as his wife after the death of Sarah.

The Dutch "Statenvertaling" gives us a slightly different translation of verse one that is significant: *"En Abraham voer voort en nam een vrouw,"* (*And Abraham continued and took a wife*). This translation indicates that after the death of Sarah, Abraham's daily life continued during which he took Keturah as wife. From the account of Keturah and her sons in verses 2-6 we are given to understand that Keturah could not take the place of Sarah. Only through Sarah, the LORD had given birth to the promised offspring. Keturah and her sons did not add to the line of the promised offspring. On the contrary, Abraham excluded the sons of Keturah from his inheritance and sent them away with gifts. This may be the reason why in I Chron. 1:32, Keturah is called Abraham's concubine. The same applies to Genesis 25:6 where both Hagar and Keturah are called concubines. *"But to the sons of his concubines Abraham gave gifts, and while he was still living he sent them away from his son Isaac, eastward to the east country."*

Of the sons of Keturah Midian is specially known to us from Numbers 22-31 and Judges 6-7. The descendants of both Ishmael and Midian were nomads of the East. The East being the Syrian Arabian Peninsula stretching from Egypt and Sur to the Wilderness of Paran as far as Ezion-geber and the Gulf of Aqaba (we will have to come back to the subject of the "East" when we come to verse eighteen).

Discussion Time

1. Explain why there is no conflict between Genesis 25:1, 6 and 1Chron. 1:32.
2. Explain how Abraham could still be *"blameless"* before the LORD (Genesis 17:1) even though he took Hagar, and later Keturah, as wives?

ABRAHAM'S DEATH VERSE 8

Abraham was 175 years old when he died. By the time Abraham died, his son Isaac had married and the grandsons Jacob and Esau were about fifteen years of age. On the way to Sodom the LORD had revealed, *"For I have chosen him, that he may command his children and his household after him to keep the way of the LORD by doing righteousness and justice, so that the LORD may bring to Abraham what he has promised him."* (Genesis 18:19). Grandfather Abraham received fifteen years in which to instruct his grandsons Jacob and Esau.

QUESTIONS

1. In the light of Genesis 18:19 explain the task Abraham had as grandfather.
2. In the light of Genesis 18:19 explain and describe the task Christian grandparents have towards their grand and great-grand children.
3. Describe the opportunities the elderly members of the congregation have to serve the other members.
4. Explain the difference between performing a task as a general human task and performing it as a task received from the LORD God.

Vs. 9-18 *"Isaac and Ishmael his sons buried him in the cave of Machpelah"*.

Abraham was buried in the cave he had purchased in hope.

QUICK QUESTIONS

1. What was Abraham's hope (see notes on ch. 23)?
2. Do we, Christians, bury our loved ones in hope?

The verses 9-18 bring back Ishmael. This time God the Holy Spirit places Ishmael beside Isaac. This side by side did not continue. In vs 18, we find Ishmael over against the descendants of Isaac. We might be surprised to see God's line of Abraham interrupted by not only the presence of Ishmael but also the genealogy of the descendants of Ishmael. The same holds true for the descendants of Keturah recorded in 25:1-4.

Several items need to be considered.

FIRST: THE LORD'S FAITHFULNESS TO ISHMAEL

The genealogy of Ishmael confirms that the LORD made true the promise he gave to Abraham concerning Ishmael. *"As for Ishmael, I have heard you; behold, I have blessed him and will make him fruitful and multiply him greatly. He shall father twelve princes, and I will make him into a great nation."* (Genesis 17:20).

SECOND: GOD THE HOLY SPIRIT INSPIRED MOSES TO INSERT THE GENEALOGIES OF ISHMAEL AND KETURAH AT THE TIME OF THE EXODUS

The Israelites in Egypt were the first addressees of the book of Genesis. Through Moses the LORD God prepared Israel for the trek through the desert and the entrance into the Promised Land. By that time the clans of Ishmael and Keturah had settled to the East and North in the Arabian Peninsula.

THIRD: THE DESCENDANTS OF BOTH ISHMAEL AND KETURAH OPPOSED THE DESCENDANTS OF ISAAC AT THE TIME OF THE EXODUS AND SETTLEMENT OF ISRAEL IN THE PROMISED LAND

Prime among the opponents of Israel's settlement in Canaan were the descendants of Ishmael and Keturah. Of Ishmael's descendants it is revealed that Ishmael *"settled over against all his kinsmen."* (Genesis 25:23). Of the descendants of Keturah, Midian became a formidable enemy of Israel.

CAUSE OF THE ENMITY AGAINST ISRAEL

The roots of the enmity of the descendants of Ishmael and Keturah against Israel go back to Isaac being the sole heir of Abraham while Ishmael and the sons of Keturah were sent away. Moreover, Isaac was not only the sole heir of Abraham's possessions but also the sole heir of the divine promise that in Abraham's seed all nations of the earth would be blessed.

CONCLUSION

As is always the case in the book of Genesis so it is with the genealogies of Ishmael and Keturah in chapter 25: The LORD is urging his people into his future by revealing the enmity that is ahead of them. In the near future Israel will face opposition and the pull of false worship of God, especially because of Midian, the son of Keturah and Kedar the son of Ishmael. By this the LORD is also urging Israel to remain true to him and his promises in his future and not join the false worship of the descendants of Ishmael and Keturah. See Numbers 25: Israel's sin with Baal Peor of the Midianites.

QUESTIONS

1. Compare the genealogies of Genesis 25 with the list of nations in Genesis 10 and find names that both have in common.
2. Explain why the LORD God inserts the genealogy of Ishmael here. Should the attention not exclusively be on Isaac?
3. Using a concordance, or computer Bible program, find passages that show Midian and Kedar harming Israel either on the way into Canaan, or while the tribes lived in Canaan.
4. The descendants of Ishmael and Keturah worshipped *El* and Israel worshipped *Yahweh*, does this mean that they worshipped the same God?
5. Evaluate the claim that Christians and Muslims worship the same God.
6. Explain how the LORD God used the genealogies of Ishmael and Midian to prepare Israel for what to expect on the trek into the Promised Land.
7. Find in the New Testament Scriptures revelation whereby the LORD God prepares us for our trek through this world to the New Jerusalem.

Vss. 19-28

THE GENERATIONS (TOLEDOTH) OF ISAAC, ABRAHAM'S SON

In Genesis 2:4 we met the term generations/toledot for the first time. Let's quote one line of that section about the term generations: *"As such it has the element of continuation, of future, in it."* We can see this confirmed in the passage we discuss right now.

This passage is all about the LORD's future with Isaac. The LORD's plan does not stop with Isaac. The LORD presses on toward the Promised Land and the Promised Seed. The LORD God is giving sons through whom the LORD carries out his plan.

QUICK QUESTION

1. Explain why we should read the Bible as a whole and not as disjointed happenings.

A MARRIAGE "IN THE LORD"

The verses 19-20 review the marriage between Isaac and Rebekah. Her ancestry is emphasised. This brings to mind the decision of Abraham not to marry his son to a Canaanite woman but to a woman from Abraham's relatives in Paddan Aram. Rebekah proved to be a gift from the LORD God. Isaac was forty years old when he married Rebekah.

ISAAC AND REBEKAH WERE TESTED IN THEIR FAITH IN GOD'S PROMISES

From verse 21 we know that Isaac and Rebekah were childless in the first twenty years of their marriage. This not only meant that the LORD was not granting them an heir to Isaac's possessions, but more so meant that there was no heir to the promise the LORD made to them, *"In you all nations of the earth shall be blessed."*

Vs. 21

ISAAC PRAYS

"Now Isaac pleaded with the LORD in front of his wife for she was barren." (my literal translation JVR). The prayer of Isaac is specific. His wife is barren, which in practical terms means that she was unable to bear children. Isaac realizes that no human effort can bring change. This is from the LORD. He is withholding fertility and only he can create in Rebekah the ability to bear the promised child. The fact that Isaac prays in front of his wife emphasizes the specific cause for which Isaac is praying to God.

God the Holy Spirit led Moses to use a Hebrew word for Isaac's prayer that fits the unchangeable situation: עָתַר (ʿātār). Several times this word is used in a situation where only the LORD God can bring change (see note in bottom margin). [46]

The LORD heard Isaac's request for change and acted in his own sovereign way: Rebekah conceived. The LORD maintained the course toward the Offspring who would become the blessing to all nations.

DISCUSSION TIME

1. Explain the special position Isaac and Rebekah had in the Counsel of the LORD.
2. We are not Isaac and Rebekah. Explain how childless couples among us should pray to the LORD God.

Once again we meet here the *times and seasons which the LORD has kept in his own authority*. With respect to the LORD God changing an impossible situation we do well to remember the word we find in this quotation: *authority*. See notes on Genesis 18 and the sovereign way in which the LORD God granted Abraham and Sarah the promised son at his time.

See also 2 Peter 3:8-9, *"But do not overlook this one fact, beloved, that with the Lord one day is as a thousand years, and a thousand years as one day. 9 The Lord is not slow to fulfill his promise as some count slowness, but is patient toward you, not wishing that any should perish, but that all should reach repentance."*

Vs. 22-23

TWO CHILDREN IN REBEKAH'S WOMB AND THE LORD'S SOVEREIGN DECISION

Rebekah was expecting twins. Rebekah was disturbed to find that the twins were struggling together inside her. She decided to go to ask the LORD about this. It had been the LORD who had created in her the possibility to conceive. These twins were the work of YHWH.

The LORD's sovereign answer: The twins in her womb were subject to the sovereign plan of the LORD. The older, and stronger, of the twins would have to serve the younger. This would continue when the two would develop into two nations. The one nation would be stronger than the other. As the LORD by sovereign decision had chosen Isaac and not Ishmael, so it was with the twins: the LORD chose the younger and weaker of the two.

QUICK QUESTION

1) Explain what Esau should do as he grew up because of the sovereign decision of the LORD to choose Jacab?

---

[46] עָתַר (ʿātar) Of the twenty occurrences of ʿatar, eight are found in the theological contest of the plagues in Ex 8–10, (viz. Ex 8:8–9, 28–30 [H 4–5, 24–26]; 9:28; 10:17-18). In Ex 8:28 [H 24] sacrifice is related to the prayer of entreaty; such a relationship seems likely throughout this episode. Sacrificial acts are associated with the making of entreaty in II Sam 24:15 (David offers burnt offerings and peace offerings to stay the plague at the direction of the prophet Gad), and perhaps in II Sam 21:14 (concerning the burial of Saul and Jonathan)
R.B.A. in: R. Laird Harris, Robert Laird Harris, Gleason Leonard Archer and Bruce K. Waltke, Theological Wordbook of the Old Testament, electronic ed. (Chicago: Moody Press, 1999, c1980), 709.

Vs. 24-26

TWO NAMES

The body of the son who came out first was covered with red hair. Because of this he was given the name Esau. The second son came out holding on to the heel of his brother. Because of this he was given the name Jacob because that name reminds us of the word heel.

Vs. 27

THE DIFFERENCE BETWEEN ESAU AND JACOB

Esau was a hunter, a man of the field. Jacob dwelt in tents. Depending on which Bible translation you are using Jacob was a quiet, or plain, or mild, man. This would make Esau rough and Jacob gentile. This, however, is a misrepresentation of what God the Holy Spirit is revealing in verse twenty seven. The Hebrew word in verse twenty seven used to describe Jacob is the same word as we find in Chapter 17:1. There the LORD God instructs Jacob's grandfather Abraham with these words, *"Walk before me and be blameless."* The Hebrew word for blameless is *tam*. The Hebrew word that describes Jacob is also *tam*. [47]

The difference between Esau and Jacob was not in occupation but in disposition before the LORD God. In spite of all his weaknesses, Jacob was blameless before the LORD. Jacob continued in the line and faith of his Grandfather Abraham. Jacob was **wholeheartedly** in the LORD's Way.

QUICK QUESTION

1. Christian believers are forgiven sinners. Christians still are weak and fall into sin. Explain how Christian believers can be *blameless* before God?
2. Vs. 28 *Isaac loved Esau for he ate of his game, but Rebekah loved Jacob.* Explain the different position Isaac and Rebekah held regarding the revelation given to Rebekah that the older would serve the younger.
3. Explain the importance for Christian parents to be one in accepting the will of the Lord for their children.

Vs 29-34

ESAU DESPISES HIS BIRTHRIGHT

This is a difficult passage. Seen from a human perspective our sympathy lies with Esau. We are inclined to call Jacob cunning. In order to understand this passage we must move away from the human, horizontal perspective to the heavenly, vertical perspective.

---

[47] W.H. Gispen, Genesis vol.III p. 15 , "rechtschapen".

We also need to avail ourselves of the principle that God the Holy Spirit, as the author, is also the interpreter. The Holy Spirit interprets Esau's action first of all in verse 34 with the words, *"Thus Esau despised his birthright."* The Holy Spirit further interprets Esau's action for us in the letter to the Hebrews, chapter 12:6, *"See to it that no one is sexually immoral or unholy like Esau, who sold his birthright for a single meal."*

QUESTIONS

1. Explain the discord in Isaac's family between Isaac and Rebekah and between Esau and Jacob.
2. Explain how Esau acted in an unholy manner by selling his birthright (Heb. 12:6).
3. Discuss why the Holy Spirit does not highlight, or even judge, the trickery of Jacob.
4. The *Quakers* say about a person who fails to wait for the Spirit to give words to speak that this person *is running ahead of his or her Guide.*
5. Discuss whether Jacob was running ahead of his Guide.
6. Explain why this did not disqualify Jacob from being *blameless.*
7. Explain the importance of the birthright in Isaac's family, starting with the sovereign will of the LORD God.

THE LORD GOD, ISAAC, A FAMINE, AND PROGRESSION

There is much similarity between chapter 20 and chapter 26. What happened to Abraham now happens to Isaac. Because of the similarity we might be inclined to speak of repetition. However, based on what the LORD God says and does we must conclude, not repetition, but *progression*. This becomes clear right from the beginning of chapter 26.

In the first verse God the Holy Spirit reveals a sequence: *"Now there was a famine in the land, besides the former famine that was in the days of Abraham."*

QUICK QUESTION

1. Which words in verse one show that here is progression and not repetition?

There is also progression in verse three, *"Sojourn in this land, and I will be with you and will bless you, for to you and to your offspring I will give all these lands, and **I will establish the oath that I swore to Abraham** your father."*

Abraham is no more, but the oath the LORD God swore to Abraham progresses from Abraham to Isaac, the son of promise. This progression of the LORD God is expressed in the words *"I will establish the oath."* This has the force of **I will continue to establish the oath.** Throughout the generations to come the LORD God will faithfully act on the oath once sworn to Abraham and his offspring.

In the heading we placed the LORD first and then Isaac. Doing this affects our interpretation of this chapter. Chapter 26 is part of the history God began at the time of creation, which spans all ages, and which God completes at the time of the triumphant return of Christ from heaven. Within the span of this history of God there is progression. In this progression of the history of God with man, we speak of *God's History of Revelation* and *God's History of Redemption*. The Bible is the record of God revealing himself to man and redeeming mankind. The LORD God progresses as he reveals to man what he plans to do in **words**. The LORD God also progresses as he acts in **redemptive acts** of salvation and judgment.

QUESTIONS

1. Explain what is meant by progression in *God's History of Revelation*.

2. Explain what is meant by progression in *God's History of Redemption*.
3. Explain what would happen to *God's History of Revelation* and *God's History of Redemption* if we would place Isaac first and the LORD God second. Whose history would it become?
4. Explain what God redeems FROM and what he redeems UNTO.
5. Explain how we, Christians, are not part of the history of Isaac but part of the history of the God of Abraham and Isaac.
6. Explain how we, Christians, benefit from knowing God's history of revelation.
7. Explain how we, Christians, benefit from knowing God's history of redemption.
8. People from Dutch descent like to compare each other's family history and call it "Dutch Bingo". Could there be a method of reading your Bible 'a la' "Dutch Bingo Method"?

Isaac and his knowledge of the revelation and redemption of the LORD

Isaac and the past.
Isaac had his historical roots in God's word revelation and redemptive acts in Abraham's household. Because of the action of the LORD God Isaac was heir of Abraham's possessions and heir to the promises of the Bond of the Covenant, *"In your offspring all nations of the earth shall be blessed."* Isaac also personally had experienced the revelation of the LORD to Abraham and himself at Mount Moriah (Genesis 22). There the LORD God had sworn an oath by himself regarding the future of Isaac and generations to come. Isaac himself had been the subject of the redemption the LORD provided: The LORD God had stopped Abraham's knife and provided a substitute. Isaac did not make an acceptable sacrifice to the LORD, rather the ram in the thicket prophetically revealed the substitute in whom all nations were to be blessed.

Discussion Time

1. Explain how, and where, Isaac personally received revelation from the LORD God.
2. Explain how, and where, Isaac personally experienced redemption from the hand of the LORD God.

Isaac and the present.
Like Abraham his father, Isaac was faced with a famine in the land. Because of the famine Isaac moved to the small City State of Gerar ruled by a king, named Abimelech. He moved to Gerar, because the LORD God had appeared to him revealing his will for Isaac and promising redemption. This redemption would take place in the present and in the future.

2 *"And the LORD appeared to him and said, "Do not go down to Egypt; dwell in the land of which I shall tell you. ³ Sojourn in this land, and I will be with you and will bless you, for to you and to your offspring I will give all these lands, and I will establish the oath that I swore to Abraham your father. ⁴ I will multiply your offspring as the stars of heaven and will give to your offspring all these lands. And in your offspring all the nations of the earth shall be blessed, ⁵ because Abraham obeyed my voice and kept my charge, my commandments, my statutes, and my laws."*

Questions

1. Why did Isaac move to Gerar?

2. Show how Isaac received revelation from the LORD God while in Gerar.
3. Show how the LORD God promised Isaac redemption while in Gerar.

The LORD God did not progress with Isaac because of Isaac's merits. On the contrary, Isaac showed himself weak in many of his dealings. The LORD God progressed with Isaac because of his sovereign choice of Isaac and his oath to Abraham.

THE LORD GOD PROGRESSES WITH HIS CHOSEN ONES IN THE BOND OF THE COVENANT

The LORD God progressed from Abraham to Isaac. The LORD God makes the same promises to the son as he made to the father. As reason for giving these same promises to Isaac the LORD God several times refers to father Abraham. In verse three, we read: *"Sojourn in this land, and I will be with you and will bless you, for to you and to your offspring I will give all these lands, and **I will establish** the oath that I swore to Abraham your father."*

The words in bold print, **I will establish** contain revelation and redemption. The LORD God reveals that he will be faithful to the oath he swore to Abraham, in the present for Isaac, and in the future for Isaac's offspring, In the same manner the LORD God makes room for Isaac and his offspring in a foreign land where they are sojourners. The opposition of Abimelech and his people turns into an acknowledgement: *"You are now the blessed of the LORD."* (vs. 29). This happens because the LORD God redeemed Isaac and his offspring from the opposing power of Satan.

DISCUSSION TIME

1. Show how the words **I will establish** contain revelation and redemption.
2. Explain how Abimelech became an instrument of the LORD for the redemption of Isaac from danger.
3. Compare this to other places in the Bible where the LORD God uses foreign powers to serve his redemptive purpose

We often read the Old Testament as if there were no redemption at all. The fullness of redemption came when the LORD God fulfilled the oath he swore to Abraham in the sending of his Son and the victory of Jesus Christ over Satan. It is because the LORD God constantly redeemed a people for himself in the past that the fullness of redemption through Christ has come.

DISCUSSION TIME

1. Explain why the LORD God constantly redeemed a people for himself.
2. Explain how this holds true today, both world-wide and specifically here in Canada.

THE PLACE THE LORD GOD ASSIGNED TO ABRAHAM IN THE BOND OF HIS HOLY COVENANT

The reason the LORD God gave to Isaac for blessing him and his offspring has been problematic for interpreters of the Bible. This is the reason the LORD God gave to Isaac:

"because Abraham obeyed my voice and kept my charge, my commandments, my statutes, and my laws." (Genesis 26:5) and again in verse 24 the LORD repeats, *"I am the God of Abraham your father. Fear not, for I am with you and will bless you and multiply your offspring for my servant Abraham's sake."*

There are two perceived problems. The one is **linguistic**. The other is **theological**.
Linguists concern themselves with the language of the Bible. Theologians concern themselves with the doctrine of the Bible.

Linguists look in verse five at the words, commands, statutes and laws, and consider them "deuteronomistic". This means that you find words like these in the book of Deuteronomy and the books of the later prophets but not in the book of Genesis. Therefore, some interpreters are of the opinion that verse five must have been inserted into chapter 26 at a later time.

Theologians become confused doctrinally by the word, *"because"*. For that word makes it look as if the LORD is dependent on Abraham's faithfulness for the fulfillment of his promise.

DISCUSSION TIME

1. Explain what linguists do with respect to the Bible.
2. Explain what theologians do with respect to the Bible.

However, is it correct to speak of problems? Are there problems? **Linguistically, there is no problem.** On page two of our discussion notes we find mention of Hammurabi. The following is a quote from page two, *"Abraham originated from the Babylonian city of Ur. A contemporary of Abraham was the Babylonian king Hammurabi at Ur[48] who wrote a book of laws consisting of a Preface, 282 commandments, and an Epilogue."* The law-terms used by the LORD God concerning Abraham are fully contemporary with the time in which Abraham lived.

QUICK QUESTION

1. Explain why linguistically there is no problem.

Doctrinally, there is no problem. Above this section we placed this caption: **The place the LORD God assigned to Abraham in the Bond of his Holy Covenant.** This is clear from how the LORD God dealt with Abraham. The LORD God had established the Bond of his Covenant with Abraham and commanded him to *"walk before me and be blameless."* (Genesis 17:1 ff.). Besides revealing the Bond of the Covenant with Abraham the LORD God revealed that he had chosen Abraham.

Genesis 18:17-19, *[17] The LORD said, "Shall I hide from Abraham what I am about to do, [18] seeing that Abraham shall surely become a great and mighty nation, and all the nations of the earth shall be blessed in him? [19] For I have chosen him, that he may command his children and his household after him to keep the way of the LORD by doing righteousness and justice, so that the LORD may bring to Abraham what he has promised him."*

In these verses, as well as in our verse (Genesis 26:5), our LORD and God reveals to us how he deals with his chosen ones. God's chosen ones live with him in the Bond of his Covenant. This places upon the chosen descendants of Abraham the obligation of love to walk before the LORD blameless, as their father Abraham had walked before the LORD blameless. This applies to all the descendants of Abraham who are his "by faith" (Gal. 3:29).

DISCUSSION TIME

1. Explain how the LORD God deals with His chosen ones.
2. What obligation do we as descendants of Abraham "by faith" have towards our revealing and redeeming God?

We find this same divine pattern of God with his chosen one David and his descendants (Psalm 89:28-36).
28 My steadfast love I will keep for him forever,
and my covenant will stand firm for him.
29 I will establish his offspring forever and his throne as the days of the heavens.
30 If his children forsake my law
and do not walk according to my rules,
31 if they violate my statutes
and do not keep my commandments,
32 then I will punish their transgression with the rod
and their iniquity with stripes,
33 but will not remove from him my steadfast love
or be false to my faithfulness.
34 I will not violate my covenant
or alter the word that went forth from my lips.
35 Once for all I have sworn by my holiness;
I will not lie to David.
36 His offspring shall endure forever,
his throne as long as the sun before me.

This same Bond of the Covenant language continues in the New Testament.
2 Tim. 2:19, *"But God's firm foundation stands, bearing this seal: "The Lord knows those who are his," and, "Let everyone who names the name of the Lord depart from iniquity."* (see also Eph. 1:1-5; Revelation 17:14).

QUICK QUESTION

1. What benefit do you receive from believing the same Bond of the Covenant language in 2 Tim. 2:19?

If Isaac would have become unfaithful to the LORD God, then he would, personally, have been excluded from the blessing. The LORD God, however, would have remained true to his oath to Abraham; the promised offspring would have come at God's appointed time in spite of Isaac's unfaithfulness.

THE PROGRESSION OF THE LORD GOD BRINGS TO ISAAC A FORETASTE OF POSSESSING THE LAND

12. *"And Isaac sowed in that land and reaped in the same year a hundredfold".*

Verse twelve introduces a new element: Isaac remains at Gerar long enough to grow crops. The LORD God had commanded Isaac not to go to Egypt but to remain in the land the LORD God showed him. There the LORD God would be with him and bless him. As a result of God's command and promise Isaac no longer roamed as a nomad but stayed at Gerar as a sojourner. Of Abraham we do not read of sowing crops but of Isaac we do. Also, this shows us progression from the LORD God. Isaac receives a foretaste of possessing the land.

DISCUSSION TIME

1. Explain why Isaac did no longer roam as a nomad but stayed at Gerar as a sojourner.
2. Explain how we find here progression from the LORD God.

THE LORD GOD SEVERED ISAAC FROM DEPENDING ON ABIMELECH

Because of the protection Isaac received from Abimelech, Isaac prospered. He did so well that Abimelech considered Isaac a threat and sent him away. Once again Isaac was a nomad looking for water and fodder. Whenever his servants dug a well the men of Abimelech disputed ownership forcing Isaac to move on. In this we see the hand of the LORD God. He prevented Isaac from depending on the people of the land. The separation led Isaac to greater dependence on the LORD.

DISCUSSION TIME

1. Explain how this principle of separation applies to Christians today in a society that increasingly is against God and His Christ.

Rehoboth *"The LORD has made room for us."*
22 And he moved from there and dug another well, and they did not quarrel over it. So he called its name Rehoboth, saying, "For now the LORD has made room for us, and we shall be fruitful in the land."

Isaac once again experienced the redeeming grace of the LORD God because of his oath to Abraham. Isaac recognized this and expressed this in the name he gave to the well of water, **Rehoboth**. Isaac made clear what he meant by this name: *The LORD has made room for us, and we shall be fruitful in the land.* The LORD God did not merely break Isaac's dependence on Abimelech. The LORD God showed Isaac that he could fully depend on the LORD God who is the total owner of the whole world and all the lands.

DISCUSSION TIME

1. Explain how the LORD God has shown us during our lives that we can depend on him and his everyday redemption.

PROGRESSION FROM THE FIRST BEERSHEBA TO THE SECOND BEERSHEBA.

23 "From there he went up to Beersheba."

We must have another look at what progression is. There are in this context two sides to progression.
The **first** is progression with increase or growth.
The **second** is progression with confirmation, faithfully holding the course.

To a great extent the latter is the case from Beersheba to Beersheba. Looking at the two happenings at Beersheba superficially there is only repetition. What happened to Abraham the father now happens to Isaac the son. Wells are no longer disputed. The LORD God appears to Isaac at Beersheba and repeats the promises made earlier to Abraham the father. Just as his father did so Isaac builds an altar to the LORD.

However, this holding the course **is big!** From one generation to the next there is a time gap. During that gap there is no absence of the presence and power of the LORD God. At the second Beersheba the LORD God surrounds Isaac with his gracious presence. In the building of the altar Isaac acknowledges the presence of the LORD God in the hostile land of Abimelech and his henchmen. Isaac trusts the LORD who showed himself true to his once given word.

DISCUSSION TIME

1. Explain the two sides of progression.
2. Explain how from Beersheba to Beersheba there is not just repetition.
3. Explain how the LORD God is "holding the course".
4. Explain why this is **big!**
5. Explain what Isaac expresses in the building of the altar.

WHEN THE LORD GOD BLESSES HIS PEOPLE IT BECOMES PUBLIC KNOWLEDGE

28 They said, "We see plainly that the LORD has been with you".

Abimelech realizes that he is not just dealing with Isaac when he makes life hard for Isaac. Abimelech is faced with the power of the LORD God. In spite of trying to reduce the wealth and power of Isaac, Abimelech sees growth. From afar, Abimelech sees the reason for Isaac's prosperity: The LORD God is blessing Isaac. Abimelech exclaims, *"You are now the blessed of the LORD."* That is the basis of the covenant Abimelech makes with Isaac.

DISCUSSION TIME

1. Explain how Abimelech has "public knowledge" of the blessing of the LORD God.
2. Explain whether the world around us has reason to publically see the "blessed of the LORD" today.
3. Explain why Christian believers may not covet the favor of the "world" to shun persecution.
4. Show where you see progression of evil against Christ and His believers in our world today.
5. Discuss whether and how we live in the "times of the end".

A TRANSITION VERSE AND MORE THAN THAT

34-35 *"When Esau was forty years old, he took Judith the daughter of Beeri the Hittite to be his wife, and Basemath the daughter of Elon the Hittite, 35 and they made life bitter for Isaac and Rebekah."*

These two verses form a transition to chapter 27 and the lifting of Jacob above Esau. Such transition from one chapter to the next happens more often. But here is more than that. **Esau is placing himself outside the progression of the LORD God.** Notice the contrast between the marriage between Isaac and Rebecca and the marriages of Esau with Hittite women.

According to the commandments and laws of the LORD God Abraham had forbidden his servant Eliezer to take a wife for Isaac from the Canaanites. The LORD God himself had provided a wife for Isaac from the family of Abraham in Padan Aram. Abraham prepared a marriage for his son in the way of the LORD revealed to him in Genesis 18:19, *"For I have chosen him, that he may command his children and his household after him to keep the way of the LORD by doing righteousness and justice, so that the LORD may bring to Abraham what he has promised him."*

Esau acted contrary to the command of the LORD God when he married Hittite women. Esau continued in the wrong way he started to take when he despised his birthright. In doing so he broke the Bond of holiness by which he was bound to the LORD God. Esau forfeited the blessing (see Malachi 2:2-3).

DISCUSSION TIME

1. Explain the contrast between the marriage of Isaac and Rebecca and the marriages of Esau with Hittite women.
2. Explain how Esau is placing himself outside the progression of the LORD God.
3. Explain how Esau forfeited the blessing by breaking the Bond of holiness.
4. Explain how our choices and the choices of our children marrying an outright unbeliever affects our status with the LORD God in the Bond of his Holy Covenant.

GENESIS 26:34 to 28:9

THE LORD GOD MAINTAINS HIS WORD TO REBECCA

The choice of the verses 26:34 to 28:22 as one passage.

The choice of chapter 26:34 to 28:9 is based on two considerations. The first consideration is that these verses reveal the sovereign work of the LORD God in the family of Isaac and Rebecca regardless of the errant actions of Isaac and Rebecca and their sons. The second consideration is that this passage begins and ends with Esau and his wives.

The older shall serve the younger
Rebecca had been disturbed when she was pregnant with the twins. She observed that the twins were struggling within her womb. The struggle was of such a nature that she found it necessary to go to the LORD for an answer. And the LORD said to her,
"Two nations are in your womb,
and two peoples from within you shall be divided;
       the one shall be stronger than the other,
the older shall serve the younger." (Genesis 25:23).
Apparently the struggle between the twins in her womb was not incidental but intentional. The effort of Esau to resist the will of the LORD began in the womb of his mother Rebecca.

QUESTIONS

1. Explain what kind of struggle there was in Rebecca's womb?
2. Explain what, and who, was behind this struggle?
3. Explain who, according to God's plan, should have come out as the firstborn?
4. In the light of God's plan, explain baby Jacob's action of holding on to Esau's heel.

We are not informed how much Isaac knew of these words of the LORD God. We do know that Isaac acted contrary to what the LORD God had decided concerning the place of Jacob. Isaac loved Esau while Rebecca loved Jacob. In doing so Rebecca was motivated by what the LORD God had told her. Isaac apparently was not only blind but was also unable to see the ungodly lifestyle of Esau. In spite of the bitterness that Isaac experienced because of Esau marrying Hittite women, he continued to favor Esau even to the extent of intending to bless him with the blessing of the firstborn. In her position as wife Rebecca was unable to overrule Isaac. Rebecca followed the way of the LORD but resorted to trickery. In this she took along her son Jacob.

In spite of these human errors, it was the word of the LORD God that prevailed. We have here the same situation as we found in Genesis 17. There, the LORD God chose Isaac as the firstborn and not Ishmael. From the notes on that chapter we quote the following: *The LORD God, who is from the beginning the Opener of the Way of Life, has chosen to push forward His Way through Isaac. The Bond of His Covenant will continue through Isaac and not through Ishmael. Not natural descent determines who God's firstborn son is but God's sovereign decision determines that.*

In the case of Jacob and Esau we once again meet the sovereign right of the LORD God to choose. This time the sovereign LORD chooses Jacob. The LORD God continues the Bond of the Covenant with its promises through Jacob instead of through Esau.

THE HOLY SPIRIT REFRAINS FROM REVEALING DISAPPROVAL OF THE ACTIONS OF REBECCA AND JACOB

We could qualify the trick actions of Rebecca and Jacob as acts of disbelief and lack of trust in the LORD God to act. Surprisingly, God the Holy Spirit refrains from instructing the Bible writers to record such a judgment over the actions of Rebecca and Jacob. Earlier, we found the same lack of recorded judgment with the actions of Abraham. There must be a reason for this, and there is a reason indeed. God the Holy Spirit wants us to focus on the sovereign actions of the LORD God instead of on the errors of Rebecca and Jacob.

QUESTIONS

1. Explain why God the Holy Spirit refrains from recording judgment over the trick actions of Rebecca and Jacob.
2. Explain why it is more important for us to focus on the actions of the LORD God then on the actions of men.
3. Explain that this silence of God the Holy Spirit does not mean that God approves of the way Rebecca and Jacob (or we!) go about things.
4. Explain what the actions of the LORD God in Isaac's family aimed at.
5. Explain that in spite of all this Jacob was still *"blameless"* before the LORD God. (To help the discussion check back to Genesis 6 on p. 38; Genesis 17 on p. 90 and Genesis 25 on pages 143-145.)
6. Explain how the LORD God is going forward with His plan of Glory today in spite of the weaknesses of believers and even of the Church.
7. Explain how we can learn from the mistakes of Isaac and Rebecca without losing focus on what the LORD God is doing.

THE LORD GOD MOVES ISAAC'S HEART TO DO WHAT IS RIGHT IN THE EYES OF THE LORD AND ISAAC OBEYS

Esau enters right after Jacob has left and Isaac is confronted with the fact that he has blessed Jacob with the blessing of the firstborn instead of Esau. Isaac *trembles violently* (vs.33), but in spite of that a remarkable change comes over Isaac. No longer does Isaac follow his own preferences but he obeys the LORD God and his leading. Realizing that he has blessed Jacob with the blessing of the firstborn does not make Isaac rebel against the leading of the LORD God. Isaac takes the consequence of his action which is evident from his answer to Esau, *"I have blessed him? Yes, and he shall be blessed."*

QUESTIONS

1. Explain that Isaac is not giving in to Rebecca but is obeying the leading of the LORD God.
2. Explain the difference between the two blessings, the one of Jacob and the one of Esau.
3. Explain how these blessings had future fulfillment.
4. What obligations did the leading of the LORD God lay upon Esau?
5. What obligations did the leading of the LORD God lay upon Jacob?
6. Explain how Esau rebelled against the leading of the LORD God.

THE LORD GOD MOTIVATES ISAAC AND REBECCA TO SET JACOB ON THE PATH OF A MARRIAGE IN THE LORD AND GODLY OFFSPRING

Up till now Isaac and Rebecca had been divided. Isaac followed tribal custom and personal favor. Rebecca had acted upon the revelation she received from the LORD God when the twins were struggling in her womb. This changed. Isaac and Rebecca became one on the Way of the LORD.

Rebecca is told of Esau's hatred for Jacob and his intent to kill Jacob. Rebecca tells Isaac of her plan to protect Jacob. Jacob is to flee to Rebecca's relatives in Haran, stay there and marry one of her brother Laban's daughters. Besides protection for Jacob, Isaac and Rebecca voice a more important reason for Jacob to go to the house of Bethuel and Laban. Rebecca voices this in a negative way, *46 Then Rebekah said to Isaac, "I loathe my life because of the Hittite women. If Jacob marries one of the Hittite women like these, one of the women of the land, what good will my life be to me?*

Isaac, this time takes the lead and positively instructs Jacob not to marry a woman of the land. The LORD God is leading Isaac to leave human desires and preferences behind and to act as heir of the promises made to Abraham. This is evident from the wording with which Isaac instructs his heir Jacob. Isaac takes his words from the words Yahweh spoke to Abraham recorded for us in Genesis 17.

Here are Isaac's words:
28 *Then Isaac called Jacob and blessed him and directed him, "You must not take a wife from the Canaanite women. ² Arise, go to Paddan-aram to the house of Bethuel your mother's father, and take as your wife from there one of the daughters of Laban your mother's brother. ³ God Almighty bless you and make you fruitful and multiply you, that you may become a company of peoples. ⁴ May he give the blessing of Abraham to you and to your offspring with you, that you may take possession of the land of your sojournings that God gave to Abraham!"*

DISCUSSION TIME:

1. Explain from Isaac's words how Isaac is acting like his father Abraham when he instructs Jacob to marry a daughter of Rebecca's brother Laban.
2. Explain Hebrews 11:20 *"By faith Isaac invoked future blessings on Jacob and Esau."*
3. Explain from Genesis 24 and 27 why it is so important to *"marry in the LORD"* (I Corinthians 7:39).

GOD THE HOLY SPIRIT HIMSELF INTERPRETS SCRIPTURE

Hebrews 12:15-17 *"See to it that no one fails to obtain the grace of God; that no "root of bitterness "springs up and causes trouble, and by it many become defiled; ¹⁶ that no one is sexually immoral or unholy like Esau, who sold his birthright for a single meal. ¹⁷ For you know that afterward, when he desired to inherit the blessing, he was rejected, for he found no chance to repent, though he sought it with tears."*

DISCUSSION TIME

1. Explain Esau's tears.

2. Explain what it means to repent.
3. Explain how God the Holy Spirit interprets Genesis 27 in Hebrews 12.
4. Explain how in Hebrews 12:15-17 God the Holy Spirit corrects our human view of feeling sorry for Esau.

Malachi 1:2 *"I have loved you," says the LORD. But you say, "How have you loved us?" "Is not Esau Jacob's brother?" declares the LORD. "Yet I have loved Jacob but Esau I hated."*

Romans 9:13 *"As it is written, "Jacob I loved, but Esau I hated."*

TWO LINES CONVERGE

In the words of Hebrews 12, Malachi 1, and Romans 9 two lines converge: The line of divine election and the line of human responsibility.

TO CONSIDER

1. Find in the three passages quoted above the line of divine election.
2. What does the word "sovereign" in sovereign election mean?
3. Find in the three passages quoted above the line of human responsibility.
4. Try to reconcile these two lines with each other using your human logic.
5. How does God the Holy Spirit teach us to submit ourselves to God's sovereignty? Turn to Romans 9. There you find the teaching of the Holy Spirit.

To aid the discussion I pass on a quote from the Commentary of Dr. A. Van Selms,[49] p. 93 in my translation:

"The author knows Jacob as an imposter, who in Beersheba left a reputation in ruins, and who will soon in Harran will meet his equal. Nevertheless, God intends to be with this imposter, not because he is an imposter, not because he also has his good characteristics, only because God wants to confirm His Covenant with the fathers with the children. Just as in 25:23 the whole history of the rivalry between the twins has been placed under the heading of predestination, so is here human sin placed under the heading of divine faithfulness and forgiveness. In other words, predestination and grace appear to be two sides of the same matter."

QUESTIONS

1. Show how Van Selms uses divine logic instead of human logic.
2. Explain the term "predestination".
3. What is the biblical meaning of "grace"?

---

[49] A. Van Selms, Genesis II, Nijkerk 1973

ESAU MARRIED MAHALATH THE DAUGHTER OF ISHMAEL, ABRAHAM'S SON, THE SISTER OF NEBAIOTH

TO CONSIDER

1) Explain the reason why Esau married a daughter of Ishmael.
2) Explain how Esau, by marrying Mahalath, failed to return to the Way of the LORD.
3) Explain how in the New Testament the Way of the LORD runs through the Body of Christ (Ephesians 1:23).

GENESIS 28:10-22

These thirteen verses form a core passage.
If one would cut these verses out of the book of Genesis, then what follows in the chapters 29 to 31 would become a mere fairy tale. This is because cutting out these verses means cutting away the presence of the LORD God from going with Jacob. These verses are the basis for what follows.

QUICK QUESTION

1. What is it that "follows"?

There is another reason why these verses form a core passage.
The place Jacob called Bethel was at that time in the **centre** of two world powers
whose rulers claimed to reach heaven. To the South East of Bethel lay Egypt where the Royal Pyramids were claimed to be gateways to heaven. To the North East of Bethel lay cities like Ur of the Babylonians with their Ziggurats. One of these was called *"The House of the Staircase of the bright Heaven"* – *"a name which itself emphasizes that the building was considered as a link between heaven and earth."*[50]

THE LORD GOD CALLED THE PROMISED LAND "THE CENTRE OF THE EARTH."

Ezekiel 5:5
*5 "Thus says the Lord GOD: This is Jerusalem. I have set her in the **center** of the nations, with countries all around her".*

Ezekiel 38:12
*12 to seize spoil and carry off plunder, to turn your hand against the waste places that are now inhabited, and the people who were gathered from the nations, who have acquired livestock and goods, who dwell at the **center** of the earth".*

---

[50] I.E.S. Edwards, The Pyramids of Egypt, Penguin Books Canada Ltd, Toronto, 1947, 1961 pp. 293-4

Quick Question

1. Discuss how the Church of Christ could be the "center" of the earth.

The presence of the LORD goes with Jacob and keeps him wherever he goes

From southern Beersheba Jacob travels North toward Harran. On the way Jacob finds a place to sleep at, or, near a place called Luz. Apparently he sleeps in the open field for he finds a stone suitable for a headrest. From pictures of headrests of that time we know that specially shaped stone headrests were quite common in Near Eastern countries.

Jacob's dream

Jacob's dream is not caused by his own state of mind. The dream comes to him from the LORD God and is close to a vision. In the dream the LORD God is sending a message to Jacob in pictures (vs. 12-13a) and in words (vs. 13b-15).

The pictures are the basis of the words of promise that follow.

The ladder, or stairway, the angels, and the LORD God standing by, are not merely pictures but revelation of realities. These are the realities: Heaven is opened and there is traffic from earth to heaven and vice versa. Angels are ascending and descending to and from heaven. It is remarkable that the angels are first seen *ascending*. The angels are already present for the LORD God himself was present on earth with Jacob.

God was surrounded by his heavenly host. The angels are specifically called *angels of God*. This is to assure us that the atmosphere is not idolatrous but holy and divine. The *"of God"* also reveals that these angels have a task from God toward Jacob. God and his angels are going with Jacob to care for him in Paddan Aram and bring Jacob back to Canaan to inherit the promises given to Abraham and Isaac.

Discussion Time

1. Discuss what kind of dream Jacob had.
2. Discuss what the realities of Jacob's dream were.
3. Discuss why dreams from God no longer happen. Or do they?

The revelation of angels being present on earth from God to serve God's chosen people is to be trusted by all who have descended from Abraham. Whenever Christians of our day read Genesis 28, God the Holy Spirit assures them that God's angels are serving them in the here and now.

See, Heb. 1:14 *"Are not all angels ministering spirits sent to serve those who will inherit salvation?"*
When Jesus, the Son of God, had endured the temptation of the Devil he was served by angels. Luke 4:11, *"Then the Devil left Him, and behold, angels came and were ministering unto Him."*
It is important to note how the Lord Jesus spoke to Nathanael:
"Truly, truly, I say unto you, you will see heaven opened, and the angels of God ascending and descending on the Son of Man." John 1:51.

Questions

1. Who all are descended of Abraham?
2. Discuss what task angels of God have towards us, Christians, today?
3. Explain what it meant to the Lord Jesus to have *"heaven opened, and the angels of God ascending and descending on the Son of Man."* It will be helpful to compare John 1:51 with Genesis 28:10-22.

The everlasting Promises

The word "everlasting" fits the words the LORD God speaks to Jacob. "Everlasting" includes the past, the present and the future. In the **past** the LORD God spoke the words of promise to Abraham and Isaac. The words of 28:13, *"I am the LORD, the God of Abraham your father and the God of Isaac,"* remind Jacob of what the LORD promised in the past.

Before the LORD God addresses Jacob's present situation, he repeats the words of promise pertaining to **future** generations: *"The land on which you lie I will give to you and to your offspring. ¹⁴ Your offspring shall be like the dust of the earth, and you shall spread abroad to the west and to the east and to the north and to the south, and in you and your offspring shall all the families of the earth be blessed."*

Lastly the LORD God addresses Jacob in his **present** situation.

Discussion Time

1. Discuss the difference between everlasting and eternal.
2. Explain why it is impossible to understand your present situation, and future times, if you neglect to know what the LORD God has said and done in the past.

Jacob's present situation

Behind Jacob is the threat of murder. His brother Esau has vowed to kill Jacob. That threat makes it humanly impossible for him to return to the promised land. Ahead of him he has a long and arduous journey to Paddan Aram. Once there he has relatives to go to but it is uncertain what kind of a welcome he will have.

Quick Question

1. Considering all this what chance does Jacob have to inherit all that is promised him and his offspring?

The LORD God places Jacob's predicament in the proper perspective. The fulfillment of the Words of Promise does not depend on Jacob. The power to make promises true belongs to the LORD.
¹⁵ *"Behold, I am with you and will keep you wherever you go, and will bring you back to this land. For I will not leave you until I have done what I have promised you."*
The LORD God will be powerfully present in all the uncertainties facing Jacob.

Matt. 28:18-20

*18 And Jesus came and said to them, "All authority in heaven and on earth has been given to me. 19 Go therefore and make disciples of all nations, baptizing them in the name of the Father and of the Son and of the Holy Spirit, 20 teaching them to observe all that I have commanded you. **And behold, I am with you always, to the end of the age.**"*

DISCUSSION TIME

1. Discuss the similarity between the words of promised presence by the LORD God in Genesis 28 and the words of the Son of God, Jesus the Christ, in Matt. 28.
2. How does that similarity comfort you?

THIS IS THE HOUSE OF GOD, THE GATE OF HEAVEN

16 "Then Jacob awoke from his sleep and said, "Surely the LORD is in this place, and I did not know it." 17 And he was afraid and said, "How awesome is this place! This is none other than the house of God, and this is the gate of heaven."
18 "So early in the morning Jacob took the stone that he had put under his head and set it up for a pillar and poured oil on the top of it".

Imperfect and erring, Jacob has seen heaven opened and the LORD God standing with him and he is overawed. He has witnessed God's heavenly host commuting between earth and an open heaven. He has seen a ladder, not placed there by human hands, but by the power and grace of the LORD God. Jacob sees this in a dream from God that represents realities from God. Jacob gets to see and hear what hundreds of thousands of people to the North, East, West and South of him search for. The Pyramids and Ziggurats and similar structures throughout the world witness to mankind's futile efforts to find the Gate to Heaven. This futile effort began with the "Tower of Babel" and continues to the present day.

QUESTIONS

1. Explain why it is not sufficient to study Pyramids and Ziggurats scientifically, mathematically, or historically.
2. What was first, the Pyramids and Ziggurats of Egypt and Babylon or the presence of God from an open heaven and on earth?
3. Discuss whether the Bible borrows from pagan idolatrous images and works.
4. Explain that pagan images, words and works are distorted caricatures of the truth.
5. Apply what you have found in regard to the above points to Jacob at Bethel.

THIS IS THE HOUSE OF GOD

Jacob concludes that the presence of the LORD God with his chosen one is not a passing incident but a lasting divine gift. This is clear from his words, *"This is none other than the house of God."* A house is a permanent dwelling. In this case the house is a temple, for Jacob makes a vow, *20 "Then Jacob made a vow, saying, 'If God will be with me and will keep me in this way that I go, and will give me bread to eat and clothing to wear, 21 so that I come again to my father's house in peace, then the LORD shall be my*

God, ²² and this stone, which I have set up for a pillar, shall be God's house. And of all that you give me I will give a full tenth to you.'"

QUICK QUESTION

1. Explain the difference between a passing incident and a lasting divine gift.

THIS IS THE GATE OF HEAVEN

With the words, *this is the Gate of Heaven,* God the Holy Spirit opens for us a wealth of divine good pleasure and revelation. God has opened his dwelling place of heaven, and is approachable for his chosen ones on earth; in his house, in his temple God will be present and is available for who seek him in true worship. "This is the House of God" and "this is the Gate of heaven" belong together. This temple will be for God's chosen ones, the Gate of Heaven, for it is via God's house on earth that God gives access to his throne in heaven. Jacob has been given to understand what the LORD God was doing and therefore he named the place properly.

QUESTIONS

1. Explain Jacob's anointing of the stone.
2. Explain how this stone could become a house of God.
3. What is the function of a pillar?

The wide range of Jacob's words
Jacob's vow of serving the LORD God on earth, at his House, at his Temple, concords with the will of God. We know from history, the House of God as the Gate of Heaven revealed throughout the Bible; The Tabernacle, the Temple, Jesus Christ, and the Church, are all House of God and Gate of Heaven. Here follow some passages of Scripture that show the progression of what was started in Genesis 28.

The temple at Jerusalem
Psalm 118:19-20 ¹⁹ *"Open to me the **gates** of righteousness, that I may enter through them and give thanks to the LORD. ²⁰ This is the **gate** of the LORD; the righteous shall enter through it."*

Jesus Christ is the Door (John 10)
⁷ *" So Jesus again said to them, 'Truly, truly, I say to you, I am the door of the sheep. ⁸ All who came before me are thieves and robbers, but the sheep did not listen to them. ⁹ I am the door. If anyone enters by me, he will be saved and will go in and out and find pasture.'"*

QUICK QUESTION

Explain Christ's "if" in the following sentence, ⁹ *"I am the door. If anyone enters by me, he will be saved and will go in and out and find pasture."*

THE CHURCH IS A HOLY TEMPLE IN THE LORD (EPH. 2:17-22)

17 "And he came and preached peace to you who were far off and peace to those who were near. 18 For through him we both have access in one Spirit to the Father. 19 So then you are no longer strangers and aliens, but you are fellow citizens with the saints and members of the household of God, 20 built on the foundation of the apostles and prophets, Christ Jesus himself being the cornerstone, 21 in whom the whole structure, being joined together, grows into a holy temple in the Lord. 22 In him you also are being built together into a dwelling place for God by the Spirit."

DISCUSSION TIME:

1. Explain that the Church is the temple of God.
2. Explain how important it is for the Church to remain faithful in love to Christ according to the Scriptures in order to remain the Temple of the Holy Spirit and Gate to Heaven.

THE CHRISTIAN BELIEVER IS A TEMPLE OF THE HOLY SPIRIT (1 CORINTHIANS 6:19)

19 "Or do you not know that your body is a temple of the Holy Spirit within you, whom you have from God? You are not your own, 20 for you were bought with a price. So glorify God in your body."

DISCUSSION TIME

1. Explain what it means for us that our body is called a "temple of the Holy Spirit". Apply what we have learned in these notes about the House of God and the Gate of heaven as you formulate your explanation.

It looked so puny but it is God's work for all times
What is Jacob's stone in comparison to Egyptian Pyramids and Babylonian Ziggurats? Jacob's stone was small and has long since disappeared but the Pyramids and Ziggurats are still there. To the present-time, scientists make an effort to unravel the mysteries of these gigantic structures. To the frustration of archeologists these so-called Gates to Heaven fail to live up to their claims. They still do not present a gate to heaven. There is no memory of reality. Our strong God, however, has preserved the memory of Jacob's anointed stone. Jacob's pillar is witness to the reality of the power of the LORD God to break open the Gate of Heaven. We believe the history of God the Father, God the Son Jesus Christ, and God the Holy Spirit of truth: from Bethel to God's Church and on to the New Jerusalem.

Matthew 16:18
"And I tell you, you are Peter, and on this rock, I will build my church, and the gates of hell shall not prevail against it."

DISCUSSION TIME

1. Compare the gates of hell with the Gates of Heaven.

Jacob's Vow ²⁰ *Then Jacob made a vow, saying, "If God will be with me and will keep me in this way that I go, and will give me bread to eat and clothing to wear, ²¹ so that I come again to my father's house in peace, then the LORD shall be my God, ²² and this stone, which I have set up for a pillar, shall be God's house. And of all that you give me I will give a full tenth to you."* Earlier, we saw that Abraham built altars to the LORD in a land promised to him but where he owned no land. He did this believing that the LORD was present in this land, and would give it to Abraham's descendants. Jacob made his vow believing the promise.

QUESTIONS

1. Should we make vows like the vow Jacob made?
2. What kind of vows do we Christians make?

Introduction: The LORD God does what he had promised to Jacob

The chapters 29 to 35 contain the history of God with Jacob from Bethel to Bethel. We consider the chapters 29-35 a unit because they contain the fulfillment of God's solemn Word of Promise spoken to Jacob at Bethel, *"Behold, I am with you and will keep you wherever you go, and will bring you back to this land. For I will not leave you until I have done what I have promised you."* (Genesis 28:15).

In our interpretation of the chapters dealing with Jacob's sojourn with Laban until his return to his father Isaac, we must make a prayerful effort to keep this promise of the LORD God to Jacob in mind. It is a time of the LORD God keeping his word, doing what he promised to do. It is easy for us to get caught up in the multiple errors of Jacob, Laban, Rachel and Leah and forget what is first in the book of Genesis: The actions of the LORD God are first.

Questions

1. There are two that travel from Bethel (ch. 28) to Bethel (Ch. 35). Who are these two?
2. What promise of the LORD God are we to keep in mind when studying chapters 29 through 35?
3. Why is it so necessary to keep this promise of the LORD God in mind during our study?
4. Has the LORD God made the same promise to you?
5. When, and at what occasion, did the LORD God promise you that he would be with you and not rest until he had fulfilled all that he had promised you?

GENESIS 29

29:1 *"Then Jacob went on his journey and came to the land of the people of the east."*
A literal translation would give us: *"Then Jacob lifted up his feet."* This portrays for us in simple words that Jacob is continuing on his journey. However, these simple words portray more to us than that Jacob continues on his journey.

Questions

1. Please read Jacob's vow once more (Genesis 28:20-22).
2. What spirit motivated Jacob when he put his foot on the ground in the direction of Laban?
3. In what direction are you traveling today?
4. Are you traveling alone?

5. Who is making sure that you will be preserved on your travels?
6. In what spirit do you move forward?
7. If an enemy of Christ would kill you, would you still arrive safely at your destination?

JACOB ARRIVES AT THE PEOPLE OF THE EAST (HARRAN)

TO CONSIDER

1. Describe how the LORD God prospered Jacob on his arrival. (Ch. 29:2-14)
2. Does this mean that when you go forward in faith and trust you will be successful in all you undertake?
3. Is there a difference between Jacob's place in God's council and yours and mine?
4. What, however, is the similarity between us and Jacob in God's council?

MAIN PERSONS IN GENESIS CHAPTERS 29-35 AND THEIR ACTIONS. AMONG THEM THE LORD GOD IS FIRST

- **The LORD God (Yahweh Elohim)**
- **The LORD's heavenly army of angels**
- **Jacob / Israel**
- **Laban and his sons**
- **The sorry state of Jacob's marriage**
- **Leah (Bilhah)**
- **Rachel (Zilpah)**
- **Reuben and his mandrakes**
- **The Man who wrestles with Jacob**
- **Esau**

The LORD brings Jacob safely to the land of the East.

The LORD's heavenly army of angels is shown to Jacob at Bethel as he flees from Esau who has vowed to kill Jacob.

The LORD leads Jacob to the correct place: Rachel and her father's household.

Jacob: From the time that Jacob left Bethel to his return to Bethel, Jacob remained faithful to the LORD God. In spite of the semi-pagan environment of Laban's family Jacob remained *"blameless"* (see notes on chapter 25:27 for *blameless*).

DISCUSSION TIME

1. Does this mean that Jacob was not held responsible for errors?
2. Find out from these chapters where Jacob acted in error.

Laban's first deceit (29:23-25): Laban cheats Jacob by substituting Leah for Rachel.
Laban's deceit (29:30) hurts Leah and gives Jacob a divided household.
The LORD judges between Leah, who is hated, and Rachel, who is loved, and Jacob who is responsible.

QUESTIONS

1. What was Jacob's place in this judgment?
2. Was this not just between Leah and Rachel?

The LORD God prospers Jacob in his good pleasure in spite of Jacob's many weaknesses.

QUICK QUESTION

1. Explain how this applies to our life before God.

The LORD protects Jacob's interest by showing Jacob how to secure his wages. **Jacob** receives in a dream from the LORD revelation concerning his wages. **Laban's** second deceit (30:35-36): Laban prevents Jacob from earning his wages by removing the rams and ewes that are spotted, black or speckled (see p.165).
Jacob rebukes Laban:

"you have changed my wages ten times. ⁴² If the God of my father, the God of Abraham and the Fear of Isaac, had not been on my side, surely now you would have sent me away empty-handed. God saw my affliction and the labor of my hands and rebuked you last night."

Jacob's words are testimony to God being faithful to his promise. Jacob does not credit himself of his being clever. **The LORD God** himself empowered Jacob to defend himself against Laban's deceit.

DISCUSSION TIME

1. Is it right to accuse Jacob of practicing magic when peeling the rods?
2. Explain what really happened?

The sorry state of Jacob's marriage:
Leah (29:17) *"Leah's eyes were soft."* Soft, or tender. There does not necessarily have to be anything wrong with Leah's eyes. The contrast between Leah and Rachel could have been that Leah's soft, tender eyes reflected her soft character. She was sexually less appealing to Jacob than her sister Rachel.

Rachel: this interpretation is based on the description of her sister Rachel: *"Rachel was beautiful in form and appearance."* This is a typical description of the outer appeal of a woman while the description of Leah was more that of the inner spirit of a woman. In today's language one would speak of sex-appeal. Reading that Leah's eyes were tender makes one wonder what Rachel's eyes were like.

QUICK QUESTION

1. When we look for a marriage partner what should be the first thing we look for in our future spouse?

Leah and the LORD God
All through the time of her being hated Leah trusted in the LORD God. When the LORD heard her plea, he judged in her favor and opened her womb. She gave birth to four sons and for each she credited the LORD God for opening her womb and praised him.

DISCUSSION TIME

1. Explain that Leah is of a humble, trusting, spirit.
2. Show that Rachel is bitter instead of trusting.
3. Are bitterness, and trusting God and his righteousness compatible with each other?

The LORD opens the womb of Leah but does not open the womb of Rachel.

Rachel without the LORD God (30:1-2).
Rachel's reaction to not giving birth contrasted with Leah's attitude. Rachel blamed Jacob instead of praying to the LORD. *"When Rachel saw that she bore Jacob no children, she **envied** her sister. She said to Jacob, "Give me children, or I shall die!"² Jacob's anger was kindled against Rachel, and he said, "Am I in the place of God, who has withheld from you the fruit of the womb?"*

QUICK QUESTION

1. Explain what was wrong in Rachel's words to Jacob.

Rachel then must have prayed in a different attitude for **the LORD** listens to Rachel and opens her womb.

Reuben's mandrakes
Mandrakes were believed to awaken lust and promote fertility. Rachel asked Leah for Reuben's mandrakes because she trusted in the fertility power of mandrakes rather than trusting in God.
The sorry state of Jacob's marriage is sharply characterized by what Leah says to Jacob.
Leah hails Jacob; when he comes home from the field she says to him,
"You must come in to me, for I have hired you with my son's mandrakes!"

QUESTIONS

1. Explain how Leah's words show the sorry state of Jacob's marriage.
2. Compare present day misuse of "lust" drugs and the use of mandrakes.
3. Under what circumstances is it allowed for a Christian couple to use fertility drugs?

Jacob lacks faithfulness in his marriage to Leah by loving Rachel and neglecting Leah.

Discussion Time

1. How should Jacob have acted in his marriage with Leah and Rachel?
2. Discuss the lawlessness of having multiple wives.
3. Discuss the disorder that corrupts a marriage with multiple partners.
4. Discuss the instructions God the Holy Spirit gives us concerning elders in the Church (see: 1 Timothy 3).

The LORD counsels Jacob to return to his father's house in Beersheba.

The LORD God commands Jacob to take his family and go back to the "land of your kindred."

Jacob tells his wives of the LORD's command (31:10-13).

Jacob also relates how the LORD appeared to him in a dream and corrected Laban's repeated deceit.
"In the breeding season of the flock I lifted up my eyes and saw in a dream that the goats that mated with the flock were striped, spotted, and mottled. 11 Then the angel of God said to me in the dream, 'Jacob,' and I said, 'Here I am!' 12 And he said, 'Lift up your eyes and see, all the goats that mate with the flock are striped, spotted, and mottled, for I have seen all that Laban is doing to you. 13 I am the God of Bethel, where you anointed a pillar and made a vow to me. Now arise, go out from this land and return to the land of your kindred.'"

Laban prevents Jacob from leaving (30:25-30) saying,
"I have learned by divination that the LORD has blessed me because of you."

Laban seeks the counsel of the LORD but in a pagan way (נחש seeking omens cf. Lev. 19:26 "You shall not interpret omens or tell fortunes.").

Quick Question

1. Explain what a Ouija board is. Is it just a toy?

Laban and his sons: (31:1-2) no longer favor Jacob.

GENESIS 31:17-21

Paganism in Laban's house.
Jacob and his wives and children flee from Laban but **Rachel** stole her father's household gods. They cross the Euphrates. This indicates that Paddan Aram was the pagan territory "across the River" that father Abraham was told to leave.
Rachel's action shows that she is not loose from paganism.

Laban and the LORD God

Laban has met the power of the LORD. He observes the power of the LORD to protect Jacob. He has also experienced the threat of the LORD to come against him. Now he calls upon the LORD to witness between him and Jacob. They are two items with the same function; both are witness to the pact between Laban and Jacob. The difference in function of the pillar might be that on a pillar one could write which were not well possible on a heap of stones.

LABAN THE ARAMEAN (31:22-30)

24 But God came to Laban the Aramean in a dream by night and said to him, "Be careful not to say anything to Jacob, either good or bad."

The designation "Aramean" tells us that Laban belonged to a pagan, or semi pagan, society. God appeared to Laban to protect Jacob. That Laban did not accept the God of Jacob as his God is clear from his own words,

*"But the **God of your father** spoke to me last night, saying, 'Be careful not to say anything to Jacob, either good or bad.' 30 And now you have gone away because you longed greatly for your father's house, **but why did you steal my gods**!"*

*Note the contrast between *the God of your father* and *but why did you steal my gods*.

The LORD appears to Laban in a dream and orders him not to speak to Jacob either good or bad.

QUICK QUESTION

1. Did the LORD appear to Laban because Laban honored God as the only LORD?

THE DIFFERENCE IN THE OATH THEY SWEAR (31:53)

Jacob: The God LORD is the *"Fear of my father Isaac."*
- What is the weight of the *"Fear of my Father Isaac"* (see Ch. 31:42 and 53)?

Laban calls on God to be Judge within an Aramean context:
"The God of Abraham and the God of Nahor, the God of their father, judge between us." ("their father" refers to Terah). *"So Jacob swore by the Fear of his father Isaac."*

QUICK QUESTION

1. Discuss the difference in the oaths they swear.

THE FEAR

Laban had experienced fear when the LORD God appeared to him telling him to leave Jacob alone.

Jacob knows the awesome deeds of the LORD God. "Anyone who has a fearsome God is also fearsome" (H.P. Muller, in ThDOT vol XI p.525).

Discussion Time

1. Discuss what kind of fear we are talking about here.
2. Using these notes explain what it means to have faith in a fearful God.
3. Discuss what the book of Proverbs means when we read, *The fear of the LORD is the beginning of wisdom.*

Heap and Pillar (31:52)

Two items with the same function; both are witness to the pact between Laban and Jacob. The difference in function of the pillar might be that on a pillar one could write which were not well possible on a heap of stones.

Quick Question

1. Discuss how the sign or seal of our baptism can be a witness between God and us.

The LORD God prepares Jacob for meeting his brother Esau. Jacob is afraid of meeting his irate brother Esau. Jacob prayed:

> "I am not worthy of the least of all the deeds of steadfast love and all the faithfulness that you have shown to your servant, for with only my staff I crossed this Jordan, and now I have become two camps. Please deliver me from the hand of my brother, from the hand of Esau, for I fear him that he may come and attack me, the mothers with the children."

The LORD's heavenly army of angels: The camp of the heavenly army of angels is shown to Jacob a second time as he prepares to meet Esau and his army of 400 men.

Discussion Time

1. Yahweh Tsavaoth means LORD of Hosts. The NIV 1984 translates this with LORD almighty. Use the camps of the heavenly army of angels to show that the translation of the NIV is incorrect and that is should be "LORD of Hosts" (see the ESV for a correct translation).
2. Find more instances in the Bible where angels form an army of God.
3. Discuss how God's armies should have helped Jacob to overcome his fear of Esau.

The camp of the heavenly army of angels is shown to Jacob as he flees from Laban and prepares to meet Esau and his army. **Esau** came to Jacob with an army of 400 men. It is understandable that Jacob took precautions.

Quick Question

1. Did Jacob trust God enough? Explain.

The LORD God once again appears to Jacob at Bethel, confirms the Abrahamic promises, repeats the name change and confirms the blessing.

The LORD God shows Jacob his heavenly army of angels and wrestles with Jacob.

DISCUSSION TIME

1. Explain the importance of God wrestling with Jacob at this point of Jacob's life.
2. Discuss whether today the Spirit of God and his Christ would wrestle with us Christians?
3. Discuss the following statement, *"After the LORD God has wrestled with you, you are a different person."*

The LORD God wrestles with Jacob in the appearance of a man, blesses Jacob and changes his name from Jacob to Israel. Then the LORD touched Jacob's hip at the sinew of the thigh. There are two aspects to the name Israel. The name reflects that Jacob wrestled with God and overcame. The way the name is pronounced in Hebrew makes it sound like *man saw God*. This refers to the fact that Jacob saw God and lived. In distinction to all other nations; the nation of Israel was the only nation whose God would appear, be seen.

QUESTIONS

1. Explain how God, appearing as a man, could be weaker than Jacob. It might help if you would think of the weakness of the Lord Jesus, the Son of Man.
2. How did God prevent Jacob from becoming proud toward God?
3. Explain what the name Israel stands for?

The LORD God who appeared to Jacob when he fled from his brother Esau orders Jacob to go to Bethel and live there.

Jacob humbles himself before his brother Esau calling Esau *"my Lord"*.

DISCUSSION TIME

1. Was it necessary for Jacob to humble himself before Esau? Explain.
2. Discuss Jacob's change of attitude toward Esau.

The LORD God changes the heart of Esau toward his brother Jacob. **Jacob** promises to follow his brother Esau to his semi-pagan environment in Seir but decides not to do so. His failing to keep his word shows that Jacob is still weak when dealing with his fellow man and weak in relying on the LORD who fights for him.

QUESTIONS

1. Explain the reason why Jacob could not join with Esau in Seir.
2. Should Jacob have come out straight and told Esau why he could not join Esau at Seir?

3. Explain how we often show a similar weakness in standing up for what we believe.

Simeon and Levi avenge the rape of their sister Dinah by treacherously killing the inhabitants of Shechem. **The LORD God** protects Jacob and his sons from the power and anger of cities that were around them so that they did not pursue the sons of Jacob.

QUICK QUESTION

1. What were the consequences for Simeon and Levi? Compare the treacherous action of Simeon and Levi against Shechem with Jacob's words about them in Genesis.

THE LORD GOD AND HIS *EXHODOS* AND *ENHODOS* MESSAGE

The origin and meaning of these two words
The two words in the heading are unfamiliar to us. However, we are familiar with the Book of Exodus. In this Bible book we receive the message that the LORD God provides a way *out* and provides a way *in*. The LORD God led Israel *out* of the house of slavery and idolatry. The LORD God also led Israel *into* the freedom of a home with the LORD in the land he promised to Abraham, Isaac and Jacob. The title "Exodus" is taken from the Greek language. Exodus is *Ex-hodos* which means the Way-out. *En-hodos* then means the Way-in (for simplicity, I have given en-hodos instead of eis-hodos).

The *exhodos* and *enhodos* message in the book of Genesis
This message of the LORD God leading *out* and bringing *in* begins in chapter three.
Through our first parents, Adam and Eve, we listened to the Devil and became his slave. In Genesis 3:15, we receive the first message; *the Seed of the Woman will crush the head of the Serpent*. The LORD God started this process of leading out and bringing in by covering the nakedness of our first parents with the skins of animals.
A Christian cannot read this message without praising God for making this promise true in the birth of his Son who leads out of the power of the Devil and into the freedom of belonging to the children of God. Other examples of the LORD God leading out and bringing in are Noah and the Flood, and Abraham from Ur of the Chaldeans.

DISCUSSION TIME

1. Discuss what idolatry has to do with being enslaved and apply this to the following discussion points.
2. Discuss from what circumstances the LORD God did lead Noah and his family out and into what he did lead them in?
3. Discuss from what circumstances the LORD God did lead Abraham and Sarai out and into what he did lead them in?
4. Discuss from what circumstances the LORD God did lead Jacob out and into what he did lead Jacob and his family in?

In Retrospect:
From the beginning of our *"Discussion Points"* we have maintained that the LORD God not only gave Moses the staff of God but also the contents of his history in the book of Genesis. During their stay in

Egypt, Israel had become Egyptianized to the point of serving their idols. They needed to be led out of Egypt and into the freedom of dwelling with the living God.

QUESTIONS

1. Discuss how the LORD God taught Israel in Egypt through Moses. Moses told the enslaved Israelites how the LORD God had led Jacob out and in (or: Moses told them of Jacob's ex-hodos and en-hodos).
2. Discuss the being led out and being led in as it applies to the Lord Jesus. Use Luke 9:30. The word *departure* in this verse is literally *exodus*.
3. Discuss how the exhodos/enhodos work of the LORD God applies to the Great Reformation when he used Luther and Calvin.
4. Discuss how the LORD God works the leading out and leading in with us personally.
5. Discuss how God's history, from Genesis 1 to Revelation 22, is a history of *exhodos* and *enhodos* (or of leading out and leading into).

Genesis 35

THE PROMISED CYCLE FROM BETHEL TO BETHEL IS MADE FULL

35:1. God said to Jacob, "Arise, go up to Bethel and dwell there. Make an altar there to the God who appeared to you when you fled from your brother Esau"

This verse contains the fulfillment of two promises, one by the LORD God and the second by Jacob. For these promises we need to page back to Genesis 28.

First, the LORD's promise:

"Behold, I am with you and will keep you wherever you go, and will bring you back to this land. For I will not leave you until I have done what I have promised you."

The LORD God made that promise to Jacob at Bethel. The LORD has kept his promise. During all these years of exile and hardships, Jacob has been provided for by the LORD. The more than twenty-year trek from Bethel to Bethel is about to be completed. The LORD God has given his marching orders: Go up to Bethel and build an altar there. That order links in to the promise Jacob had made to the LORD God.

Second, Jacob's promise:

20 *"Then Jacob made a vow, saying, "If God will be with me and will keep me in this way that I go, and will give me bread to eat and clothing to wear, 21 so that I come again to my father's house in peace, then the LORD shall be my God, 22 and this stone, which I have set up for a pillar, shall be God's house. And of all that you give me I will give a full tenth to you."*

It is at Bethel that the LORD God appeared to Jacob and Jacob exclaimed, *"the LORD is at this place and I did not know it. ... This is the house of God."* At that holy place the LORD God commands Jacob to build an altar to the Lord. Because of the holiness of the LORD Jacob prepares his household to be holy before the LORD God at Bethel. He instructs all of them: *"Put away the foreign gods that are among you and purify yourselves and change your garments. 3 Then let us arise and go up to Bethel, so that I may make there an altar to the God who answers me in the day of my distress and has been with me wherever I have gone." 4 So they gave to Jacob all the foreign gods that they had, and the rings that were in their ears. Jacob hid them under the terebinth tree that was near Shechem.* (Compare Josh. 24:26 and Judges 9:6).

QUESTIONS

1. What is the significance of Jacob building an altar and calling upon the Name of the LORD? He was still a stranger in a strange land with only a promise (cf. section on Abraham building an altar).
2. Is there no altar when we worship? Discuss Heb. 13:10.
3. Are Christians strangers in a strange land?
4. Discuss the similarity between Jacob meeting God at the House of God in Bethel and our Christian Congregation meeting God in worship on the Sunday.
5. Discuss which sentence describes more accurately what we do on Sunday:
6. 1."We are going to Church." Or: 2. "We are going with God's people to come before him in worship".
7. Discuss how we offer sacrifices to God (Heb. 13:15,16; 1Peter 2:5).
8. Discuss the following: Do we really meet in God's presence on the Sunday?
9. Discuss how we and our children should prepare before going to meet the LORD on the Sunday. How would we put away idols?
10. Discuss what we can learn from Jacob's family. They changed their clothes and purified their bodies in preparation for coming before our holy God to worship.

Genesis 35:16-21

RACHEL GIVES BIRTH AND DIES

TO CONSIDER

1. **Ephrath**: well-known from Micah 5:2; Matt. 2:5,6.
2. Discuss the difference in meaning of the names Ben-oni and Ben-jamin.
3. Discuss how the difference in name-giving reflects the attitudes of Rachel and Jacob.
4. Discuss how God the Holy Spirit interprets Rachel's attitude in Jeremiah 31:15-17.

"While Israel lived in that land, Reuben went and lay with Bilhah his father's concubine. And Israel heard of it."

QUESTIONS

1. Discuss the consequence of Reuben's sin (See Gen 49:3-4).
2. Where was Isaac buried?
3. Discuss the cooperation between Esau and Jacob as they buried their father.

"Esau that is Edom"

The keyword to the understanding of chapter 36 is **"Edom" (9x).** Superficial reading of chapter 36 may lead us to questioning the importance of the information we receive in this chapter. Is there really a message for God's people here? The records of Esau and his family might fit at this point but why are the Horites and the later nation of Edom included?

The previous chapter ended with the death of Isaac and his burial by his sons Esau and Jacob. This makes it plausible for chapter 36 to begin with the records of the oldest son, Esau. However, this is more than a list of the descendants of Esau. Besides the history of Esau's family we find here the history of the family of Hori, chief of the land of Seir, whose history antedates that of Esau. Esau arrives at Seir with his family and all his possessions and integrates himself with Hori and his descendants. Together they form what becomes the nation of Edom.

We will find the message when we remember who were the first recipients of the message of "Genesis". Throughout our discussion of the book of Genesis we have maintained that Yahweh, the LORD God, had equipped Moses to lead his people Israel out of Egypt and into the Promised Land. God equipped Moses in two ways. The equipment was not only the Rod of God but also the revelation contained in the book of Genesis. Israel no longer knew the LORD. By his miracles, and by his historic divine records in the book of Genesis, the LORD made himself known to ignorant Israel. Genesis 36 belongs to that record. The record concerning the land of Edom was needed to let Israel know what they would meet at the entrance into the Promised Land.

The first nation Israel would meet at the border of the Promised Land was to be the land of Edom (Numbers 20:14 ff.). The character of that nation was made known clearly to Israel well before they would arrive at Edom's border. The descendants of Esau had settled among the pagan Horites in Seir and intermarried with them. This explains the hostility of the Edomites to Israel and the opposition to the worship of Yahweh. Genesis 36 prepared Moses and Israel for this hostility.

Read Numbers 20:14-28 and Habakkuk 3 for more information on Edom. These chapters help us in the ongoing discussion of who the Horites were. In many commentaries on the book of Genesis the possibility is considered that these Horites were *Hurrians*. The area where Esau arrived and where Aaron died was mountainous. Aaron died on *Mount Hor.* The word Hor is the Hebrew word for *mountain.* The man Hori and his people were named after the mountains – possibly caves – where they lived. Below I have inserted an article on the Horites by J. Wiseman.

Horites, Horim.

The ancient inhabitants of Edom, defeated by Chedorlaomer (Gn. 14:6), said to be the descendants of Seir the Horite (Gn. 36:20), and an ethnic group distinct from Rephaim. They were driven out by the sons of Esau (Dt. 2:12, 22). Esau himself seems to have married the daughter of a Horite chief, Anah (Gn. 36:25). The Horites (Heb. *ḥōrî*, Gk. *chorraios*) also occupied some places in central Palestine, including Shechem (Gn. 34:2) and Gilgal (Jos. 9:6–7), the LXX reading 'Horite' in both passages (AV; RSV, 'Hivite').

The E Horites cannot be identified as Hurrians either archaeologically or linguistically (Semitic personal names in Gn. 36:20–30). Some think the pre-Edomites to have been cave-dwellers (*ḥōr*) and equate this with the Egyptian name for Palestine (*hr* = *hurru*) cited with Israel on the Merenptah stele *c.* 1225 BC.

The pre-Israelite Jebusites ruled by Abdi-hepa during the *AMARNA period seem to be Hurrians, as was *ARAUNAH (Ornan, *'rwnh, 'wrnh*, 2 Sa. 24:16; *'rnn* (1 Ch. 21:18), the Hurrian word for 'the king/lord' (*ewirne*).

Hurrian, a non-Semitic (Caucasian?) language was spoken by a people who formed part of the indigenous population of N Syria and Upper Mesopotamia from *c.* 2300 BC. From the 18th century they are well attested at Mari and *Alalaḫ* as well as in the Hittite archives where from *c.* 1500 to 1380 BC Hurrian myths and literature are found.

At this time the Hurrian kingdom of Mitanni, ruled by kings with Indo-Aryan names, corresponded with Egypt (*e.g. Tušratta-Amenophis* IV), and influenced Assyria (*e.g.* *NUZI). Hurrian personal names are found throughout Syro-Palestine (*ALALAH, *TAANACH, *SHECHEM) and some biblical names may best be considered of Hurrian origin: Anah, Ajah, Dishon, *SHAMGAR, Toi and Eliahba (D. J. Wiseman, *JTVI* 72, 1950, p. 6).

Hori was also the personal name both of an Edomite (Gn. 36:22; 1 Ch. 1:39) and of a Simeonite (Nu. 13:5).

BIBLIOGRAPHY. I. J. Gelb, *Hurrians and Subarians*, 1944; E. A. Speiser, *Introduction to Hurrian*, 1941; E. A. Speiser, *JWH* 1, 1953, pp. 311–327; H. G. Gütterbach, *JWH* 2, 1954, pp. 383–394; F. W. Bush, *A Grammar of the Hurrian Language*, 1967; H. A. Hoffner *POTT*, 1973, pp. 221–226. D. J. WISEMAN.[51]

Discussion Time

1. Discuss what message Genesis 36 carries to the descendants of Abraham, enslaved in Egypt.
2. Discuss how Genesis 36, Matt. 24, Mark 13, Luke 17, and the Book of Revelation prepare us for the warfare that awaits us at our Exodus into the New Heaven and Earth.

---

[51] Wiseman, D. J. (1996). Horites, Horim. In D. R. W. Wood, I. H. Marshall, A. R. Millard, & J. I. Packer (Eds.), New Bible dictionary (3rd ed., p. 481). Leicester, England; Downers Grove, IL: InterVarsity Press.

Caption to chapters 37-50

Joseph through suffering to glory. Or, the LORD leading Joseph out of suffering and into glory (the ex-hodos and en-hodos of Joseph). During all this, from being sold into slavery to becoming viceroy of Egypt, Joseph remains the firstborn and is revealed as the opener of the way of life. [52]

The chapters 37 to 50 form a unit. This is indicated by verse two of chapter 37, *"These are the generations of Jacob."* (in the Hebrew the word *toledot* is used).
The heading, *"these are the generations,"* is used ten times in the book of Genesis. This is the last of the ten "toledots".
Although the generations of Jacob begin with Joseph and end with Joseph, father Jacob is the bearer of the promises made to Abraham and Isaac. As God's chosen "firstborn" Jacob governs his family. The chapters 37 – 50 begin and end with Joseph because father Jacob has appointed Joseph as his firstborn son.

DISCUSSION TIME

1. Research in the Bible how the LORD God himself confirms Joseph as the firstborn son.

JACOB'S FIRSTBORN SON BY RACHEL WAS JOSEPH

Interpreters frequently put Joseph in an unfavorable light. He is spoiled by his father. Joseph has dreams in which his whole family bows down before his greatness. Joseph rats on his brothers. An example of such an interpretation is this quote from K Strassner, "Opening Up Genesis", *"Instead, he used the dreams simply as wind to further inflate his already puffed-up self-opinion. Joseph took gifts from God—his dreams—and turned them into tools of self-promotion!"*

Anyone who is of the same low opinion of Joseph is actually agreeing with his brothers and their hatred for Joseph. However, do we find proof in this part of God's revelation that God agrees with the brothers? On the contrary! Even if it would be true that Joseph acted as a spoiled kid, the Bible contains no record of it. God the Holy Spirit is not focusing on Joseph's good or bad character but on the LORD God who chooses Joseph as the firstborn in his plan.

Within the Bible, God the Holy Spirit himself helps us to the right understanding of this passage. We go to **I Chronicles 5:1-2.** There God the Holy Spirit gives this revelation: *"The sons of Reuben the firstborn*

---

[52] See my future essay God's Firstborn Son, the Opener of the Way of Life, to be mailed out on this list.

of Israel (for he was the firstborn, but because he defiled his father's couch, his birthright was given to the sons of Joseph the son of Israel, so that he could not be enrolled as the oldest son; ² though Judah became strong among his brothers and a chief came from him, yet the birthright belonged to Joseph)."

The whole of Scripture, from Genesis to Revelation, has only one divine author and that is God the Holy Spirit (1 Tim. 3:16). In 1 Chronicles, God the Holy Spirit gives us the key to understanding Genesis 37. That key is **the right of the firstborn son.** [53] Joseph did not take this right. Father Jacob gave Joseph the right of the firstborn. The cloak Jacob gave him set Joseph apart and above his brothers. The tasks Jacob gave Joseph to do also set him apart above his brothers.

QUICK QUESTION

1. Discuss and evaluate Joseph by the light of Scripture.

JOSEPH THE PROPHET

The LORD God confirmed Jacob's action of declaring Joseph the firstborn son. The LORD God set Joseph apart by sending Joseph dreams. These dreams were prophetic. In this manner the LORD God set Joseph apart in the whole of the family of Jacob. There would come a time when all members of his family would prostrate themselves before Joseph as before a king. This made his father think, but it made the brothers hate Joseph. The prophet Joseph was not honored in his own family (compare the words of the Lord Jesus in Luke 4:24).

DISCUSSION TIME

1. Discuss and evaluate Joseph as prophet.
2. Discuss who the first author of the whole of the Bible is.
3. Discuss from the Bible the biblical doctrine of inspiration
4. Discuss whether also the formatting of the whole of the Bible is the work of the first Author.

JOSEPH'S DREAMS FORETELL OF ROYAL KINGSHIP

Joseph's brothers understood the dreams to mean that Joseph was to rule over them.

QUESTIONS

1. Read Genesis 41:32. Then discuss what it meant that Joseph received two dreams from the LORD.
2. Discuss how the dreams of Joseph foretell royal kingship.
3. Discuss who could reveal this about Joseph so long beforehand.
4. Discuss what purpose the dreams could serve?

---

[53] I found one author who agrees with me concerning Joseph and that is G. Van Groningen in Messianic Revelation in the Old Testament p. 149 n. 12, Baker, Grand Rapids MI, 1990

THE DIVINE 'LEAD-UP' TO JOSEPH THE FIRSTBORN SON

We do not come to Joseph's position as firstborn son in Jacob's house unprepared. God the Holy Spirit, as the divine author of the Bible, structures the preceding chapters so that we might understand why the LORD God chose Joseph from among his brothers.

Genesis 35:21, Reuben disqualified from being the firstborn son.
Genesis 34, Simeon and Levi disqualified from being the firstborn son.
Genesis 35, The LORD God confirms Jacob as the firstborn son.
Genesis 36, Esau (Edom) disqualified from being the firstborn son.
Genesis 37, The LORD God in his sovereign good pleasure appoints Joseph as the firstborn son.

DISCUSSION TIME

1. Discuss what disqualified Reuben from being honored as the firstborn son.
2. Discuss what disqualified Simeon and Levi from being honored as the firstborn son.
3. Discuss the so-called "divine right of kings" in human history.

THE COMING CHRIST FORESHADOWS HIS OWN ROAD, 'FROM SUFFERING TO GLORY'. HE DOES THAT IN JOSEPH'S ROAD, WHICH WAS 'FROM SUFFERING TO GLORY'

Foreshadowing and typology [54]

It is not uncommon to find commentators on the Old Testament Scriptures speaking of *'types of Christ'*. This is understandable, for God the Holy Spirit inspired the apostle Paul to write in Romans 5:14, *"Yet death reigned from Adam to Moses, even over those whose sinning was not like the transgression of Adam, who was a **type** of the one who was to come."* Taking our cues from Romans 5:14 we may consider Joseph to be a type of Christ. Joseph is the firstborn son, the prophet and the royal prince, who comes to his glory through suffering. In his glory the LORD God uses him to keep a great people alive.

IN ADDITION TO "TYPE" WE FIND IN THE BIBLE THE CONCEPT OF *SHADOW*

In the following quotes we receive revelation from God the Holy Spirit about how Christ was **foreshadowed in the Old Testament dispensation.** We find the progression from Old Testament shadow to New Testament substance in **Col. 2:16-17,** *"Therefore let no one pass judgment on you in questions of food and drink, or with regard to a festival or a new moon or a Sabbath. 17 These are a **shadow** of the things to come, but the **substance** belongs to Christ."*

We find the progression from Old Testament shadow to New Testament true form of realities, and especially body, in **Heb. 10:1-7,** *"For since the law has but a **shadow** of the good things to come instead of the **true form** of these **realities**, it can never, by the same sacrifices that are continually offered every year, make perfect those who draw near. 2 Otherwise, would they not have ceased to be offered, since the worshipers, having once been cleansed, would no longer have any consciousness of sins? 3 But in these sacrifices there is a reminder of sins every year. 4 For it is impossible for the blood of bulls and goats to*

---

[54] G. Van Groningen, Messianic Revelation in the Old Testament, Grand Rapids 1990, has an extensive overview on Messianic Typology, p. 153-167.

take away sins. ⁵ *Consequently, when Christ came into the world, he said, "Sacrifices and offerings you have not desired, but* **a body** *have you prepared for me;* ⁶ *in burnt offerings and sin offerings you have taken no pleasure.*⁷ *Then I said, 'Behold, I have come to do your will, O God, as it is written of me in the scroll of the book.'"*

The reality, or substance, of what was foreshadowed in Joseph is Jesus Christ, God's firstborn son, the chief prophet and the royal prince, who comes to his glory through suffering. As the substance, he is the promised Son of God, the Son of David, the Son of Abraham, the Son of Adam.

DISCUSSION TIME

1. Discuss what the term *foreshadow* means
2. Discuss what we mean by the LORD God *progressing* (a help is L.D. 6 Q.A. 17 which also speaks of foreshadowing).
3. Discuss how the LORD God progressed in the chapters 1-36 of Genesis.
4. Looking ahead in Genesis the chapters 37-50, discuss how the LORD God is progressing towards his final glory.
5. Discuss what it means that God must come to his glory.
6. On his way to his final glory the LORD God chooses one and rejects another. Carefully discuss God's Sovereignty.
7. Discuss how the LORD God comes to his glory in our personal Christian life today.

THE SALE OF THE PROPHET AND FUTURE RULER IN JACOB'S HOUSE

Father Jacob sent Joseph to see if all is well with his brothers who are pasturing the flock. When he meets up with his brothers they conspire to kill him. Reuben convinces his brothers not to kill Joseph so he can restore Joseph to his father. The brothers then cast Joseph in a pit. While Reuben is absent the brothers sell Joseph to passing Ishmaeli/Midian traders for twenty shekels.

DISCUSSION TIME

1. Discuss Reuben's position among his brothers.
2. Discuss Reuben's action to restore Rachel's firstborn to his father.
3. Discuss why Reuben would cry out "and I, where would I go?' and not "where will we go?"
4. Discuss where in Genesis we already earlier discussed Ishmaelites and Midianites. This may solve the confusion of the two names together as traders.
5. Twenty shekels is the price of a slave in the Bible. Discuss the twenty shekels as a shadow of the sale of Jesus our Savior.

GENESIS 38 IS NOT AN INTERMEZZO

The account of Judah and Tamar comes in between the account of Joseph. This raises the question why this chapter is at this place and not before chapter 37. It looks as if this is a mere interruption. However, we have confessed above that God the Holy Spirit is not only the author of the spiritual contents of Scripture but also the one who formatted the Bible. He has a purpose with what he does.

QUICK QUESTIONS

1. Discuss once more the role of God the Holy Spirit in bringing us the Bible as we have the Scriptures today.
2. Critically discuss this 'academic' statement: *What we find in the Old Testament Scriptures is the expression of **the faith of Israel**.*

We found earlier the purpose and consequence of the actions of Reuben and Simeon and Levi. In chapter 38, God the Holy Spirit reveals the place of Judah in the Generations (Toledot) of Jacob. Judah's part in selling the prophet and future ruler to the Midianites has consequences. Judah also is excluded from being Jacob's firstborn heir.

Because of this Judah has no rest. His guilty conscience drives him away from the obedience to the God of Jacob and faith in his promises. Judah wanders. Judah seeks the company of Hirah, an Adullamite. Judah marries Shua, who is called a *certain* Canaanite. The word *certain* emphasis the erratic action of Judah. There is no longer a firm and faithful line in Judah's life. There is lust instead of love. The result is that the sons born to him by Shua live wicked lives. The wickedness in Judah's family causes the LORD God to act against Judah. In sequence, his sons die in their wickedness. Tamar, who was wife by levirate marriage to each of them, remains a widow in her father's house because Judah refuses to give her to his last son, Shelah.

Tamar devises a scheme by which she will have offspring from her father in law, Judah. Tamar disguises herself as a prostitute along the way where Judah must pass. On the way to his sheepshearers, and in the company of his friend Hirah, the Adullamite, Judah goes in to Tamar. Tamar is promised a goat as payment. She asks for, and receives in pledge, Jacobs signet ring, cord and staff.

It becomes known to Judah that Tamar is expecting a child out of wedlock and Judah self-righteously makes know his verdict: Tamar is to be burned. Tamar defends herself by proving that Judah himself is the father of the child she is expecting: She shows the pledge Judah gave her. Tamar is pregnant by the man who owns this signet ring and the cord and the staff. Judah is forced to admit, *"She is more righteous than I, since I did not give her to my son Shelah."*

THE LORD GOD, AS SOVEREIGN KING, BREAKS THROUGH JUDAH'S SINFUL LIFE: PEREZ

Tamar gives birth to twins.

"27 When the time of her labor came, there were twins in her womb. 28 And when she was in labor, one put out a hand, and the midwife took and tied a scarlet thread on his hand, saying, "This one came out first." 29 But as he drew back his hand, behold, his brother came out. And she said, "What a breach you have made for yourself!" Therefore, his name was called Perez. 30 Afterward his brother came out with the scarlet thread on his hand, and his name was called Zerah."

DISCUSSION TIME

1. Discuss whether the breakthrough of Perez was, or was not, the result of a natural process.
2. Discuss what it means that God, as LORD of the Covenant, has the right to act contrary to our idea of what is right or wrong.
3. Discuss the fact that the LORD God did not reject Judah.

Zerah *shone first*, that is why he was called *Zerah*. Against expectation his twin brother broke through and came out first, that is why he was called *Perez*. Throughout the Bible God the Holy Spirit shows that the breakthrough of Perez was not a freak incident but according to God's sovereign plan. The following quotes show that the LORD God chose Perez, faithful to his Covenant Oath to Abraham: "In your offspring all nations of the earth shall be blessed."

Ruth 4:12, *"Through the offspring the LORD gives you by this young woman, may your family be like that of Perez, whom Tamar bore to Judah."*

Ruth 4:18-31, *"This, then, is the family line of Perez: Perez was the father of Hezron, 19 Hezron the father of Ram, Ram the father of Amminadab, 20 Amminadab the father of Nahshon, Nahshon the father of Salmon, 21 Salmon the father of Boaz, Boaz the father of Obed, 22 Obed the father of Jesse, and Jesse the father of David.*

Nehemiah 4: 1 and 6, *"And in Jerusalem lived certain of the sons of Judah and of the sons of Benjamin. Of the sons of Judah: Athaiah the son of Uzziah, son of Zechariah, son of Amariah, son of Shephatiah, son of Mahalalel, of the sons of Perez. 6, All the sons of Perez who lived in Jerusalem were 468 valiant men".*

Matthew 1:3, *"and Judah the father of Perez and Zerah by Tamar, and Perez the father of Hezron, and Hezron the father of Ram.*

DISCUSSION TIME

1. In the light of the texts quoted above, discuss the place of Perez in God's plan of salvation.

Matthew 1:3 shows that Perez is one of the forefathers of the Lord Jesus according to God's plan. The place of Perez in God's plan was revealed when God caused Perez to "break through" from his mother's womb. In the line of Judah, Perez was a firstborn son.

The LORD God bent the heart of Judah

The following chapters bear witness to the change in Judah's life. The LORD God used Tamar and Perez to shock Judah into seeing his own unfaithfulness. Judah returned to the way of God's Covenant in Jacob's house.

RIGHTEOUS JOSEPH IS POTIPHAR'S SLAVE BUT MORE SO HE IS SOJOURNER WITH THE LORD GOD OF THE COVENANT

QUESTIONS

1. Discuss which Covenant we are talking about here.
2. Discuss the promises the LORD God made in this Covenant.
3. Discuss what it means to be a sojourner with the LORD of the Covenant using these texts: **Psalm 15:1,** "O LORD, who shall **sojourn** in your tent? Who shall dwell on your holy hill?
4. **Psalm 39:12,** "Hear my prayer, O LORD, and give ear to my cry; hold not your peace at my tears! For I am a **sojourner** with you, a guest, like all my fathers."
5. Are you a **sojourner** with the LORD God of the Covenant? Discuss what this means for you (1 Peter 2:11-12 *"Beloved, I urge you as **sojourners and exiles** to abstain from the passions of the flesh, which wage war against your soul. 12 Keep your conduct among the Gentiles honorable, so that when they speak against you as evildoers, they may see your good deeds and glorify God on the day of visitation"*).
6. Discuss how Joseph benefitted from being a **sojourner** with the LORD God of the Covenant while he was a slave of Potiphar.
7. Discuss how the LORD God was faithful to his promises to Joseph in Egypt.

In Pagan Egypt, no one experienced the nearness of Amon the "hidden" god.
Yahweh, however, was able to reveal himself to Potiphar through Joseph his chosen one.

Genesis 39:3

"His master saw that the LORD was with him and that the LORD caused all that he did to succeed in his hands." This is a remarkable statement coming from a highly placed Egyptian official. The captain of the guard does not credit Egypt's gods because of Joseph, but rather the LORD Yahweh. Egypt's gods supposedly were somewhere but they were neither seen nor heard. Joseph supposedly has no god for he is an Asiatic nomad. Yet, against all Egyptian expectation, Potiphar is forced to admit that Joseph not only has a god but is in the favor of Yahweh, the God of all creation, who showed himself powerfully present to bless.

QUICK QUESTION

1. There is a reason for Potiphar's crediting the presence of Yahweh to bless. What is that reason?

THE LORD'S WORK IN AND THROUGH RIGHTEOUS JOSEPH COULD NOT REMAIN HIDDEN

The work the LORD God began through Joseph continued where ever the LORD sent Joseph. Joseph's position from the LORD God remains prophetic and royal just as when Joseph lived in Jacob's house. This is what Potiphar sees. Potiphar sees something that cannot be accredited to pagan gods. This can only be the work of Yahweh, the God who is and who is the only one able to make himself known.

DISCUSSION TIME

1. Discuss how the work of the LORD God, in and through Joseph, foreshadows the work of God in and through his Son when he had become Jesus of Nazareth.
2. Look up what the people said when they saw the works Jesus of Nazareth did.
3. Discuss how the work of the LORD God becomes visible in and through his believers in today's world.
4. Discuss the visible work of God the Holy Spirit in and through us with respect to us winning our neighbor for Christ.
5. Discuss the importance of not obstructing the work of God the Holy Spirit in us.

Potiphar's wife aims to seduce Joseph

TO CONSIDER

1. Discuss how Satan was at work in Potiphar's house to make righteous Joseph fall.
2. Discuss how the LORD God tested Joseph but how Satan tempted Joseph.
3. Discuss why a Christian believer should not be surprised when unbelievers tempt you to find out whether you are for real or not (whether you are a hypocrite).

JOSEPH REMAINS THE SLAVE OF POTIPHAR IN THE ROYAL JAIL WHICH IS IN POTIPHAR'S HOUSE

39:20 *And Joseph's master took him and put him into the prison, the place where the **king's prisoners** were confined, and he was there in prison."*
39:23 *The keeper of the prison paid no attention to anything that was in Joseph's charge, because the LORD was with him. And whatever he did, the LORD made it succeed."*
40:2-4 *And Pharaoh was angry with his two officers, the chief cupbearer and the chief baker, ³ and he put them in custody **in the house of the captain of the guard, in the prison where Joseph was confined**. ⁴ **The captain of the guard** appointed Joseph to be with them, and he attended them. They continued for some time in custody."*

These quotes show:
Potiphar continues to be Joseph's master.

Potiphar's position as captain of the guard includes being responsible for Pharaoh's prisoners in the royal jail.

Potiphar continues to entrust responsibility to Joseph for he sees Yahweh blessing him because of Joseph, even here in the jail.

ON THE WAY TO FULFILLMENT OF JOSEPH'S OWN DREAMS THE LORD GOD ONCE MORE EQUIPS JOSEPH AS HIS PROPHET

Misfortune after misfortune had befallen Joseph. Nothing had become true of his grandiose dreams. Instead of royal ruler he had become an imprisoned slave. Yet, during all this the LORD God obviously had not forgotten Joseph. Because of him the LORD God had continually blessed Potiphar so that his master remained favorably inclined toward Joseph.

QUICK QUESTION

1. Discuss the fact that Joseph was neither killed nor cast away but rather remained with Potiphar.

That the LORD God had not forgotten Joseph, nor the promises he made him, became evident in what happened to Joseph while in the royal jail. In jail Joseph is given the care of two high ranking officials of Pharaoh: Pharaoh's personal baker and personal chief cupbearer. Both officials have dreams that make them uneasy, even sad.

Notice how Joseph speaks to the officials. He does not tell them that he is able to interpret their dreams for them. Joseph said to them, *"Do not interpretations belong to God? Please tell them to me."* Joseph trusts and gives glory to the God of Abraham, and the LORD God gives Joseph the ability to understand and interpret their dreams.

QUICK QUESTION

1. Discuss the difference between a diviner and a true prophet.

The LORD God reveals to Joseph the meaning of the dreams: The cupbearer is going to be restored to his position with Pharaoh and the baker is going to be condemned to death and hanged. All this means that, in a nation with only fake gods, the only true living God reveals his faithful love to Joseph a descendant of Abraham, the 'friend of God'. Egypt will be held responsible for having witnessed the power and faithfulness of Yahweh.

QUICK QUESTION

1. Discuss the previous line and apply it to today

THE LORD GOD ELEVATES HIS PROPHET JOSEPH TO SECURE THE FUTURE OF THE OFFSPRING OF ABRAHAM AS HE HAD PROMISED

In Genesis 41, The LORD God fulfills the royal dream he earlier sent Joseph and Jacob and the brothers. The LORD God starts this fulfillment by sending two dreams to Pharaoh. In the first dream seven ugly skinny cows eat seven fat cows. In the second dream seven blighted ears of grain devour seven fat ears of grain. Pharaoh orders his diviners to explain the dreams to him but they are unable to do so. It is then that the cupbearer belatedly remembers Joseph. The cupbearer recommends Joseph to Pharaoh and Joseph is summoned to the palace. There Pharaoh commands Joseph to interpret the dreams for him.

FAITHFUL TO HIS SENDER, JOSEPH STEPS BACK FROM THE LIMELIGHT AND GIVES GLORY TO YAHWEH, THE GOD OF THE COVENANT WHICH HE PROMISED TO ABRAHAM, ISAAC AND JACOB AND THEIR DESCENDANTS

Joseph answered Pharaoh, 41:16 *"It is not in me; God will give Pharaoh a favorable answer."*

Genesis 41:25, "Then Joseph said to Pharaoh, *'The dreams of Pharaoh are one;* **God** *has revealed to Pharaoh what he is about to do.'"*

Genesis 41:28, "It is as I told Pharaoh; *'**God** has shown to Pharaoh what he is about to do.'"* God will give Pharaoh a favorable answer.

QUESTIONS

1. Discuss how Joseph this time does not say that interpretation of dreams belongs to God. Rather discuss how Joseph immediately confronts Pharaoh with the authority of the only true, living God.
2. Discuss why it was amazing that the true God revealed something to a Pagan Egyptian who himself was looked upon as a god.
3. Discuss what purpose the LORD had with addressing Pharaoh. Was God's purpose only to elevate Joseph, or was there more?
4. Joseph showed Pharaoh how to care for his people during the seven-year famine. Discuss from where Joseph got this wisdom.
5. Discuss what present day governors of the nation should do when faced with economic depression or danger.
6. Discuss what the Church should do when the nation is faced with economic depression or danger.

Genesis 41:44-50 (ESV)

44 Moreover, Pharaoh said to Joseph, "I am Pharaoh, and without your consent no one shall lift up hand or foot in all the land of Egypt." 45 And Pharaoh called Joseph's name Zaphenath-paneah. And he gave him in marriage Asenath, the daughter of Potiphera priest of On. So Joseph went out over the land of Egypt. 46 Joseph was thirty years old when he entered the service of Pharaoh king of Egypt. And Joseph went out from the presence of Pharaoh and went through all the land of Egypt. 47 During the seven plentiful years the earth produced abundantly, 48 and he gathered up all the food of these seven years, which occurred in the land of Egypt, and put the food in the cities. He put in every city the food from the fields around it. 49 And Joseph stored up grain in great abundance, like the sand of the sea, until he ceased to measure it, for it could not be measured. 50 Before the year of famine came, two sons were born to Joseph. Asenath, the daughter of Potiphera priest of On, bore them to him.

Genesis 41:51-57 (ESV)

51 Joseph called the name of the firstborn Manasseh. "For," he said, "God has made me forget all my hardship and all my father's house." 52 The name of the second he called Ephraim, "For God has made me fruitful in the land of my affliction."

53 The seven years of plenty that occurred in the land of Egypt came to an end, 54 and the seven years of famine began to come, as Joseph had said. There was famine in all lands, but in all the land of Egypt there was bread. 55 When all the land of Egypt was famished, the people cried to Pharaoh for bread. Pharaoh said to all the Egyptians, "Go to Joseph. What he says to you, do."

56 So when the famine had spread over all the land, Joseph opened all the storehouses and sold to the Egyptians, for the famine was severe in the land of Egypt. 57 Moreover, all the earth came to Egypt to Joseph to buy grain, because the famine was severe over all the earth.

PLEASE USE THE SPECIAL SECTION BELOW AS MATERIAL TO DISCUSS THE FOLLOWING POINTS

1. Discuss the meaning of Zaphenath-paneah
2. Discuss what the city of ON stands for.
3. Discuss what it means that God made Joseph "Father to Pharaoh".
4. Discuss the difference between Potiphar and Potiphera.
5. Discuss the fact that Joseph, Zaphenath-paneah, and Father to Pharaoh, was nevertheless slave to Pharaoh.
6. Discuss the consequence of being a slave and being given in marriage to an Egyptian wife. Whose decision was this?
7. Discuss Ezekiel 23:1-3 and 19-21(ESV) and Joseph's marriage to Asenath, daughter of the priest of ON.

    The word of the LORD came to me: 2 'Son of man, there were two women, the daughters of one mother. 3 They played the whore in Egypt; they played the whore in their youth; there their breasts were pressed and their virgin bosoms handled. 4 Oholah was the name of the elder and Oholibah the name of her sister. They became mine, and they bore sons and daughters. As for their names, Oholah is Samaria, and Oholibah is Jerusalem.'"

    19 "Yet she increased her whoring, remembering the days of her youth, when she played the whore in the land of Egypt ²⁰ and lusted after her lovers there, whose members were like those of donkeys, and whose issue was like that of horses. ²¹ Thus you longed for the lewdness of your youth, when the Egyptians handled your bosom and pressed your young breasts."

8. Discuss the providence of the LORD God and Joseph's ties to ON.
9. Discuss the importance of placing Joseph in the time of Asiatic and Hyksos domination of Egypt.

A SPECIAL SECTION ON GENESIS 41-51 AND THE EARLY DATE OF THE EXODUS

Donald B. Redford writes,
"In spite of the fact that the basic plot of the story, as pointed out, is in no special way tied to a Nilotic setting, a number of details that color the present version of this plot motif do, indeed, point to Egypt. Most obvious are the Egyptian personal names, of which four are produced in passages rather tangential to the main story line (Genesis 39:1, 41:45): Saphnathpane'afu, Asenath, Potiphar, and Potipherah. The last two being variants of one name, we are left with three Egyptian names in the story Saphnathpane'ah is unanimously agreed to be the transliteration of an Egyptian name-type that means "God N speaks (or spoke) and he lives." [55]

This quote from Donald Redford is quite representative for the opinion of most Egyptologists and their regard for the book of Genesis. The book of Genesis may have some hints as to an Egyptian setting but that is all. Don't look for any links to true historical settings. However, we intended to look and we did find links. In the last ten chapters of the book of Genesis there are definite links to the historical times of Israel's sojourn in Egypt and even the time of the Exodus.
The links we found point to the time of the Hyksos rule over lower Egypt.

Zaphenath-paneah, God speaks and he lives.

Genesis 41:45, "And Pharaoh called Joseph's name Zaphenath-paneah." Pharaoh concludes the appointment of Joseph by recognizing the God of Joseph who spoke to Joseph and through Joseph and Joseph did not die but lived. We must take note of the difference between this Hyksos Pharaoh and his attitude toward the God of Joseph and the New Kingdom Pharaoh who rejected the God of Moses saying, "I do not know Yahweh".

THE HYKSOS (SOMETIMES CALLED AMURUH, THE BIBLICAL AMORITES)

E.T.Campbell, Jr. writes in "The Amarna Letters and the Amarna Period" p. 17, *"Indeed, Joseph may better fit into the preceding Hyksos period ... ."* [56]
P.Montet, *Lives of the Pharaohs*, p171, *"East of the city of Avaris there began the land of Goshen: the Hyksos king had granted it to the children of Israel when they had been authorized to live in Egypt."* [57]

The title **Hyksos** means "rulers of foreign lands". For centuries, Semites from the East had entered Lower Egypt and settled there. They became so numerous that they were able to take over the government of (mainly) Lower Egypt. Hyksos kings were in power from 1650-1550 B.C. However, the process of

---

[55] Donald B. Redford, Egypt, Canaan and Israel in Ancient Times, P. 424, Princeton 1992

The Biblical Archaeologist (Vol. XXIII. 1960, 1).

[57] P. Montet, lives of the Pharaohs, Spring Books, London/New York, 1968/1974

Hyksos domination leading up to 1650 B.C. started earlier. John Van Seters and Nicolas Grimal make mention of two Pharaohs who were called "Asiatic" and who reigned in the period leading up to the Hyksos domination.[58]

The centre of priestly service of the Hyksos in Lower Egypt was **ON** (Heliopolis). The priests there were serving the gods **Re, Set-Baal,** and **Astarte**. Egyptian gods with Semitic names. The people that moved from Canaan and the Eastern Desert into Lower Egypt brought their own idols along and mixed them with the idols of Egypt.

By marriage Joseph became integrated into a Hyksos priestly family.
Pharaoh gave Joseph in marriage "Asenath, the daughter of Potiphera priest of On". Genesis 41: 45. Potiphera priest of On. On is Heliopolis, city of Re, or city of the Sun. Is it possible that the ending "ra" of potiphe**ra** was there since he was a priest to Ra?
This fits the period of the Hyksos. The Hyksos were enemies of the Theban king and did not worship Amon Re. The Hyksos worshiped Seth-Baal the protégé of Re. On (Heliopolis) was the centre of worship for the Hyksos. It was a Hyksos king that took Joseph in his service.

Joseph, Father to Pharaoh a priestly rank
Genesis 45:8, "So it was not you who sent me here, but God. He has made me **a father to Pharaoh**, and lord of all his house and ruler over all the land of Egypt."

James Wasserman, The Egyptian Book of the Dead,[59]
2nd col. *"God's Father": Priestly rank.*
Idem: **Arielle Kozloff p. 41 bottom,** *"Yuya's characteristic title is 'god's father', a priestly title often given in the New Kingdom to senior officials – viziers ... generals, but also men of lower ranks – who were 'like a father' to the king (such as royal tutors), this is the only case in which it demonstrably refers to a royal father-in law."* **P.52 top,** *(Aper-El) "its burial chamber contained objects bearing the names of Amenhotep III and Tiy as well as Amenhotep IV (Akhenaten). In addition to the vizier's title, Aper-el was god's father, child of the nursery, and high priest (bak tepy) of the Aten."*

The fact that Joseph was made "Father to Pharaoh" and "Ruler of all Egypt" means that Joseph had the position of a vizier and had a priestly title. This may also be connected to the fact that Joseph married into the priestly family of the high priest of On (Heliopolis).

Genesis 46:33-34 (ESV)

33 When Pharaoh calls you and says, 'What is your occupation?' 34 you shall say, 'Your servants have been keepers of livestock from our youth even until now, both we and our fathers,' in order that you may dwell in the land of Goshen, for every shepherd is an abomination to the Egyptians."

---

[58] John Van Seters, The Hyksos, A New Investigation, Yale Univ. Press, 1967
Nicolas Grimal, A History of Ancient Egypt, Oxford 1994

[59] Arielle P. Kozloff and Betsy M. Bryan with Lawrence M. Berman and an Essay by Elisabeth Delange, Egypt's Dazzling Sun, Amenhotep III and his World. Publisshed by he Cleveland Museum of Art in cooperation with the Indiana Universty Press 1992

Genesis 47:5-6 (ESV)

5 Then Pharaoh said to Joseph, "Your father and your brothers have come to you. 6 The land of Egypt is before you. Settle your father and your brothers in the best of the land. Let them settle in the land of Goshen, and if you know any able men among them, put them in charge of my livestock."

A PHARAOH WHO HAS LIVESTOCK

Shepherds are an abomination to the Egyptians but this Pharaoh has livestock and is in need of shepherds. This must be one of the Pharaohs who originated in the Near East and therefore is called Hyksos, or Asiatic. This is one more indication that Israel was in Egypt during the Second Intermediary Period and that the time of oppression came during the early New Kingdom. That is approximately between 1550 B.C and 1440 B.C.

CONCLUSION

Joseph entered Egypt at the age of seventeen and died there at the age of one hundred and ten. Joseph's life in Egypt coincided with the reign of Hyksos Pharaohs, or possibly with the period leading up to that time. With slight variation, the period of the Hyksos rule is considered from 1675 B.C. to 1550 B.C. The reign of the two Asiatic kings, mentioned above, would have been between 1750 and 1675 B.C. The first kings of the New Kingdom, Kamose and Ahmose, expelled the Hyksos. From that time on the Israelites were cruelly treated. These early dates leave us room to date the Exodus early.

Genesis 48:13-21

13 "And Joseph took them both, Ephraim in his right hand toward Israel's left hand, and Manasseh in his left hand toward Israel's right hand, and brought them near him. 14 And Israel stretched out his right hand and laid it on the head of Ephraim, who was the younger, and his left hand on the head of Manasseh, crossing his hands (for Manasseh was the firstborn). 15 And he blessed Joseph and said, 'The God before whom my fathers Abraham and Isaac walked, the God who has been my shepherd all my life long to this day, 16 the angel who has redeemed me from all evil, bless the boys; and in them let my name be carried on, and the name of my fathers Abraham and Isaac; and let them grow into a multitude in the midst of the earth.'"

"17 When Joseph saw that his father laid his right hand on the head of Ephraim, it displeased him, and he took his father's hand to move it from Ephraim's head to Manasseh's head. 18 And Joseph said to his father, 'Not this way, my father; since this one is the firstborn, put your right hand on his head.' 19 But his father refused and said, 'I know, my son, I know. He also shall become a people, and he also shall be great. Nevertheless, his younger brother shall be greater than he, and his offspring shall become a multitude of nations.' 20 So he blessed them that day, saying, 'By you Israel will pronounce blessings, saying, 'God make you as Ephraim and as Manasseh.' Thus he put Ephraim before Manasseh."

JOSEPH RECEIVES A DOUBLE BLESSING, EPHRAIM AND MANASSEH

1 Chronicles 5:2, *"… and though Judah was the strongest of his brothers and a ruler came from him, the rights of the firstborn belonged to Joseph."*

QUICK QUESTION

1. In the light of this revelation discuss the impact of Joseph's receiving a double blessing.

Hebrews 11:21 *"By faith Jacob, when dying, blessed each of the sons of Joseph, bowing in worship over the head of his staff."*

QUICK QUESTION

1. Discuss God speaking through Jacob and why yet Jacob needed "faith".

Jeremiah 31:9 "They will come with weeping; they will pray as I bring them back. I will lead them beside streams of water on a level path where they will not stumble, *because I am Israel's father, and Ephraim is my firstborn son."*

31:20 "Is Ephraim my dear son? Is he my darling child? For as often as I speak against him, I do remember him still. Therefore, my heart yearns for him; I will surely have mercy on him, declares the LORD."

DISCUSSION TIME

1. In the light of the quote from Jeremiah discuss how the LORD God Himself confirmed Jacob's blessing of Ephraim as the firstborn.
2. In the light of this revelation discuss the position of the tribe of Ephraim among Israel.

THE LORD GOD, HIS PROMISE TO ABRAHAM, AND A DEFILED ISRAEL IN EGYPT

The defilement began when the slave Joseph became a Father (priest) to Pharaoh and was given a daughter of the priest of On (Heliopolis) as wife. Joseph married into a priestly family that served Re, Seth-Baal and Astarte. From the LORD's revelation to Ezekiel we learn of the extent of the defilement of the descendants of Abraham in Egypt:

Ezekiel 20:5–9 (ESV)
5 "… and say to them, Thus says the Lord GOD: On the day when I chose Israel, I swore to the offspring of the house of Jacob, making myself known to them in the land of Egypt; I swore to them, saying, I am the LORD your God. 6 On that day I swore to them that I would bring them out of the land of Egypt into a land that I had searched out for them, a land flowing with milk and honey, the most glorious of all lands. 7 And I said to them, 'Cast away the detestable things your eyes feast on, every one of you, and do not defile yourselves with the idols of Egypt; I am the LORD your God.' 8 But they rebelled against me and were not willing to listen to me. None of them cast away the detestable things their eyes feasted on, nor did they

forsake the idols of Egypt. Then I said I would pour out my wrath upon them and spend my anger against them in the midst of the land of Egypt. ⁹ *But I acted for the sake of my name, that it should not be profaned in the sight of the nations among whom they lived, in whose sight I made myself known to them in bringing them out of the land of Egypt."*

THE DEFILEMENT OF ISRAEL STARTED IN EGYPT AND CONTINUED FOR CENTURIES AS WE READ IN THE PROPHECIES OF ISAIAH, JEREMIAH, EZEKIEL AND DANIEL

DISCUSSION TIME

1. Discuss whether the LORD depends on having a perfect, faithful, people in order to fulfill his promise to Abraham, *"In your Seed shall all the nations be blessed."*
2. Discuss why the LORD God puts up with his rebellious people.
3. Discuss the "way-stations" on the road the LORD God went with his rebellious people until he brought his Son Jesus to save his people from their sins.
4. Discuss why Egypt was mentioned in Revelation 11:8, *"and their dead bodies will lie in the street of the great city that symbolically is called Sodom and **Egypt**, where their Lord was crucified."*
5. Discuss whether the one God, Father, Son, and Spirit, depends on a perfect Church in order to come to his full Glory at Christ's return.
6. Discuss whether we are a perfect congregation of the LORD.
7. Discuss our need as Congregation of the Lord to receive admonishment with respect to defilement.
8. Why is the LORD God putting up with us?

Genesis 49:1-27

THE LORD GOD REVEALS THROUGH JACOB WHAT WILL HAPPEN IN THE "LATTER DAYS"

The "Latter Days" The "Latter Days" in the heading of this section is placed between quotation marks and capitalized. That is done with a purpose. It is to indicate the specific place these words have in God's revelation. Moreover, the translation "latter days" is chosen, rather than the phrase "in days to come", which is general, rather than specific. In the flow of the biblical revelation we discern three specific time periods. The time from creation till Israel's Exodus from Egypt is "The Days".

The time from the Exodus till the coming of the Christ is "The Latter Days". The time from the coming of the Christ till his return on the clouds of heaven is "The Last Days". It is important for understanding the Scriptures to recognize this flow in God's revelation. By paraphrasing the term "Latter Days" into "days to come", we hide God's revelation of the flow of his history of redemption and judgment. I use the word history because these three revealed time periods determine the way we teach and study history.

The term "Latter days" appears frequently in Scripture. Some examples are: Num. 24:14; Deut. 4:30; 31:29; Isaiah 2:2; Jer. 23:20; Dan. 2:28; 10:14; Hos. 3:5.

What times was Jacob referring to when he spoke of the latter days? The verses 1-27 contain references to two different phases in the time period of the latter days. First there is the prophecy regarding the settling of Jacob's descendants in Canaan. Then there is the prophecy regarding Shilo and the Messianic Period in the far future. The coming of Shilo will also be the transition into the "Last Days".

Here follow some examples of verses in Scripture on the three time periods

DAYS

Isaiah 51:9
"Awake, awake, put on strength,
O arm of the LORD; awake, as in days of old,
the generations of long ago.
Was it not you who cut Rahab in pieces,
who pierced the dragon?"

Genesis 47:9

"And Jacob said to Pharaoh, "The days of the years of my sojourning are 130 years. Few and evil have been the days of the years of my life, and they have not attained to the days of the years of the life of my fathers in the days of their sojourning."

When we speak of "Days" in the history of God and his created world then we cannot fail to speak with awe of God's great deeds in the time of the patriarchs.

DISCUSSION TIME

1. Discuss God's great deeds in the days of Noah, Abraham, Jacob, and Joseph.
2. Discuss how we should speak with awe of God's great deeds in our personal history.
3. Discuss with awe how God is still doing great deeds in the Church and in society/nations in our days.

LATTER DAYS

Numbers 24:14 "And now, behold, I am going to my people. Come, I will let you know what this people will do to your people in the latter days."

Deuteronomy 4:30 "When you are in tribulation, and all these things come upon you in the latter days, you will return to the LORD your God and obey his voice."

Micah 7:20 "You will show faithfulness to Jacob and steadfast love to Abraham, as you have sworn to our fathers from the days of old."

LAST DAYS

(ἔσχατο, eschatos, JVR well-known from the subject of *eschatology*)
Acts 2:17 "And in the last days it shall be, God declares, that I will pour out my Spirit on all flesh, and your sons and your daughters shall prophesy, and your young men shall see visions, and your old men shall dream dreams."
2 Timothy 3:1 "But understand this, that in the last days there will come times of difficulty."
2 Peter 3:3 "Knowing this first of all, that scoffers will come in the last days with scoffing, following their own sinful desires."

DISCUSSION TIME

1. Discuss why it is better to translate "latter days" then "in days to come" in 49:1.
2. Discuss what this has to do with the flow of the history of God's redemption and judgment in the Bible
3. Discuss signs and events that show that we live in the "Last days".
4. Discuss the means with which God provides us in these "Last days" to endure and persevere in the faith. (Rom. 15:4; 1 Corinthians 10:14; Col. 1: 10-11; Revelation 14:12.)

THE LORD GOD SETS THE STAGE THROUGH JACOB'S PROPHECY

DISCUSSION FOREVER

1. Discuss how God set the stage for the settlement of the tribes under Joshua through Jacob's prophecy.
2. Discuss how Jacob's blessings take into account the previous history of each of his sons.
3. Discuss the consequences our actions have.
4. Discuss how Jacob's prophecy concerning Reuben was fulfilled when they lived in Canaan.
5. Discuss the same with respect to Simeon. Was Simeon an independent tribe?
6. Discuss the tribe of Levi. How was Jacob's prophecy fulfilled?
7. Discuss the surprising place of holiness the tribe of Levi received.
8. Discuss the surprising place of holiness Christian believers receive.
9. Discuss how the prophecy concerning Judah was fulfilled in the days of the trek through the desert (limit the discussion for we will discuss Judah and the "Latter Days" a little later).
10. Discuss the fulfillment of the prophecy concerning Zebulun and Issachar in the time of the Judges.
11. Discuss the fulfillment of the prophecy concerning Dan in the time of the Judges.
12. Discuss why Jacob would follow the prophecy regarding Dan with the exclamation "*I wait for your salvation, O LORD.*" (vs 18) There are two ways of explaining this.
13. Discuss by whom Joseph was set apart Genesis 49:26 "*The blessings of your father are mighty beyond the blessings of my parents, up to the bounties of the everlasting hills. May they be on the head of Joseph, and on the brow of him **who was set apart from his brothers**.*"
14. Discuss why the LORD God set Joseph apart among his brothers.
15. Discuss the position of Joseph as Ephraim among the tribes in the latter times.
16. Discuss the prophecy concerning Gad, Asher and Naphtali and their geographical Northern locations
17. Relate the fact that Dan is missing in the Sealing of the 144,000 of Israel in Revelation 7:1-8 to Jacob's prophecy.
18. Discuss the warning the prophecy concerning the missing of the tribe of Dan holds for us and our time.
19. Discuss this warning as it applies to the Canadian Reformed Churches.
20. Discuss this warning as it applies to the teaching at our Theological Seminary in Hamilton.
21. Discuss this warning as it applies to our nation's parliamentarians.
22. Discuss this warning as it applies to our Christian elementary and high schools.
23. Discuss how the prophecy concerning Benjamin was fulfilled both in the time of the Judges and in the time of the kings.
24. Discuss the opinion of many of today's theologians who hold that the prophecy of Genesis 49 is not really foretelling but rather hindsight. This is also called a re-writing of history.

THE LORD GOD APPOINTS JUDAH IN DIVINE DISREGARD OF JUDAH'S PAST SINS

Judah was the fourth son of Jacob by Leah. Jacob had disqualified the first three sons, Reuben, Simeon and Levi. As such one would expect Judah to be given the rights of the firstborn son. From **I Chronicles 5:1-2** we learn that this is not so. There God the Holy Spirit gives this revelation:

"*The sons of Reuben the firstborn of Israel (for he was the firstborn, but because he defiled his father's couch, his birthright was given to the sons of Joseph the son of Israel, so that he could not be enrolled as the oldest son; ² though Judah became strong among his brothers and a chief came from him, yet the birthright belonged to Joseph.).*"

The Scriptures do not tell us that also Judah was disqualified. We could expect him to be disqualified when we look at Judah's previous wayward life. Through Jacob the LORD God appoints Judah to bring about the promises God made to Abraham.

QUESTIONS

1. Discuss Judah's past sins.
2. Discuss Judah's unworthiness to qualify for the birthright.
3. Discuss how we, who believe, can be found worthy to belong to the assembly of the firstborn. Are we better than Judah? About the assembly of the firstborn see Hebrews 12:23 *"… and to the assembly of the firstborn who are enrolled in heaven, and to God, the judge of all, and to the spirits of the righteous made perfect."*
4. We can put the foregoing also in these words: The LORD God appoints Judah to lead the tribes of Israel, to Shilo. The consequence of this is that the LORD God, by appointing Judah, is bringing Shilo from the tribe of Judah to Israel and the nations.
5. Discuss how the Lord Jesus Christ came from Judah to us.

Genesis 49:10 (Literal translation)

"The scepter shall not depart from Judah, nor the ruler's staff from between his feet, until Shilo comes and to him shall be the obedience of the peoples."

SHILO

Most modern Versions of the English Bible do not leave "Shilo" untranslated but choose to give a paraphrase. An example of such a paraphrase is how the ESV translates chapter 49:10 *"The scepter shall not depart from Judah nor the ruler's staff from between his feet, until tribute comes to him; and to him shall be the obedience of the peoples."*

Two remarks must be made about such a paraphrase, one of appreciation and the other of correction. It is appreciated that such a paraphrase maintains the prophetic reference to the coming of the Lord Jesus Christ as the great son of David. The critical note is to point out that the title Shilo should be maintained to be linked to other prophetic titles for the Lord Jesus, "seed /offspring", "shoot" and "branch". Some examples of these prophetic titles have been listed below.

Genesis 22:18 "…and in your offspring (seed) shall all the nations of the earth be blessed, because you have obeyed my voice."
Isaiah 4:2 "In that day the branch of the LORD shall be beautiful and glorious, and the fruit of the land shall be the pride and honor of the survivors of Israel."
Isaiah 11:1 "There shall come forth a shoot from the stump of Jesse, and a branch from his roots shall bear fruit."
Jer. 23:5 "Behold, the days are coming, declares the LORD, when I will raise up for David a righteous Branch, and he shall reign as king and deal wisely, and shall execute justice and righteousness in the

land.⁶ In his days Judah will be saved, and Israel will dwell securely. And this is the name by which he will be called: 'The LORD is our righteousness.'"

Micah 5:4 "And he shall stand and shepherd his flock in the strength of the LORD, in the majesty of the name of the LORD his God. And they shall dwell secure, for now he shall be great to the ends of the earth."

Zechariah 3:8 "Hear now, O Joshua the high priest, you and your friends who sit before you, for they are men who are a sign: behold, I will bring my servant the Branch."

John 15:5 "I am the vine; you are the branches. Whoever abides in me and I in him, he it is that bears much fruit, for apart from me you can do nothing."

DISCUSSION TIME

1. Discuss these prophetic titles, other than Shilo as they are used for the Lord Jesus in the Bible.
2. Discuss the possible meaning of Shilo as "Rest Bringer" (be at rest HAL, DB.Shilo = Rest-bringer שלה).

Genesis 49:28 to 50:26

JACOB AND JOSEPH GIVE ORDERS TO BE BURIED IN THE LAND OF PROMISE

49:29 "Then he commanded them and said to them, "I am to be gathered to my people; bury me with my fathers in the cave that is in the field of Ephron the Hittite."

49:31 "There they buried Abraham and Sarah his wife. There they buried Isaac and Rebekah his wife, and there I buried Leah."

Genesis 50:24-25 "And Joseph said to his brothers, "I am about to die, but God will visit you and bring you up out of this land to the land that he swore to Abraham, to Isaac, and to Jacob. ²⁵ Then Joseph made the sons of Israel swear, saying, "God will surely visit you, and you shall carry up my bones from here."

Jacob is referring to what is recorded for us in Genesis 23. In our notes on that chapter we noted that Abraham arranged for a burial place "in hope". Abraham was a stranger in the land of Canaan as yet owning nothing but having the oath of promise from the LORD God that his descendants would inherit the land.

QUESTIONS

1. Using the verses quoted above, discuss the different circumstances of: Abraham making the arrangement for burial "in hope"
   1. Jacob making the arrangement for burial "in hope"
   2. Joseph making the arrangement for burial "in hope"
2. Discuss the basis the patriarchs had for being buried in the Promised Land.
3. Discuss our Christian hope at the grave.
4. Discuss today's pessimistic prevailing *Nihilism*.
5. Compare and discuss the pessimistic *Nihilism* of our day with Revelation 21:5 *"And he who was seated on the throne said, 'Behold, I am making all things new.' Also, he said, 'Write this down, for these words are trustworthy and true.'"*

6. Discuss the effect the message of Moses should have had on enslaved Israel when he reminded them of the hope their "fathers" expressed in choosing their place of burial.
7. Discuss the effect the message of God *"making all thing new"* should have on our style of everyday life.

Genesis 50:1-15

JACOB' FUNERAL

Joseph needs permission from Pharaoh to go outside Egypt to bury his father Jacob.

QUICK QUESTION

1. Discuss why Joseph the ruler of Egypt under Pharaoh needs this permission. Why can he not ask for this permission himself?

The inhabitants of Canaan express their opinion that this is a *"grievous mourning by the Egyptians."*

DISCUSSION TIME

1. Discuss how the LORD God uses the power of Egypt to bury Jacob in the Promised Land.
2. Discuss how God uses Jacob's burial in the cave of Magpelah to keep Joseph and his brothers on the path to the Promised Land.
3. Discuss how the LORD God is keeping the Church on the path to the promised New Earth.
4. Discuss the necessity to see the Glory of God at work in our turbulent times.
5. Discuss ways and means to keep our eye of faith sharp so we may reach the promised goal.

JOSEPH, "RULER BY THE GRACE OF GOD" GENESIS 50:15-21

Joseph's brothers fear the power of Joseph to take revenge for the wrong they did to

him in the past. As ruler under Pharaoh, Joseph indeed has that power and opportunity. Joseph refuses to take revenge. His refusal of revenge is not to come out on top and serve his own glory. Joseph gives glory to the LORD God: Genesis 50:20 *"As for you, you meant evil against me, but God meant it for good, to bring it about that many people should be kept alive, as they are today."*

QUESTIONS

1. Discuss what you read in the heading of this paragraph: **Joseph, "Ruler by the Grace of God"**.
2. How does it show in Genesis 50:15-21 that Joseph ruled by the Grace of God?
3. Discuss whether we still can say that our present-day rulers are rulers "by the Grace of God".
4. Must we call them that?

Joseph's words, "God will visit you", correspond to the Lord's words to Abraham

Genesis 15:13-14 *"Then the* LORD *said to Abram, 'Know for certain that your offspring will be sojourners in a land that is not theirs and will be servants there, and they will be afflicted for four hundred years. ¹⁴ But I will bring judgment on the nation that they serve, and afterward they shall come out with great possessions'"*.

Genesis 50:24 *"And Joseph said to his brothers, "I am about to die, but God will visit you and bring you up out of this land to the land that he swore to Abraham, to Isaac, and to Jacob."*
Joseph's use of the verb to **visit** shows that Joseph knows that the time has come for God to fulfill his words spoken to Abraham. The visit of the LORD is not a social visit, it is a divine power visit. The visit is to come at a time of Israel's deliverance from affliction.

We are used to hearing in the Law about the LORD visiting the *"iniquity of the fathers upon the children."* That, however, is only one meaning of the LORD visiting his people.
Here, in Genesis 50:24, the LORD God is coming to rescue from oppression and so renew his promise to Abraham, Isaac, and Jacob through Joseph and fulfill it.

Questions

1. Discuss the two uses of the LORD God visiting his people.
2. Discuss how Joseph's use of the word "visit" shows that the favor of the Egyptians toward the Israelites was changing into oppression.
3. Discuss how the LORD God visited his people in the sending of his Son.
4. Discuss these promises of the Lord Jesus Christ:
5. **John 14:18** *"I will not leave you orphans. I will come to you."*
6. **John 14:23** *"If anyone loves me he will keep my word, and my Father will love him and make our home with him."*
7. **Matt. 28:20** *"And behold, I am with you to the end of the age."*
8. Discuss how these promises of the Lord Jesus Christ relate to the prophecy of Joseph in Genesis 50:24.
9. Discuss how all these promises of God's visitation comfort you today.

Joseph's death at age 110 coincides with the end of the reign of Hyksos Pharaohs and the beginning of the oppression of the Israelites

Joseph's lifespan roughly corresponds with the length of time that the Hyksos pharaohs ruled in Egypt. The power of the Hyksos pharaohs was favorable for Joseph and Abraham's descendants. The end of the Asiatic Hyksos rulers meant also the end of the protected status Israel enjoyed. We receive a glimpse of this situation from the text of the so-called *Kamose Stela*. Kamose was the Middle Egypt pharaoh who was able to drive the Hyksos pharaoh and his Asiatics from power around 1550 B.C.

*"His majesty spoke in his palace to the council of nobles who were in his retinue: 'Let me understand what this strength of mine is for! (One) prince is in **Avaris**, another is in Ethiopia, and (here) I sit*

*associated with an Asiatic and a Negro! Each man has his slice of this Egypt, dividing up the land with me. None can pass through it as far as Memphis (although it is) Egyptian water! See he (even) has Hermopolis! No man can settle down, when despoiled by the taxes of the **Asiatics**. I will grapple with him, that I may rip open his belly! My wish is to save Egypt and to smite the **Asiatic**!"*

TAXES, THE FIRST THING TO NOTICE IN THIS QUOTE

Upon the advice of Joseph, the Hyksos pharaohs subsequently had become owner of all persons and lands of the Egyptians that had bought grain during the famine. After the famine a fifth from the proceeds of the crops had to be paid to Pharaoh as taxes. From the above quote from the Kamose Stela you can taste the bitterness of the Egyptians against the Asiatics, including Israel in Goshen because of their loss of ownership and person.

When Kamose overcame the Asiatics he became king of all Egypt from North to South up to the cataracts. In the position as victor, Kamose, as the last Pharaoh of a divided Egypt, heralded a united Egypt under the rule of the Pharaohs of the New Kingdom or eighteenth Dynasty. From then on the pharaohs oppressed the people of Israel in Goshen.

GOD THE HOLY SPIRIT SLOTS THE BOOK OF GENESIS WITH THE BOOK OF THE EXODUS

We accept the whole Bible as inspired by God the Holy Spirit. **2 Peter 1:21** *"For no prophecy was ever produced by the will of man, but men spoke from God as they were carried along by the Holy Spirit."*

It is because of this revelation in 2 Peter 1:21 that we conclude that the Book of Genesis slots with the Book of the Exodus. The oppression and redemption by Yahweh is foretold and already signaled in the last chapters of the Book of Genesis. The oppression and redemption of the people of Israel becomes a reality in the Book of the Exodus. The unity of the two books is underlined by the fact that Yahweh makes the fulfillment of his oath to Abraham central in the Book of Genesis as well as in the Book of the Exodus.

See Genesis 15:12–16. *"As the sun was going down, a deep sleep fell on Abram. And behold, dreadful and great darkness fell upon him.* **13** *Then the* LORD *said to Abram, "Know for certain that your offspring will be sojourners in a land that is not theirs and will be servants there, and they will be afflicted for four hundred years.* **14** *But I will bring judgment on the nation that they serve, and afterward they shall come out with great possessions.* **15** *As for you, you shall go to your fathers in peace; you shall be buried in a good old age.* **16** *And they shall come back here in the fourth generation, for the iniquity of the Amorites is not yet complete."*

DISCUSSION TIME

1. Discuss how the inspiration of the Books of Genesis and the Exodus is from God the Holy Spirit.
2. Discuss how the Book of Genesis slots into the Book of the Exodus.
3. Discuss the comfort and assurance of faith we receive when we accept that the LORD God truly did what he promised to Abraham.

4. Discuss what God's giving us the Book of Genesis has to do with the Way, the Truth and the Life present in Jesus Christ our only Savior.

Genesis 50:24-25

JOSEPH AND THE BEGINNING OF OPPRESSION

24 And Joseph said to his brothers, "I am about to die, but God will visit you and bring you up out of this land to the land that he swore to Abraham, to Isaac, and to Jacob." 25 Then Joseph made the sons of Israel swear, saying, "God will surely visit you, and you shall carry up my bones from here."

These verses show that Joseph clearly is aware of a change in the attitude of the Egyptians toward him and the Israelites. Joseph is not expecting that the Israelites will be able to freely leave Egypt. It is God who has to visit them and bring them up out of Egypt.

The Pharaoh who did not know Joseph

Joseph's words to his brothers harmonize with what we read in Exodus 1:8. "Now there arose a new king over Egypt, who did not know Joseph".

The new king is radically different in his attitude toward the Semitic descendants of Jacob and Joseph. Egypt no longer has a Hyksos king. The native Egyptian king owes no debt to Joseph. The change of kings means a change from the Second Intermediate period to the New Kingdom period and a united Egypt.

AFTERMATH OF THE HYKSOS ERA IN THE NEW KINGDOM

D.B.Redford, Egypt, Canaan and Israel in Ancient Times p. 148 " … and well into the 18th Dynasty the perception of himself as launching a pre-emptive strike against "the foreign rulers who had attacked him" or " who were intending to destroy Egypt" and "were on the march against him" dominated the 18th Dynasty monarch's thinking. And so it was appropriate and necessary to "extend the frontiers of Egypt" and turn the territory thus engulfed into a buffer zone. Those within it would be transformed into Egypt's "serfs" and "Asia (would) become His Majesty's tenant," swearing fealty on Pharaoh's name." [60]

JVR Take note of the "Those within it". This also would apply to the Israelites who were at that time within the Delta region of Goshen.

---

[60] D.B.Redford, Egypt, Canaan and Israel in Ancient Times p. 148 Princeton, New Jeersey 1992

www.ingramcontent.com/pod-product-compliance
Lightning Source LLC
Chambersburg PA
CBHW081354290426
44110CB00018B/2378